INTELLECTUAL PROPERTY IN THE 21ST CENTURY

INTELLECTUAL PROPERTY

TRADE CONSIDERATIONS AND PROTECTION EFFORTS

INTELLECTUAL PROPERTY IN THE 21ST CENTURY

Additional books in this series can be found on Nova's website under the Series tab.

Additional E-books in this series can be found on Nova's website under the E-book tab.

INTELLECTUAL PROPERTY IN THE 21ST CENTURY

INTELLECTUAL PROPERTY

TRADE CONSIDERATIONS AND PROTECTION EFFORTS

NICHOLAS D. MELARK
EDITOR

Nova Science Publishers, Inc.
New York

For permission to use material from this book please contact us:
Telephone 631-231-7269; Fax 631-231-8175
Web Site: http://www.novapublishers.com

Library of Congress Cataloging-in-Publication Data

Intellectual property : trade considerations and protection efforts / Editor, Nicholas D. Melark.

p. cm.

Includes index.

ISBN 978-1-61470-506-2 (hardcover)

1. Intellectual property (International law). 2. Intellectual property --United States. I. Melark, Nicholas D.

K1401 .I57755 2011 +

2011024417

Published by Nova Science Publishers, Inc. † New York

CONTENTS

PREFACE

This book provides background on intellectual property rights (IPR) and discusses the role of U.S. international trade policy in enhancing IPR protection and enforcement abroad. IPR are legal rights granted by governments to encourage innovation and creative output by ensuring that creators reap the benefits of their inventions or works, and they may take the form of patents, trade secrets, copyrights, trademarks or geographical indications. U.S. industries that rely on IPR contribute significantly to U.S. economic growth, employment, and trade with other countries. Counterfeiting and piracy in other countries may result in the loss of billions of dollars of revenue for U.S. firms as well as the loss of U.S. jobs.

Chapter 1- This report provides background on intellectual property rights (IPR) and discusses the role of U.S. international trade policy in enhancing IPR protection and enforcement abroad. IPR are legal rights granted by governments to encourage innovation and creative output by ensuring that creators reap the benefits of their inventions or works, and they may take the form of patents, trade secrets, copyrights, trademarks, or geographical indications. U.S. industries that rely on IPR contribute significantly to U.S. economic growth, employment, and trade with other countries. Counterfeiting and piracy in other countries may result in the loss of billions of dollars of revenue for U.S. firms as well as the loss of U.S. jobs. Responsibility for developing IPR policy, engaging in IPR-related international negotiations, and enforcing IPR laws cuts across several different U.S. government agencies.

Chapter 2- A patent, which is a form of intellectual property right (IPR), is a legal, exclusive right granted for the invention of a new product, process, organism, design, and plant. It allows the right holder to exclude others from making, using, or selling the protected invention for a period of 20 years. Patents constitute the most common method for governments to encourage research and development (R&D) in order to find pharmaceutical treatments and cures for diseases and other illnesses.

Chapter 3- Many businesses have developed proprietary information that provides a competitive advantage because it is not known to others. As the United States continues its shift to a knowledge- and service-based economy, the strength and competitiveness of domestic firms increasingly depends upon their know-how and intangible assets. Trade secrets are the form of intellectual property that protects this sort of confidential information.

Chapter 4- Intellectual property (IP) plays a significant role in the U.S. economy. Enforcing IP laws involves many U.S. agencies, making coordination essential. Under the Prioritizing Resources and Organization for Intellectual Property Act of 2008 (PRO-IP Act), Congress required the U.S. Attorney General, through the Department of Justice (DOJ), to devote additional resources and undertake other specific IP efforts. The PRO-IP Act also created the position of the Intellectual Property Enforcement Coordinator (IPEC) to enhance interagency coordination. The act mandates that GAO provide Congress with a report on the efforts of DOJ and the IPEC.

Chapter 5- In October 2008, Congress passed the Prioritizing Resources and Organization for Intellectual Property Act of 2008 (PRO-IP Act), to improve the effectiveness of U.S. government efforts to protect intellectual property (IP) rights such as copyrights, patents, and trademarks. The act also directed GAO to provide information on the quantification of the impacts of counterfeit and pirated goods. GAO (1) examined existing research on the effects of counterfeiting and piracy on consumers, industries, government, and the U.S. economy; and (2) identified insights gained from efforts to quantify the effects of counterfeiting and piracy on the U.S. economy.

In: Intellectual Property
Editor: Nicholas D. Melark

ISBN: 978-1-61470-506-2

Chapter 1

INTELLECTUAL PROPERTY RIGHTS AND INTERNATIONAL TRADE

Shayerah Ilias and Ian F. Fergusson

SUMMARY

This report provides background on intellectual property rights (IPR) and discusses the role of U.S. international trade policy in enhancing IPR protection and enforcement abroad. IPR are legal rights granted by governments to encourage innovation and creative output by ensuring that creators reap the benefits of their inventions or works, and they may take the form of patents, trade secrets, copyrights, trademarks, or geographical indications. U.S. industries that rely on IPR contribute significantly to U.S. economic growth, employment, and trade with other countries. Counterfeiting and piracy in other countries may result in the loss of billions of dollars of revenue for U.S. firms as well as the loss of U.S. jobs. Responsibility for developing IPR policy, engaging in IPR-related international negotiations, and enforcing IPR laws cuts across several different U.S. government agencies.

Promoting the enforcement of IPR is an important component of U.S. international trade policy. Since the 1995 Agreement on Trade-Related Aspects of Intellectual Property Rights (TRIPS Agreement) at the World Trade Organization (WTO), trade policy has been used to promote enforcement of IPR abroad. The United States and several trading partners have been negotiating the Anti-Counterfeiting Trade Agreement (ACTA), which would surpass TRIPS Agreement commitments.

The United States also pursues international IPR support through regional and bilateral free trade agreements (FTAs), which often include IPR commitments by U.S. partners exceeding their TRIPS Agreement obligations. However, the May 10, 2007 bipartisan trade agreement led to a scale-back of some of the IPR requirements in the Peru, Panama and Colombia FTAs, in an effort to bolster bipartisan support for the FTAs. Other trade policy tools also are available for U.S. efforts to advance international IPR. Pursuant to Section 182 of the Trade Act of 1974 as amended (P.L. 93-618), the Office of the U.S. Trade Representative (USTR) identifies countries providing inadequate IPR protection in its annual "Special 301" report. Section 337 of the amended Tariff Act of 1930 authorizes the U.S.

International Trade Commission (ITC) to prohibit U.S. imports of infringing products. Additionally, under the Generalized System of Preferences (GSP), the United States may consider a developing country's IPR policies and practices as a basis for offering or suspending preferential duty-free entry to certain products from the country.

IPR protection and enforcement has been a focal point of legislative activity in recent sessions of Congress. In the 110th Congress, legislation was enacted to establish a new entity to coordinate intellectual property activities within the federal government (P.L. 110-403). In the 111th Congress, legislation was introduced calling for greater U.S. international IPR enforcement efforts and increased prioritization of resources devoted to such activities (H.R. 496 and related bill S. 1466; H.R. 2410 and H.R. 2475).

Given the role of IPR in the U.S. economy and its contribution to U.S. employment and trade, IPR issues related to international trade policy may figure prominently in the 112th congressional agenda. Congress may choose to consider whether or not FTAs are an appropriate vehicle for boosting intellectual property protection and enforcement. Congress also may balance IPR protection and enforcement with other public policy goals such as access to medicine in poor or developing countries. In addition, Congress may examine the effectiveness of the current U.S. coordinating structure for promoting international IPR support.

INTRODUCTION

Intellectual property rights (IPR) traditionally have been matters of national concern. Individual nation states have developed IPR regimes reflecting their domestic needs and priorities. Over time, intellectual property protection and enforcement have come to the forefront as a key international trade issue for the United States, figuring prominently in the multilateral trade policy arena and in regional and bilateral U.S. free trade agreements (FTAs).

The protection and enforcement of IPR in the United States and abroad is of key interest to Congress. Intellectual property is an increasingly critical component of the U.S. economy. Industries that rely on intellectual property protection in the United States claim to lose billions of dollars each year due to overseas IPR infringement. In light of the recent international financial crisis and global economic downturn, congressional interest has grown in the role of IPR in advancing U.S. industrial competitiveness and contributing to U.S. economic recovery following the recent international crisis. Members of Congress also have expressed concern about the potential health and safety consequences of counterfeit pharmaceutical drugs and other products, as well as the possible link between terrorist groups and traffic in counterfeit and pirated goods.

This report discusses the different kinds of IPR and forms of IPR infringement; importance of IPR to the U.S. economy; estimated losses associated with IPR infringement; organizational structure of IPR protection in multilateral, regional, bilateral arenas; U.S. government agencies involved with IPR and trade; and issues for Congress regarding IPR and international trade.

INTELLECTUAL PROPERTY RIGHTS BASICS

This section provides definitions of the various kinds of intellectual property rights (patents, trade secrets, copyrights, trademarks, and geographical indications) and intellectual property rights misappropriation (infringement, piracy, and counterfeiting).

Types of IPR

IPR are legal rights granted by governments to encourage innovation and creative output. They ensure that creators reap the benefits of their inventions or works and may take the form of patents, trade secrets, copyrights, trademarks, or geographical indications. Through IPR, governments grant a temporary legal monopoly to innovators by giving them the right to limit or control the use of their creations by others. IPR may be traded or licensed to others, usually in return for fees and or royalty payments. Although the World Trade Organization (WTO) Agreement on Trade-Related Aspects of Intellectual Property Rights (TRIPS) provides minimum standards for IPR protections, such rights are granted on a national basis and are, in general, enforceable only in the country in which they are granted. However, countries are obliged to abide by WTO rules and their IPR enforcement practices can be challenged by other countries at the WTO.

Patents

The Patent Act (35 U.S.C. 101 *et seq*) governs the issuance and use of patents in the United States. Patents are granted for inventions of new products, processes, or organisms (known as utility patents). Patents also may be granted for designs and plants. For an invention to be patentable, it must be new, "non-obvious" (involving an inventive step), and have a potential industrial or commercial application. The patent provides the holder with the exclusive right to sell the invention for a period of 20 years, or to prevent the incorporation of the invention into other products without the permission of the rights-holder. The patent right is based on the proposition that inventors must be granted a temporary monopoly over their invention in order to encourage innovation and to promote the expenditure of money on research and development. The patent holder recoups these up-front costs through a temporary monopoly over sale of the invention. In return for this economic rent, the patent holder must disclose the content of the patent along with test data and other information concerning the invention. This is meant to spur further creativity by those seeking to build on the patent after its expiration. Domestically, patents are granted by the Patent and Trademark Office (PTO) of the Department of Commerce.

Trade Secrets

A trade secret is any type of valuable information, including a "formula, pattern, compilation, program device, method, technique, or process," that derives independent economic value from not being generally known or readily ascertainable and is subject to reasonable efforts by the owner to maintain its secrecy.[1] Examples of trade secrets include blueprints, customer lists, and pricing information. While protection of patents and copyright is a matter of federal law, trade secret protection is found also in state law. However, most states subscribe to the Uniform Trade Secret Act (UTSA).

There are important differences between trade secrets and patents. Individuals do not have to apply for trade secret protection as they would for patents. Protection of trade secrets originates immediately with the creation of the trade secret; there is no process for applying for or registering trade secrets. Trade secret protection does not expire unless the trade secret becomes known. In contrast, patent applicants must disclose information about their innovation to the PTO in order to acquire a patent. Patents offer rights holders stronger protection but for a limited period of time. While applying for a patent can be a costly and lengthy process, patents are valuable if the confidentiality of the innovation is fragile or if the area of research is highly competitive.

Copyright

Protection of copyrights in the United States is based on the Copyright Act (17 U.S.C. 101, *et seq*). Copyrights protect original expressions of authorship. Such protections include literary or artistic works such as books, music, sound recordings, movies, paintings, architectural works, and computer software and databases (though not individual bits of data). Traditionally, copyrights differed from patents in that there was no claim to industrial applicability or novelty of the idea. The expression of the idea, not the underlying idea, was being copyrighted. While some of the criteria for copyrights differ from those of patents, the objective is the same: investments of time, money, and effort to create work of cultural, social and economic significance should be protected to encourage further creativity. U.S. law protects authorship for life plus 70 years for personal works, or 120 years from creation (or 95 years from publication) for corporate works. Copyrights may be registered by the Copyright Office of the Library of Congress, or acquired through creating and fixation of the work of authorship.

Trademarks

Trademark protection in the United States is governed jointly by state and federal law. The main federal statute is the Lanham Act of 1946 (15 U.S.C. 1051, *et seq*). Also known as service marks, trademarks permit the seller to use a distinctive name, mark, or symbol to identify and market a product, service, or company. The trademark allows quick identification of the seller's product, and for good or ill, can become an indicator of a product's quality. If for good, the trademark can be valuable in the introduction of new products by conveying an instant assurance of quality. The trademark is designed to prevent other companies with similar merchandise from free-riding on the association of quality with the trademarked item. Thus, a trademarked good may command a premium in the marketplace because of its reputation. For trademarks, distinctiveness is at a premium because a trademark must capture the consumer's imagination to be effective as generic names of commodities cannot be trademarked. Trademark rights are acquired through use or through registration with the PTO.

A related concept to trademarks is the geographic indication, which is also protected by the Lanham Act. The geographic indication acts to protect the quality and reputation of a distinctive product originating in a certain region; however, the benefit does not accrue to a sole producer, but rather the producers of a region. Geographic indications are generally sought for agricultural products, or wines and spirits. Protection for geographical indications is acquired in the United States by registration with the PTO, through a process similar to trademark registration.[2]

Infringement of IPR

IPR infringement is the misappropriation or violation of the IPR. In the case of patents, infringement of a patent owner's exclusive rights (as afforded by patent laws) involves a third party's unauthorized use of the patented device. As relates to international trade, the greatest challenge to the patent right is infringement in foreign countries, or non-observance by WTO member states to the minimal standards of the TRIPS Agreement. Copyright infringement occurs when a third party engages in reproducing, performing, making sound or visual recordings of, or broadcasting a copyrighted work without the consent of the copyright owner.

Piracy

The term "piracy" has applications to both copyrights and trademarks. The major challenge facing copyright protection is piracy, either through physical duplication of the work, illegal dissemination of copyrighted material (such as computer software, music, or movies) over the Internet, and/or participation in commercial transactions of copyrighted materials without the consent of the copyright owner. With respect to trademarks, piracy involves the registration or use of a famous foreign trademark that is not registered in the country or is invalid because the trademark has not been used.

Counterfeiting

An imitation of a product is referred to as a "counterfeit" or a "fake." Counterfeit products are manufactured, marketed, and distributed with the appearance of being the genuine good and originating from the genuine manufacturer.[3] The purpose of counterfeit goods is to deceive consumers about their origin and nature. Counterfeiting and copying of original goods are major challenges for trademarked products. The counterfeited product can be sold for a premium because of its association with the original item, while reducing the sales of the original items. Furthermore, consumer experience with a counterfeited good of inferior quality, can damage the reputation of the trademark product. Popular examples of counterfeit products in fake fashionwear, such as Louis Vuitton bags or Rolex watches, or fake pharmaceutical products, such as popular brand-name prescription medicines.

A related issue is the imitation of labels and packaging of trademarked goods. In this situation, the imitator uses a trademark that is confusingly similar to a well-known trademark in order to benefit from the reputation of the product with which he is competing.

GLOBAL INTELLECTUAL PROPERTY HOLDINGS

The total number of patent filing applications received under the Patent Cooperation Treaty (PCT), an international patent filing system administered by the World Intellectual Property Organization (WIPO), has grown in recent years. After peaking in 2008, international patent filings under the PCT fell by 4.5% in 2009, reflecting the international financial crisis. The contraction of the global economy has been associated with a decline in investment and spending on research and development.[4] In 2010, international patent filings grew by 4.8% to 162,900—nearly 2008 levels (see Table 1).[5]

Intellectual property holdings that are protected by international agreements are highly concentrated in certain countries. The United States continues to be the source of the world's largest number of patent filing applications under the PCT, accounting for nearly one-third of such filings in 2010. However, the U.S. growth rate of patent filings has been negative in recent years. The United States, along with Germany and Japan, accounted for about 60% of all patent applications filed in 2010 under the PCT. China ranked as the fourth largest source of international patent filings under the PCT in 2010, representing about 8% of global filings. China had the highest growth rate in such filings, at about 56% in that year.

Contribution of Intellectual Property to U.S. Economy

Intellectual property is an important source of comparative advantage for the United States. Nearly every industry depends on IPR for its businesses. Among the industries that are dependent on patent protection are the aerospace, automotive, computer, consumer electronics, pharmaceutical, and semiconductor industries. Copyright-based industries include the software, data processing, motion picture, publishing, and recording industries. Other industries that indirectly benefit from IPR protection include retailers, traders, and transportation businesses, which support the distribution of goods and services derived from intellectual property.[6]

The role of IPR in the U.S. economy has been longstanding. Some evidence suggests that factors linked to innovation account for about three-fourths of the United States' post-World War II growth rate.[7] In recent years, the role of IPR in the U.S. economy has grown. Various studies suggest that IP-related industries are one of the largest source of jobs in the United States. One study using data from 2000-2007 found that, among tradable industries, IP-intensive industries surpass non-IP-intensive industries on a range of economic measures, including job creation, wages, output and sales per employee, and exports. During this time period, according to the study, IP-intensive industries paid both their low- and highly skilled employees close to 60% more than non-IP-intensive industries. The report also found that IP-intensive industries represented nearly 60% of total U.S. exports during 2000-2007.[8] More broadly, IPR-intensive industries may contribute positively to the U.S. economy through productivity gains and other spillover effects.

Industry-specific figures may further demonstrate the importance of IP to the U.S. economy. For example, in 2007, the business and entertainment software, motion picture, recording, and publishing industries, which rely on copyright protection, were estimated to contribute about $889 billion to the U.S. economy ("value-added" to current GDP), or about 6.44% of the U.S. economy. This was an increase from 2006, during which the value-added of these copyright industries to the U.S. GDP totaled $837 billion, or 6.35% of the U.S. economy. These copyright industries also accounted for nearly 23% of real U.S. annual economic growth in 2007, up from about 13% in 2006. In terms of U.S. employment, the copyright industries represented 4% of U.S. workers (5.6 million workers) in 2007, similar to the prior year. Foreign sales and exports from these industries amounted to $126 billion in 2007, up from $116 billion in 2006.[9]

The pharmaceutical industry, which is patent-intensive, provides another illustration of intellectual property contributions to the U.S. economy. In 2009, domestic sales by research-based pharmaceutical companies that are members of Pharmaceutical Researchers and Manufacturers of America (PhRMA) reached an estimated $183 billion, while sales abroad by PhRMA member companies totaled about $103 billion.[10]

The intellectual property industries contribute positively to the overall U.S. trade balance through royalties and licensing fees. Rights-holders may authorize the use of technologies, trademarks, and entertainment products that they own to entities in foreign countries, resulting in revenues through royalties and license fees.[11] In 2009, U.S. receipts from cross-border trade in royalties and license fees (relating to patent, trademark, copyright, and other intangible rights) totaled $89.8 billion, down from $93.9 billion in the previous year. Also in 2009, U.S. payments of royalties and license fees to foreign countries amounted to $25.2 billion, down from $25.8 billion in the year before. Industrial processes, computer software, and trademarks accounted for the bulk of U.S. international trade in intangible assets.[12]

Table 1. Global Intellectual Property Filings Through the PCT, 2006-2009.

Country	**2008**	**2009**		**2010**	
	Filings	**Filings**	**Filings**	**Percent of**	**Growth from**
Country	**2008**	**2009**		**2010**	
				Total	**Previous Years**
United States	51,637	45,618	44,855	27.5%	-1.7%
Japan	28,760	29,802	32,156	19.7%	7.9%
Germany	18,855	16,797	17,171	10.5%	2.2%
China	6,120	7,900	12,337	7.6%	56.2%
South Korea	7,899	8,035	9,686	5.9%	20.5%
France	7,072	7,237	7,193	4.4%	-0.6%
United Kingdom	5,466	5,044	4,857	3.0%	-3.7%
Netherlands	4,363	4,462	4,097	2.5%	-8.2%
Switzerland	3,799	3,671	3,611	2.2%	-1.6%
Sweden	4,137	3,567	3,152	1.9%	-11.6%
Canada	2,976	2,527	2,707	1.7%	7.1%
Italy	2,883	2,652	2,632	1.6%	-0.8%
Finland	2,214	2,123	2,076	1.3%	-2.2%
Australia	1,938	1,740	1,736	1.1%	-0.2%
Spain	1,390	1,564	1,725	1.1%	10.3%
All Others	13,725	12,659	12,909	7.9%	2.0%
Total	**163,234**	**155,398**	**162,900**		

Source: World Intellectual Property Organization.

Some advocates of civil liberties assert that empirical analysis on the role of IPR in the U.S. economy may not be fully evaluating the economic and commercial benefits of lawful exceptions and limitations to exclusive rights. For example, by one estimate, businesses that rely on "fair use" exceptions to U.S. copyright law contribute $2.2 trillion to the U.S.

economy. The "fair use" doctrine permits limitations and exceptions to the exclusive right afforded by copyright law. It permits limited use of copyrighted works without requiring permission from the right holder in certain cases, examples of which may include news reporting, research, teaching, and library use.[13]

Prevalence and Economic Consequences of IPR Infringement

Advances in information and technology and declining costs of transportation and communication, spurred by globalization, have fundamentally changed information and trade flows. Such changes have created new markets for U.S. exporters, but at the same time, have been associated with the proliferation of counterfeiting and piracy on a global scale.

Several factors contribute to the growing problem of IPR infringement. While the costs and time for research and development are high, IPR infringement is associated with relatively low costs and risks and a high profit margin. According to PhRMA, it takes a pharmaceutical company about 10 to 15 years of research and development to create a new drug. PhRMA member companies collectively spent an estimated $46 billion for research and development (domestic and abroad) in 2009.[14] In contrast, drug counterfeiters can lower production costs by using inexpensive, and perhaps dangerous or ineffective, ingredient substitutes.

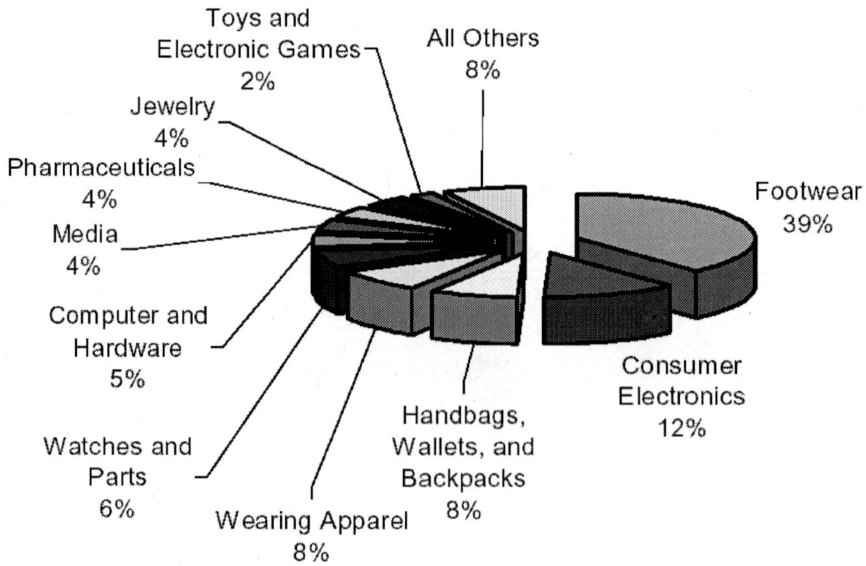

Sources: U.S. Customs and Border Protection and U.S. Immigration and Customs Enforcement.

Figure 1. Border Seizures of Counterfeit and Pirated Goods: FY2009.

The development of technologies and products that can be easily duplicated, such as recorded or digital media, also has led to an increase in counterfeiting and piracy. Increasing Internet usage has contributed to the distribution of counterfeit and pirated products. Additionally, civil and criminal penalties often are not sufficient deterrents for piracy and counterfeiting. The United States is especially concerned with *foreign* IPR infringement of

U.S. intellectual property. Compared to foreign countries, IPR infringements levels in the United States are estimated to be relatively low.

Seizures

Because of the secretive, illicit nature of IPR infringement, it is difficult to estimate the magnitude of its impact on U.S. producers and exporters. However, customs data on seizures of counterfeit and pirated goods may offer some idea of the magnitudes involved. One study by the Organization for Economic Cooperation and Development (OECD) indirectly extrapolated available customs data on seizures to conclude that world trade in counterfeit and pirated goods may have amounted to about $200 billion in 2005. In particular, the study used the customs information to estimate the probability that imports of particular goods from particular countries would be pirated or counterfeit. The OECD estimate does not include the counterfeit and pirated goods produced and consumed within a country and does not include infringing goods distributed over the Internet. If these figures were included, the trade estimate likely would be higher.[15] Updated estimates from the OECD suggest that trade in IPR-infringing goods may have totaled up to $250 billion in 2007. During that same time period, the share of counterfeiting and pirated goods in world trade also is estimated to have increased—from 1.85% in 2000 to 1.95% in 2007.[16]

Data on pirated and counterfeit seizures of imports at the U.S. border shed light of the magnitude of the issue in the U.S. context (see **Figure 1**). In FY2009, the Customs and Border Protection (CBP) and Immigration and Customs Enforcement (ICE) agencies of the Department of Homeland Security (DHS) made 14,841 IPR-related seizures, more than double the FY2005 level of 8,022. Between FY2005-FY2008, the domestic value of IPR-related seizures grew by more than 25% each year. The domestic value of seizures peaked at $272 million in FY2008 and then dropped by 4% to about $261 million in FY2009.[17]

Of all U.S. trading partners, China continues to account for the majority of counterfeits intercepted at the U.S. border. In FY2009, seizures of goods originating from China represented 79% of all seizures and $205 million in value. Other top trading partners from which IPR-infringing goods were seized include Hong Kong, India, Taiwan, and Korea. [18]

A top priority for the CBP is seizing counterfeit imports that endanger the health and safety of consumers, such as fake healthcare products, pharmaceutical products, and consumer electronics. The total value of IPR-related seizures of commodities that represent potential safety and security risks was $32 million in FY2009. Pharmaceutical goods were the top commodity posing safe and security risks, accounting for 34% ($11 million in domestic value) of such commodities intercepted at U.S. borders. Imports from China represented 62% of IPR-related goods that were intercepted at U.S. borders and identified as presenting safety and security risks, followed by such imports from India at 9%.[19]

Sectoral Infringement

U.S. industries that rely on IPR protection claim to lose billions of dollars in revenue annually due to piracy and counterfeiting. In addition, beyond the direct losses faced by U.S. intellectual property-based firms, the U.S. economy may face additional "downstream" losses from IPR infringement. According to this view, counterfeiting and piracy losses to U.S. firms, for example, also result in the loss of jobs that would have been created if the infringement did not occur, which translates into lost earnings by U.S. workers. This, in turn, translates into lost tax revenues for federal, state, and local governments from lost personal income, corporate income, and production taxes.[20]

Attempts have been made in some economic sectors to quantify the IPR infringement levels and related losses to legitimate U.S. businesses. Two intellectual property-based sectors that have calculated the extent of infringement in their industries and related costs are copyrights and pharmaceuticals. A discussion of estimated losses from these two sectors follows.

Copyright Industry

The International Intellectual Property Alliance (IIPA), a coalition of seven member associations representing over 1,900 U.S. copyright-based companies, provides annual estimates of U.S. trade loss associated with copyright infringements in selected countries.[21] For 2009, IIPA estimated that copyright piracy in 43 countries resulted in $14.3 billion in U.S. business software losses and $1.4 billion in U.S. records and music losses. China was the leading culprit in terms of trade losses due to copyright piracy, contributing to $3.4 billion in business software losses and $466 million in records and music losses to U.S. businesses.[22]

There is not always a direct relationship between IPR infringement rates and the costs to U.S. firms (see **Figure 2**). The size of a country's market and U.S. industries' access to the market affect the extent to which infringement rates translate into costs to U.S. IPR-based industries. Thus, estimated losses from IPR infringement may be lower in a country with high piracy rates but a small market for the United States, compared to a country with lower piracy rates but a bigger market for United States.

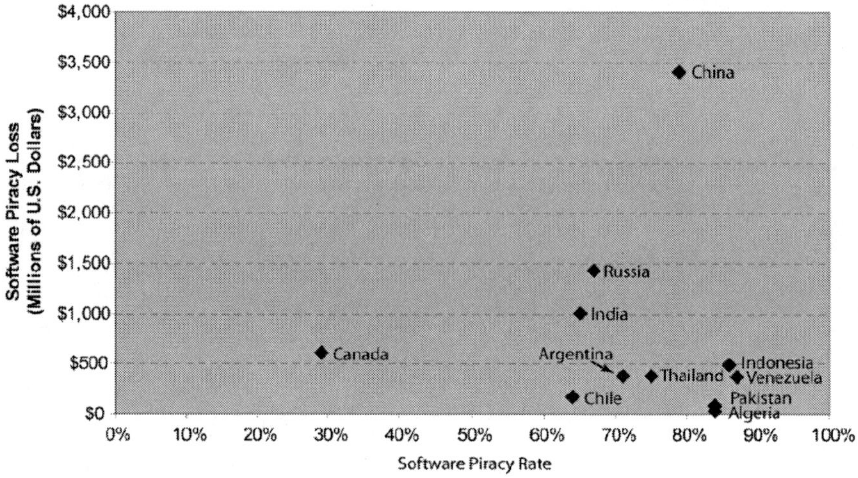

Source: Business Software Alliance.

Notes: The countries listed were identified as Priority Watch List countries in the 2010 "Special 301" report released by the Office of the U.S. Trade Representative.

Figure 2. Estimated Software Piracy Rates in Selected Countries and Estimated Related Software Piracy Losses to U.S. Businesses.

Table 2. Estimated Damages for PhRMA Member Companies From Data Exclusivity and Patent Protection Violations.

	2006 Submission (Oct. 2004 - Sept. 2005)	2007 Submission (Oct. 2005 - Sept. 2006)
Total Damages	$13.9 million	$21.7 million
Total Sales	$74.6 million	$172.1 million
Damages as a Percentage of Sales	19%	13%

Source: PhRMA 2006 and 2007 Special 301 Submissions.

Pharmaceutical Industry

In previous years, PhRMA has provided annual estimates of U.S. pharmaceutical industry losses from foreign violations of data exclusivity and patent protection.[23] In its 2007 Special 301 submission to the USTR, PhRMA contended that its member companies sustained damages totaling an estimated $21.7 million from data exclusivity and patent violations in 24 countries (see Table 2).[24] Damages reported in the 2007 submission were nearly double those reported in the prior year's submission. While the total loss associated with IPR infringement grew, damages as a percentage of sales declined from the 2006 submission to the 2007 submission.[25] At the time of reporting for submissions for subsequent years, PhRMA was not able to provide estimates of damages resulting from trade barriers associated with intellectual property protection and market access.[26]

Limitations on Data Estimating IPR Infringement Costs

There may be limitations to data estimating the impact of counterfeiting and piracy on the U.S. economy. According to a study conducted by the U.S. Government Accountability Office (GAO), the U.S. government does not systematically collect data or analyze the impacts of counterfeiting and piracy on the U.S. economy. In many cases, the federal government relies on estimates conducted by industry groups. However, industry associations may not always release their proprietary data sources and methods, complicating efforts to verify such estimates.[27] Some critics point out that many of the estimates for losses associated with IPR infringement are generated by industry groups that may have self-interested motivations.[28]

There is a possibility that such IPR infringement loss estimates may overestimate the extent to which sales of pirated and counterfeit goods displace legitimate sales. Methods for calculating data on counterfeiting and piracy often involve certain assumptions. Estimates of losses from IPR infringement can be highly sensitive to how these assumptions are derived and weighted. Some analysts question the proposition that sales of pirated goods translate directly into revenue losses for legitimate firms. The basic economic model employed in such estimates assumes that there is perfect substitutability between pirated and legitimate goods, which would equate sales of pirated goods to revenue losses of legitimate U.S. copyright businesses. Some analysts suggest that legitimate firms face a competition threat *only* if the individuals purchasing counterfeit products would be able and willing to purchase the legitimate product at the price offered when piracy is not present.[29] For consumers in poor developing countries, especially, this assumption may not be tenable. Others also question the statistical techniques used to develop these estimates.[30]

At the same time, there is a possibility that some IPR infringement loss estimates may underestimate the losses to U.S. businesses. For example, U.S. trade losses due to copyright infringement may be higher than reported because estimates oftentimes do not account for all forms of piracy, such as Internet piracy, which is an increasingly significant contributor to copyright piracy.[31] One study estimates that nearly 24% of global internet traffic infringes upon copyright.[32]

THE ORGANIZATION STRUCTURE OF IPR PROTECTION

Given the importance of intellectual property to the U.S. economy and the economic losses associated with counterfeiting and piracy, the United States is a leading advocate of strong global IPR standards and enforcement. Increasingly, the United States has integrated IPR policy in its international trade policy activities, pursuing enhanced IPR laws and enforcement through multilateral, regional and bilateral trade agreements, and national trade laws.

Multilateral IPR System

World Trade Organization (WTO)

At the center of the present multilateral trading system is the World Trade Organization (WTO), an international organization established in 1995 as the successor to the General Agreements on Tariffs and Trade (GATT). The WTO was established as the result of the Uruguay Round of trade negotiations (1986-1994), which resulted in numerous agreements on trade in goods, services, investment and other non-tariff barriers to trade. One of the Uruguay Round agreements was the Agreement on Trade-Related Aspects of Intellectual Property Rights (TRIPS Agreement), which sets minimum standards on intellectual property rights protection and enforcement with which all WTO member states must comply. The United States, the European countries, and the IPR business community were instrumental in including IPR on the Uruguay Round agenda. Many developing countries were wary of including IPR in trade negotiations, preferring to discuss them under the World Intellectual Property Organization (WIPO) (see below) instead. However, developing countries acceded, after being granted delayed compliance periods, and after achieving negotiating goals on other issues such as textiles and clothing, and savoring the prospect of operating under a rules-based trading system.

While previous international agreements on intellectual property rights continue to exist (see Table 2), the TRIPS Agreement was the first time that intellectual property rules were incorporated into the multilateral trading system. Two basic tenets of the TRIPS Agreement are national treatment (signatories must treat parties of other WTO members no less favorably in terms of IPR protection than the party's own nationals) and most-favored-nation treatment (any advantage in IPR protection granted to the party of another WTO member shall be granted to nationals of all other WTO member states).

Much of the TRIPS Agreement sets out the extent of the agreement's coverage of the various types of intellectual property: copyrights, trademarks, geographical indications, industrial designs, patents, layout of circuitry design, trade secrets, and test data. The TRIPS Agreement provisions build on several existing IPR treaties administered by the WIPO (discussed below). Another part provides standards of enforcement for IPR covered by the agreement. It enumerates standards for civil and administrative procedures and remedies, the application of border measures, and criminal procedures. A Council for the TRIPS Agreement was established to monitor the implementation of the agreement and transition arrangements were devised for developing countries. Finally, the agreement provides for the resolution of disputes under the Uruguay Round Agreement's Dispute Settlement Understanding (DSU). The binding nature of the DSU, with the possibility of the withdrawal of trade concessions (usually the re-imposition of tariffs) for non-compliance, sets this agreement apart from previous IPR treaties that did not have effective dispute settlement mechanisms.

U.S. WTO Cases against China on IPR

In April 2007, the United States filed two WTO dispute settlement cases against China, alleging inadequacies in China's enforcement of IPR laws and its barriers to market access for U.S. copyright businesses.[33]

- In January 2009, the DSU issued its final ruling on the case centering on IPR enforcement issues. The WTO panel ruled in the United States' favor that China's denial of copyright protection to works without censorship approval is inconsistent with the TRIPS Agreement. The panel also agreed with the United States that it is impermissible for China to publicly auction IPR-infringing goods seized at the border, with the only requirement being that fake brands and trademarks be removed from the goods. The WTO panel ruled that more evidence was needed before deciding whether or not China's threshold values for prosecuting counterfeiting and piracy permit commercial scale IPR infringement. China agreed to implement the WTO ruling.[34]
- In August 2009, a WTO panel ruled that a number of China's restrictions on trading rights and distribution of IPR-related products were inconsistent with WTO rules. However, the WTO panel did not address whether China's censorship policies or import limitations on foreign films violate WTO rules. China agreed to implement the WTO ruling.[35]

The TRIPS Agreement also seeks a balance of rights and obligations between the private right, enumerated above, and the obligation "to secure social and cultural development that benefits all."[36] Article 7 declares that:

> ... the protection and enforcement of IPR should contribute to the promotion of technological innovation and to the transfer and dissemination of technology, to the mutual advantage of producers and users of technological knowledge and in a manner conducive to social and economic welfare and to a balance of rights and obligations.

This paragraph attempts to link the protection of IPR with greater technology transfer, including technology covered by IPR protection, to the developing world. The language itself has been interpreted in various ways. Developed countries have tended to consider this language exhortatory, but developing countries have tried, without much success, to make technology transfer a meaningful obligation within the TRIPS Agreement system. Article 66.2 of the agreement requires developed country members to provide incentives to their enterprises and institutions to promote technology transfer to least-developed countries to assist them in establishing a viable technology base. Developed countries report annually on their efforts to encourage technology transfer (LDCs).

Complying with international IPR standards may impose greater burdens on developing countries than developed countries. Developing countries generally have to engage in greater efforts to bring their laws, judicial processes, and enforcement mechanism into compliance with the TRIPS Agreement. Consequently, developing countries were given an extended period of time in which to bring their laws and enforcement mechanisms into compliance with the TRIPS Agreement. Developing countries and post-Soviet states were given an additional four years from the entry into force of the agreement (January 1, 1995). For products that were not covered by a country's patent system (such as pharmaceuticals in many cases), an additional five years was granted to bring such products under coverage. For developing countries, all provisions of the TRIPS agreement should now be in force. For the least developed countries (LDCs), the phase-in period was set at 10 years (January 1, 2006), and for pharmaceuticals, the compliance period was later extended to 2016.[37]

Declaration on TRIPS Agreement and Public Health [38]

In agreeing to launch the Doha Round of WTO trade negotiations, trade ministers adopted a "Declaration on the TRIPS Agreement and Public Health" on November 14, 2001.[39] The Declaration sought to alleviate developing country dissatisfaction with aspects of the TRIPS regime. It delayed the implementation of patent system provisions for pharmaceutical products for least developed countries (LDCs) until 2016. The declaration committed member states to interpret and implement the agreement to support public health and to promote access to medicines for all. The Declaration recognized certain "flexibilities" in the TRIPS agreement to allow each member to grant compulsory licenses for pharmaceuticals and to determine what constitutes a national emergency, expressly including public health emergencies such as HIV/AIDS, malaria, and tuberculosis or other epidemics.

Paragraph 6 of the Declaration directed the WTO members to formulate a solution to a corollary concern, the use of compulsory licensing by countries with insufficient or inadequate manufacturing capability. Compulsory licenses are issued by governments to authorize the use or production of a patented item by a domestic party other than a patent holder. They are authorized by Article 31 of TRIPS, which places certain limitations on their use, scope, duration. A provision that predominantly restricted production authorized by compulsory license to the domestic market became the focal point of the negotiations because it, in effect, conveys the right of compulsory licensing only to countries with the capability to manufacture a given product. Countries without a domestic manufacturing capability were essentially precluded from using this flexibility of the TRIPS agreement.

On the eve of the Cancun Ministerial in August 2003, WTO members agreed on a Decision[40] to waive the domestic market provision of the TRIPS article on compulsory licensing (Article 31(f)) for exports of pharmaceutical products for "HIV/AIDS, malaria, tuberculosis and other epidemics" to least developed countries (LDCs) and countries with insufficient manufacturing capacity. This Decision was incorporated as an amendment to the TRIPS agreement at the Hong Kong Ministerial in December 2005.

The amendment must be ratified by two-thirds of the 153 WTO member states. The deadline for ratification has been extended to December 30, 2011. Until then, the 2003 waiver continues in force. To date, the following WTO members have ratified the amendment: the United States, Switzerland, El Salvador, South Korea, Norway, India, the Philippines, Israel, Japan, Australia, Singapore, Hong Kong, China, the 27 countries of the European Union, Mauritius, Egypt, Mexico, Jordan, Brazil, Morocco, Albania, Macau, Canada, Bahrain, Colombia, Zambia, Nicaragua, Pakistan, the Former Yugoslav Republic of Macedonia, Uganda, Mongolia, Croatia, and Senegal.[41]

The system established by the WTO allows LDC and countries without sufficient manufacturing capacity to issue a compulsory license to a company in a country that can produce such a product. After a matching compulsory license is issued by the producer country, the drug can be manufacturing and exported subject to various notification requirements, quantity and safeguard restrictions. While several exporting countries have established laws and procedures for implementing this system, only Rwanda has availed itself to use the system to import HIV/AIDS medicines from a generic manufacturer in Canada.[42]

INTELLECTUAL PROPERTY PROTECTION AND DEVELOPMENT

The controversy over the relationship between IPR and development was engaged by the advent of the TRIPS Agreement, which for the first time placed IPR obligations on developing countries. Some hold that expansion of IPR is an obstacle to growth and development in less advanced countries, while others, with a diametrically opposing view, maintain that IPR are beneficial to both developed and developing countries.

Some IPR critics believe that a strong IPR regime may reduce developing countries' access to technology from advanced countries by imposing higher fees for technology licenses and production right, limiting their innovation and economic growth and development. For instance, Japan, Singapore, Taiwan, and South Korea enhanced their technological abilities and developed their economies through "reverse engineering" of foreign technologies.

Others claim that IPR promote technology transfer through increased trade, foreign investment, and licensing in the long-run by making a country more attractive to foreign partners. A 2002 OECD study concluded that stronger IPR laws, particularly enhanced patent standards, may be associated with increased foreign direct investment (FDI) and trade for developing countries over time, with variation by industries and level of development.[43] For instance, India experienced an increase in foreign investment and technology transfer once it expanded its patent protection. China offers a counterexample of a country with a weak IPR regime but high FDI and trade levels.

There is also evidence that IPR's impact on developing countries may vary by the level of development. One study suggests that IPR protection may offer more benefits for the more industrialized developing countries, such as Brazil and India, compared to other developing countries. Such industrializing economies could experience economic growth of as much as 0.5% annually through increased trade, FDI, and licensing.[44] Another study finds that rapid economic growth is associated with weak intellectual property regimes, but that developing countries with higher levels of per capita income may benefit economically from stronger IPR regimes.[45]

There is also concern that strengthened patent protection may drive up prices for medicines or delay the entry of generic drugs into the market, reducing access to HIV/AIDS treatments and other drugs. IPR supporters argue that strong IPR is critical to creating incentives for pharmaceutical innovations and suggest that reduced prices are no guarantee that needed goods will make it into the hands of individuals in developing countries due to political corruption, poverty, and poor social infrastructure.

World Intellectual Property Organization (WIPO)

In addition to the WTO, the other main multilateral venue for addressing IPR issues is the World Intellectual Property Organization (WIPO), a United Nations agency. Established in 1967, WIPO is charged with fostering the effective use and protection of intellectual property globally. WIPO's mandate focuses exclusively on intellectual property, in contrast to the WTO's broader international trade mandate. WIPO's antecedents are the 1883 Paris Convention for the Protection of Industry Property and the 1886 Berne Convention for the Protection of Literary and Artistic Work. Most of the substantive provisions of these two treaties are incorporated in the WTO's TRIPS Agreement. WIPO's primary function is to administer a group of IPR treaties which put forth minimum standards for member states (shown in Table 3). All international IPR treaties, save TRIPS, are administered by WIPO.

In order to address digital technology issues not dealt with in the TRIPS Agreement, WIPO established the WIPO Copyright Treaty (WCT) and WIPO Performance and Phonograms Treaty (WPPT) in 1996.[46] Recent WIPO efforts have focused on patent law. In June 2000, WIPO signatories adopted the Patent Law Treaty (PLT), which called for harmonization of patent procedures. This agreement went into force on April 28, 2005. Discussions began in May 2001 for the Substantive Patent Law Treaty (SPLT), which targets issues specifically related to patent grants, but stalled in 2006. Government leaders participating in the Group of 8 (G8) meeting in July 2008 called for "accelerated discussions" of the SPLT.[47]

WIPO's other functions include assisting member states through training programs, legislative information, intellectual property institutional development, automation and office modernization efforts, and public awareness activities. WIPO's enforcement activities are more limited than those of the WTO. Through its Advisory Committee on Enforcement (ACE), WIPO cooperates with member states to promote international coordination on enforcement activities.

With the emergence of the TRIPS Agreement, some observers question the relevance of WIPO. However, others contend that the TRIPS Agreement has given WIPO a new and stronger role. Through a 1996 agreement between the WTO and WIPO, the two organizations have agreed to work closely together to ensure the implementation of the TRIPS Agreement by member states through legal and technical assistance and technical cooperation.[48] In 1998, WIPO and WTO began a joint initiative based on the 1996 agreement to enhance their coordination of technical cooperation activities in order to assist developing countries, in particular, to fulfill their TRIPS commitments.[49]

Table 3. Summary of WIPO-Administered IPR Treaties.

Treaty	Date Concluded	Provisions
Intellectual Property Protection Treaties		
Paris Convention for the Protection of Industrial Property (Paris Convention)	1883 (entered into force 1884)	Protects industrial property (includes patents, marks, industrial designs, utility models, trade names, and geographic indications)
Berne Convention for the Protection of Literary and Artistic Works (Berne Convention)	1886 (entered into force 1886)	Protects literary and artistic works, providing right to control and receive payments for use
Madrid Agreement for the Repression of False and Deceptive Indications of Source on Goods (Madrid Agreement - Indications of Source)	1891	Requires States to seize imported goods with false/deceptive indications of source or to prohibit importation of such goods; open to States party to Paris Convention (1883)
Rome Convention for the Protection of Performers, Producers of Phonograms and Broadcasting Organizations (Rome Convention)	1961	Protects rights of performers against certain acts to which they have not agreed; protects rights of producers of phonograms, and broadcasting organizations to authorize/prohibit certain acts; open to States party to Berne Convention (1886)
Convention for the Protection of Producers of Phonograms Against Unauthorized Duplication of their Phonograms (Phonograms Convention)	1971	Protects producers of phonograms against unauthorized reproduction of their phonograms or importation of duplications for public distribution
Brussels Convention Relating to the Distribution of Programme-Carrying Signals Transmitted by Satellite (Brussels Convention)	1974	Protects against the unauthorized distribution of program-carrying signals transmitted by satellite
Nairobi Treaty on the Protection of the Olympic Symbol (Nairobi Treaty)	1981	Protects Olympic symbol against unauthorized commercial uses
Treaty on the International Registration of Audiovisual Works (Film Register Treaty)	1989	Establishes International Register for Audiovisual Works
Treaty on Intellectual Property in Respect to Integrated Circuits (Washington Treaty)	1989	Protects layout designs which display electrical components of an integrated circuit
Trademark Law Treaty (TLT)	1994	Streamlines national and regional trademark registration processes
WIPO Copyright Treaty (WCT)	1996 (entered into force 2002)	Special agreement under Berne Convention; grants exclusive rights to owners of copyright in computer programs and compilations of data/other material

Table 3. (Continued)

Treaty	Date Concluded	Provisions
WIPO Performances and Phonograms Treaty (WPPT)	1996 (entered into force 2002)	Grants exclusive rights to performers and phonogram producers
Patent Law Treaty (PLT)	2000 (entered into 2005)	Aims to harmonize and streamline national and regional patent application procedures and patents
Singapore Treaty on the Law of the Trademarks	2006 (not yet in force)	Builds on TLT (1994); aims to harmonize trademark registration procedures; has wider scope (includes communication technology developments)
Global Protection System Treaties		
Budapest Treaty on the International Recognition of the Deposit of Microorganisms for the Purposes of Patent Procedure (Budapest Treaty)	1977 (entered into force 1980)	Special agreement under Paris Convention (1883); requires States to recognize the deposit of a microorganism with any "international depositary authority"
Madrid Agreement Concerning the International Registration of Marks (Madrid Agreement -Marks)	1891	Requires seizure of imported goods with false/deceptive indication of source or prohibition of importation of such goods; open to States party to Paris Convention (1883)
Hague Agreement Concerning the International Registration of Industrial Designs (Hague Agreement)	1925 (entered into force 1928)	Allows protection of industrial designs in all member states on basis of single application with WIPO; three acts currently in force: 1934, 1960, and 1999 Acts
Lisbon Agreement for the Protection of Appellations of Origin and their International Registration (Lisbon Agreement)	1958	Provides international protection for geographical indications
Patent Cooperation Treaty (PCT)	1970 (entered into force 1978)	Establishes an international patent filing system; allows a single international patent application to have legal standing in all countries signatory to PCT; open to States party to Paris Convention (1883)
Protocol Relating to the Madrid Agreement (Madrid Protocol)	1989 (entered into force 1995)	Relates to Madrid Agreement (1891); seeks to make Madrid system more amenable to domestic laws of certain who are not yet signatories to Madrid Agreement; open to States party to Paris Convention (1883)
Classification Treaties		
Nice Agreement Concerning the International Classification of Goods and Services of the	1957 (entered into force 1961)	Establishes a classification of goods and services in order to register trademarks and service marks; open to

Table 3. (Continued)

Treaty	Date Concluded	Provisions
Purposes of the Registration of Marks (Nice Agreement)		States party to Paris Convention (1883)
Locarno Agreement Establishing an International Classification for Industrial Designs	1968 (entered into force 1971)	Establishes a classification for industrial designs; open to States party to Paris Convention (1883)
Strasbourg Agreement Concerning the Industrial Patent Classification (Strasbourg Agreement)	1971 (entered into force 1975)	Establishes the International Patent Classification (IPC); open to States party to Paris Convention (1883)
Vienna Agreement Establishing Classification of the Figurative Elements of Marks (Vienna Agreement)	1973 (entered into force 1985)	Establishes a classification for marks which consist/contain figurative components; open to States party to Paris Convention (1883)

Source: WIPO.

Free Trade Agreements

In recent years, the United States increasingly has focused on free trade agreements (FTAs) as an instrument to promote stronger IPR regimes by foreign trading partners. In general, the United States has viewed the TRIPS Agreement and WIPO-administered treaties as a minimum standard and has pursued higher IPR protection and enforcement levels through regional and bilateral agreements.

Trade Promotion Authority and Negotiating Objectives

Under Trade Promotion Authority (TPA), Congress delegates its constitutional authority to regulate foreign commerce to the President to negotiate and enter into certain free trade agreements (FTAs), and to have their implementing bills considered under expedited legislative procedures (no amendment, up-or-down vote), provided the President follows the guidelines, objectives, reporting, and consultation requirements mandated by Congress. IPR have become important negotiating objectives in grants of trade promotion authority; the most recent extension of that authority expired on July 1, 2007.

IPR negotiating objectives for FTAs were first enacted in trade promotion authority (then known as fast-track authority) by the Omnibus Trade and Competitiveness Act of 1988 (P.L. 100-418).

The act sought enactment and enforcement of adequate IPR protection from negotiating partners. It also sought to strengthen international rules, dispute settlement, and enforcement procedures through the GATT and other existing intellectual property conventions. This negotiating mandate led to the establishment of the TRIPS Agreement during the Uruguay Round and the IPR provisions in the North American Free Trade Agreement (NAFTA). In the intervening period since the 1988 Act, the TRIPS agreement came into force and the IPR provisions of NAFTA became the template for future bilateral or regional FTAs. Thus, the focus of IPR negotiating objectives shifted from creating to strengthening the IPR trade regime.

More recent FTA negotiations have been conducted under the Trade Promotion Authority Act of 2002 (P.L. 107-210), which included two broad IPR negotiating objectives. One broad objective was to apply the existing IPR protection to digital media. The negotiating objectives contained provisions to extend IPR protection to new and emerging technologies and to methods of transmission and dissemination. The language called for standards of enforcement to keep pace with technological change and to allow rights-holders the legal and technological protections for their works over the Internet and other new media.

A second broad objective of the Trade Promotion Authority Act of 2002 was to negotiate trade agreements in terms of IPR that "reflect a standard of protection similar to that found in U.S. law."[50] This phrase opened the door to the negotiation of provisions that go beyond the level of protection provided in the TRIPS agreement. Often referred to as "TRIPS-plus" provisions, these obligations include expanding coverage to new sectors; establishing more extensive standards of protection; and reducing the flexibility options available in TRIPS. Some of the new measures also address technological innovations that have come about since the TRIPS Agreement.

In May 2007, the Bush Administration and Congress concluded a bipartisan agreement on trade policy that addressed some Members' concerns about the implications of enhanced IPR on developing countries' ability to meet public health needs.[51] In particular, congressional leadership sought to ensure that pending FTAs allowed trading partners to have enough flexibility to meet their IPR obligations and to be able to promote access to life-saving medicines, while otherwise meeting their international IPR protection and enforcement obligations. IPR language previously negotiated in the FTAs with the developing countries of Peru, Panama, and Colombia subsequently were modified to reflect the agreement. Because Korea is an industrialized country, the United States did not significantly scale-down the patent protection obligations in the U.S.-Korea FTA.

Current IPR-Related U.S. FTA Activity

In 2011, the Obama Administration may ask Congress to approve a free trade agreement (FTA) with South Korea, as well as FTAs with Colombia and Panama. These three FTAs were negotiated by the Bush Administration, but have not been implemented.

Meanwhile, the Obama Administration has entered into negotiations with participants in the Trans-Pacific Partnership (TPP) Agreement—Australia, Brunei, Chile, New Zealand, Peru, Malaysia, Singapore, and Vietnam. The objective is to build on U.S. trade ties in the region already established in FTAs with Australia, Chile, and Singapore and to provide a high-standard framework for expanded free trade in the region.[20] IPR, particularly in the area of pharmaceuticals, may prove to be a contentious issue in the negotiation of the TPP.

In addition, the Obama Administration has been conducting negotiations on the Anti-Counterfeiting Trade Agreement (ACTA), a proposed agreement being negotiated by Australia, Canada, the 27 member states of the European Union, Japan, South Korea, Mexico, Morocco, New Zealand, Singapore, Switzerland, and the United States. Negotiations on the ACTA Agreement began under the Bush Administration. The ACTA would build on the minimum standards for IPR protection and enforcement set forth by the TRIPS Agreement. It is being crafted independent of any existing international organization or agreement. The eleventh and final round of negotiations concluded on October 2, 2010, and the ACTA participants released to the public a draft text of the agreement. ACTA participants are working to resolve outstanding issues in the agreement.[52]

Central IPR Standards in U.S. FTAs

What follows is a discussion of some of the central patent and copyright standards sought in FTAs that are currently in force or have been signed by the United States (see Table 4).[53]

Patents

Patent protection is arguably the most contentious area of U.S. FTA negotiations on IPR issues. While the United States and other developed countries advocate for strong patent protections in order to promote innovation, there is concern that such stringent protections may delay developing countries' access to generic drugs and increase prices. Many of the FTAs in force include TRIPS-plus patent provisions, the most prominent of which are patent term length extensions, linkages between regulatory authority and patent status, data protection, compulsory licensing and parallel importation. The FTAs with Peru, Panama, and Colombia respond to the concerns of some Members of Congress over provisions that could restrict access to medicines in these countries and contain less ambitious standards for pharmaceutical patents, compared to previously negotiated FTAs. Pharmaceutical industry advocates express concern that this scale-down in patent protection in these FTAs may set a precedent for future FTA negotiations.[54]

Patent Term Extensions: Many FTAs include provisions for mandatory patent term length extensions beyond the TRIPS Agreement obligation of patent protection terms of twenty years from the filing date. These FTAs allow for extensions in cases of "unreasonable" delays in the issuance of patents due to the regulatory review or administrative process. Patent holders contend that such measures enhance the ability of rights-holders to recoup the costs of research and development of new products. However, there is concern that patent terms extensions may delay the entry of generic drugs into a market. In a scale-down from TRIPS-plus obligations, FTAs with Peru, Colombia, and Panama state that patent term restorations for pharmaceutical products are optional.

Patent Linkages: In general, the term "patent linkage" refers to the attachment of regulatory approval for the marketing of a drug with the status of a patent. If a patent exists, the FDA and its counterparts in other countries may not grant marketing approval for a generic version of a drug that is patented in the country without the permission of the patent holder. Patent linkage is a common provision in the trade agreements obtained by the United States. This presents a departure from TRIPS, under which generic drug manufacturers are able to apply for marketing approval without the patent owner's permission and prior to the expiration of the patent; this may reduce the time it takes for generic drugs to enter a market once the patent expires.[55] In light of developing country concerns about delays in access to generic versions of drugs, FTAs signed with Peru, Panama, and Colombia do not tie marketing approval for a generic drug with the patent status of its brand name drug.

Data Protection: In cases where the patent holders must submit undisclosed data regarding the safety or effectiveness of new pharmaceutical or agricultural products in order to market them, the TRIPS Agreement requires members to take measures to protect such data from disclosure and unfair commercial use. The TRIPS agreement does not prescribe any time period for this protection. Recent U.S. FTAs take these standards a step further, generally requiring a five-year period of marketing exclusivity for the patent holder, which typically begins from the date the product is approved in the country. Under this TRIPS-plus provision, generic drug manufacturers who want to market and distribute a generic version of a drug while the data exclusivity period is in effect must conduct their own clinical trials and submit their own findings to the national drug regulatory authority; they cannot rely on the findings submitted by the patent holder. Some critics contend that such provisions may raise the cost of manufacturing generic versions of patented drugs, as well as delay access to generic forms of drugs. The FTAs with Peru, Panama, and Colombia now include provisions that may reduce data exclusivity terms of five years by a minimum of six months in practice.[56]

Compulsory Licensing: A compulsory license is an authorization by a government for third parties (such as a company or the government itself) for the manufacture or use of a product under patent without the permission of the rights- holder. The TRIPS Agreement permits signatories to issue compulsory licenses for patented devices and provide compensation to the owner of the patent and does not limit the situations in which such licenses may be issued. The third party must have attempted to obtain permission from the patent holder, although this requirement is waived in times of national emergency or other extenuating circumstances. U.S. FTAs with Australia and Singapore limit attaining compulsory licenses only for domestic use and to situations of remedying antitrust violations or in situations of public non-commercial use, national emergency, or other cases of extreme need. Also under these FTAs, the patent holder is under no obligation to provide test data, technical know-how or other undisclosed information for the patent subject to compulsory license. The compulsory license provisions have not been included in FTAs with developing countries.

Parallel Importation: Parallel imports, also known as grey-market goods, refer to goods imported into a country without permission of the rights-holder after those goods were legitimately sold elsewhere. Parallel importation relates to the concept of territorial exhaustion of IPR, which governs the extent of IPR after the first sale. Under a national system of exhaustion practiced in the United States, IPR are exhausted domestically after the first sale, but not abroad, thus prohibiting trade in those goods without permission of the rights-holder. Under an international system, IPR are exhausted at the first sale for any destination, and such goods can be exported freely. Article 6 of the TRIPS specifically excludes issues arising from exhaustion of IPR from WTO dispute settlement, allowing each member to adopt different exhaustion regimes. Thus, TRIPS does not address the issue of parallel imports. Some developing countries contend that parallel importation is an alternative method for governments to increase access to medicines in the absence of a compulsory license.[57] Pharmaceutical companies have voiced concerns that this practice threatens their ability to engage in price differentiation between different markets. U.S. FTAs negotiated with Australia, Singapore, and Morocco disallow parallel importing of patented products. Subsequent U.S. negotiated FTAs have not included this provision, due to language included in the Science, State, Justice, and Commerce, and Related Agencies, Appropriations Act of 2006 (P.L. 109-108), which prohibited the use of such provisions.

BIODIVERSITY AND TRADITIONAL KNOWLEDGE

International trade negotiations increasingly have focused on the protection of plant and animal inventions, new plant varieties, traditional knowledge, and folklore. Some indigenous communities in developing countries and international non-governmental organizations have expressed concern about the use of patents to provide private rights for traditional knowledge and genetic material; the commercial use of such resources by entities other than the indigenous communities or countries from which such resources are derived; and the distribution of benefits from commercial use. The United States, other advanced countries, and business groups favor treating traditional knowledge and genetic material as intellectual property and protecting these resources through an IPR framework.

Article 27.3(b) of the TRIPS Agreement permits Member states to exempt "plants and animals other than microorganisms, and essentially biological processes" from patentability. TRIPS requires Members to protect plant varieties through patent protection, some other system ("sui generis"), or a combination of the two. Paragraph 19 of the Doha Declaration added another dimension to the issue by requiring the TRIPS Council to probe the relationship between the TRIPS Agreement, the UN Convention on Biological Diversity (CBD), and traditional knowledge and folklore. These issues also are being discussed in WIPO's Intergovernmental Committee on Intellectual Property and Genetic Resources, Traditional Knowledge, and Folklore (IGC).

India, Brazil, and Peru, among other countries, contend that patent applicants should be required to disclose the source of genetic materials, including plant life and traditional knowledge, before obtaining patents. The United States and the European Union have advocated for national systems in which companies are granted permission to research genetic materials and are obligated to share benefits from patents derived from those genetic products.

Some earlier U.S. FTAs have required signatories to provide protection for plants, animals, and plant varieties. The recent FTAs with Peru, Panama, and Colombia do not mandate patentability for plants and animals, but state that the countries should take efforts to expand patent coverage to these areas and to maintain this protection once it is offered. Side-letters in the three FTAs state the signatories' recognition of the importance of biodiversity and traditional knowledge and pledge the countries to work together to address these issues through the IGC.

Copyright

In the area of copyright protection, the United States has pursued certain TRIPS-plus measures in FTAs, such as extending copyright terms; including anti-circumvention provisions; and protecting rights-management information in its FTAs. The TRIPS Agreement does not mention any obligations regarding rights-management information, which is "electronic information that identifies a protected work, its author, and terms and conditions of use,"[58] perhaps due to the fact these technologies were not available at the time. In contrast, U.S.-negotiated trade agreements prohibit the removal or alteration of such information.

While patent protection has experienced policy shifts in the FTAs with Peru, Panama, and Colombia, copyright protection provisions have remained fairly consistent through the

FTAs. In general, FTA signatories are obligated to provide an additional twenty years of copyright protection. This brings the minimum copyright term to seventy years from the death of the author or authorized publication, compared to fifty under the TRIPS Agreement. Responding to technological innovations not discussed in the TRIPS Agreement, many of the FTAs require trading partners to outlaw circumvention of copyrighted works. These provisions build on the U.S. Digital Millennium Copyright Act (DMCA) of 1998.[59] Also based on the DMCA, many FTAs contain provisions that regulate the liability of Internet service providers (ISPs) for copyright infringement that occurs within their networks. Under the FTAs, ISPs are provided limited immunity from copyright liability in certain kinds of infringing activities if they comply with regulations. For instance, ISPs must block access to or remove infringing materials as soon as they are aware of the infringement. Copyright holders argue that it is necessary for ISPs to assist in enforcing copyright for copyright laws to be effective. However, critics claim that these provisions impose excessive burdens on ISPs, reduce the rights of internet users, and limit the policy flexibility of FTA signatories in determining their own IPR regimes.

Table 4. Patent and Copyright Provisions in the TRIPS Agreement and U.S. FTAs.

Intellectual Property Forms	TRIPS Provisions	General TRIPS-Plus Provisions in FTAs	Scale-down of TRIPS-Plus Standards
Patents			
Patent term extensions	No provisions	Mandatory extensions in cases of unreasonable delays in patent grants/ regulatory approval *Jordan (Article 4.23.a), Chile (Article 17.9.6; 17.9.2a), Singapore (Article 16.7.7; 18.8.4a), Australia (Article 17.9.8; 17.10.4), Morocco (Article 15.9.7; 15.10.3), CAFTA-DR (Article 15.9.6; 15.10.2), Bahrain (Article 14.8.6),Oman (Article 15.8.6), Korea (Article 18.8.6)*	Optional extensions in cases of unreasonable delays in patent grants/Regulatory approval *NAFTA (Article 1709.12) Peru (Article 16.9.6), Panama (Article 16.9.6), Colombia (Article 16.9.6)*
Market approval linked to patent status	No provisions *NAFTA (no mention), Jordan (no linkage, but patent owner must be notified if another entity is seeking marketing approval for generic version of patented product, Article 4.23.b)*	National regulatory authorities cannot provide marketing approval for a generic version of a patented drug without permission from rights-holder; also requires notification of rights-holder if marketing permitted *Chile (Article 17.10.2b), Singapore (16.8.4c), Australia (Article 17.10.4), Morocco (Article 15.10.4), CAFTA-DR (Article 15.10.2), Bahrain (Article*	Eliminates mandate that regulatory authorities cannot approve a generic drug for marketing if patent for drug in place *Peru (Article 16.10.4), Panama (Article 15.10.4), Colombia (Article 16.10.4)*

Table 4. (Continued)

Intellectual Property Forms	TRIPS Provisions	General TRIPS-Plus Provisions in FTAs	Scale-down of TRIPS-Plus Standards
		14.9.4), Oman (15.9.4), Korea (Article 18.9.5)	
Protection for undisclosed test or other data	Members must protect data from unfair commercial use (Article 39.3) *Jordan (Article 4.22)*	Provides for at least five years of data exclusivity from date of approval in country for pharmaceuticals that contain new chemical products *NAFTA (Article 1711.6), Bahrain (Article 14.9.1), Oman (Article 15.9(1-2), CAFTA-DR (Article 15.10.1), Singapore (Article 16.8(1-3)), Australia (Article 17.10.1), Morocco (Article 15.10.1), Chile (Article 17.10.1), Korea (Article 18.9(1-2))*	Provides for at least five years of marketing exclusivity from date of approval in country of first filing if new drug is granted marketing approval within six months in country of second filing *Peru (Article 16.10.2), Panama (Article 15.10.4), Colombia (Article 16.10.2)*
Issuance of compulsory licenses	Some restrictions in issuance of compulsory licenses; circumstances under which licenses can be issued not limited (Article 13) *NAFTA (Article 1709.10),*	Limits issuance of compulsory license to specific cases: Correcting anti-competitive practices, public noncommercial contexts, national emergencies, and other extremely urgent situations *Jordan (Article 4.20), Singapore (Article 16.7.6), Australia (Article 17.9.7)*	Not discussed *Chile (no mention), Morocco (no mention), CAFTA-DR (no mention), Bahrain (no mention), Oman (no mention) Peru (no mention), Panama (no mention), Colombia (no mention), (no mention)*
Parallel importing of patented products	TRIPS will not be used to discuss IPR exhaustion (Article 6) *Jordan (no mention), Chile (no mention), CAFTA-DR (no mention), Bahrain (no mention), Oman (no mention)*	Parallel importation can be restricted or prohibited *NAFTA (Article 1709.5, 1709.9), Singapore (Article 16.7.2), Morocco (Article 15.9.4), Australia (Article 17.9.4)*	Not discussed *Peru (no mention), Panama (no mention), Colombia (no mention), Korea (no mention)*
Biodiversity and traditional knowledge	Members may exclude plants and animals from patentability (microorganisms and non-biological and micro-biological processes must be eligible for patents); must provide protection of plant varieties (Article 27.3(b))	Countries shall make patents available for plants and animals *Morocco (Article 15.9.2, plants 7and animals mentioned, plant varieties are not mentioned)*	Members may exclude plants and animals from patentability, but shall take reasonable effort to provide patent protection for plants or animals and maintain protection once offered *Chile (Article 17.9.2, mentions plants but not animals), CAFTADR (Article 15.9.2), Peru (Article 16.9.2), Panama (Article 15.9.2), Colombia (Article 16.9.2)*

Table 4. (Continued)

Intellectual Property Forms	TRIPS Provisions	General TRIPS-Plus Provisions in FTAs	Scale-down of TRIPS-Plus Standards
	NAFTA (Article 1709.3), Bahrain (Article 14.8.(1-2)), Oman (Article 15.8.2, plants not discussed), Jordan, (no mention), Singapore (no mention), Australia (no mention), Korea (no mention)		
Copyrights			
Rights-management information	Not discussed *NAFTA (no mention), Jordan (no mention)*	Outlaws removal or alternation of information *Chile (Article 17.5.6), Australia (Article 17.4.8), Singapore (Article 16.4.8), Morocco (Article 15.5.9), CAFTA-DR (Article 15.5.8), Bahrain (Article 14.4.8), Oman (Article 15.4.8), Peru (Article 16.7.5), Panama (Article 15.5.8), Colombia (Article 16.7.5), Korea (Article 18.4.8)*	
Term of protection	No less than 50 years from authorized publication (Article 12) *NAFTA (Article 1705.4), Jordan (no mention)*	No less than 70 years from death of author or authorized publication *Chile (Article 17.5.4), Singapore (Article 16.4.4), Australia (Article 17.4.4), Morocco (Article 15.5.5), CAFTA-DR (Article 15.5.4), Bahrain (Article 14.4.4), Oman (Article 15.4.4), Peru (Article 16.5.5), Panama (Article 15.5.4), Colombia (Article 16.5.5), Korea (Article 18.4.4)*	
Circumvention of copyrighted work	Not discussed *NAFTA (no mention)*	Signatories must agree to prohibit circumvention *Jordan (Article 4.6), Chile (Article 17.5.5), Singapore (Article 16.4.7), Australia (Article 17.4.7), Morocco (Article 15.5.8), CAFTA-DR (Article 15.5.7), Bahrain (Article 14.4.7), Oman (Article 15.4.7), Peru (Article 16.7.4), Panama (Article 15.5.7), Colombia (Article 16.7.4), Korea (Article 18.4.7)*	
ISP Liability	Not discussed *NAFTA (no mention), Jordan (no mention)*	ISPs are provided with limited liability in certain situations of copyright infringement on their servers if they comply with regulations *Chile (Article 17.11.23), Singapore (Article 16.9.22), Australia (Article 17.11.29), Morocco, CAFTA-DR (Article 15.11.27), Bahrain, Oman (Article 15.10.29), Peru (Article 16.11.29), Panama (Article 15.11.27), Colombia (Article 16.11.29), Korea (Article 18.10.30)*	

Note: When there is no mention of an issue in an FTA, the TRIPS standard generally holds.

U.S. TRADE LAW

Special 301

Section 301 of the Trade Act of 1974 (P.L. 93-618), as amended, is the principle U.S. statute for identifying foreign trade barriers due to inadequate intellectual property protection. The 1988 Omnibus Trade and Competitiveness Act (P.L. 100-418) strengthened section 301 by creating “Special 301” provisions, which require the USTR to conduct an annual review of foreign countries' intellectual property policies and practices. By April 30th of each year, the USTR must identify countries that do not offer "adequate and effective" protection of IPR or "fair and equitable market access to United States person that rely upon intellectual property rights." According to an amendment to the Special 301 provisions by the Uruguay Round Agreements Act (P.L. 103-465), the USTR can identify a country as denying sufficient intellectual property protection even if the country is complying with its TRIPS commitments. These findings are submitted in the USTR's annual "Special 301" report.

Special 301 Country Lists

Within 30 days of submitting the annual National Trade Estimates of Foreign Trade Barriers report, the USTR must determine which of the identified countries are "Priority Foreign Countries." Countries that "have the most onerous or egregious acts, policies or practices that deny intellectual property protection and limit market access to U.S. persons or firms depending on intellectual property rights protection" and "have the greatest adverse impact (actual or potential) on the relevant United States products" may be identified as "Priority Foreign Countries." These countries may be investigated under section 301 provisions of the Trade Act of 1974. The USTR cannot identify countries as Priority Foreign Countries if they have entered into good faith negotiations or have made significant progress in improving their intellectual property protection record.[60]

If a country is named as a "Priority Foreign Country," the USTR must launch an investigation into that country's IPR practices. This investigation is conducted in a manner similar to a "Section 301" investigation; the USTR must determine a course of action within six months (9 months if a determination of complex circumstances is made). The USTR may suspend trade concessions and impose import restrictions or duties, or enter into a binding agreement with the priority country that would eliminate the act, policy, or practice that is the subject of the action to be taken. Since the advent of the WTO and its recourse to dispute settlement, the use of the first option may lead to the initiation of dispute settlement proceedings at the WTO for member countries, rather than unilateral retaliation. For countries outside the WTO, the possibility of trade sanctions remain.

The USTR also has created several administrative categories for country identification in the Special 301 Report. "Priority Watch List" countries are those whose acts, policies, and practices warrant concern, but do not meet all of the criteria for identification as a Priority Foreign Country. The USTR may place a country on the Priority Watch List when the country lacks proper intellectual property protection and has a market of significant U.S. interest. "Watch List" countries have intellectual property protection inadequacies that are less severe than those on the Priority Watch List, but still attract U.S. attention. Just being on one of the Special 301 lists may induce countries to improve their IPR protection. Finally, countries identified for "Section 306" are monitored for compliance with bilateral intellectual property agreements used to resolve investigations under section 301. Additionally, the USTR launches out-of-cycle reviews (OCRs) on countries to monitor their progress on intellectual property issues. OCRs are conducted on countries that USTR considers to require further review and may result in status changes for the following year's Special 301 report.

SPECIAL 301 REPORT FOR 2010

For the *2010 Special 301 Report*, the USTR reviewed the IPR policies and practices of 77 countries. [61]

- Despite some improvements, China and Russia remain top concerns for the Administration due to their inadequate IPR regimes.
- The USTR placed eleven countries on the Priority Watch List: Algeria, Argentina, Canada, Chile, China, India, Indonesia, Pakistan, Russia, Thailand, and Venezuela.
- The USTR placed another 29 countries were placed on the Watch List.
- No countries were designated as Priority Foreign Countries. Paraguay was identified for Section 306 monitoring.
- The USTR announced that it would conduct OCRs for the Philippines and Thailand to monitor these nations' progress on IPR and to evaluate their Special 301 status.
- Israel's status in the Special 301 Report is pending, following the conclusion of an OCR and an understanding reached by the United States and Israel on several issues in Israel's IPR regime for pharmaceutical products.[62]
- The USTR removed the Czech Republic, Hungary, and Poland from the Special 301Watch List for significant improvement in their protection and enforcement of IPR. Following an OCR on Saudi Arabia, the USTR decided to remove Saudi Arabia from the Watch List on the basis of improvements in IPR enforcement, prosecution, and transparency issues.

Country Identification Factors

Identification of countries for the "Special 301" lists is a lengthy process of information gathering and analysis based on the USTR's annual trade barriers report and consultations with a wide variety of sources, including government agencies, industry groups, other private sector representatives, Congressional leaders, and foreign governments. The Special 301 statute is the overall guideline for identifying countries for the various lists. However, placements are country-specific and, according to a USTR official, take into consideration a host of factors, several of which are mentioned in the Special 301 report.[63] These include the level and scope of the country's IPR infringement and their impact on the U.S. economy. Other considerations include the strength of the country's IPR laws and enforcement of IPR laws. The USTR also evaluates progress made by the country in improving IPR protection and enforcement in the past year. However, even significant progress oftentimes does not change the position or inclusion of a country on the lists. For instance, the USTR may decide not to upgrade a country from the Priority Watch List to the Watch List so that it can continue monitoring the country's intellectual property practices. Also, the USTR may note significant progress made by a country but not remove the country from the Special 301 list in order to continue highlighting concerns about the country's practices and limit backsliding. Another consideration for the USTR is the sincerity of the country's commitment to multilateral and bilateral trade agreements. There is no weighting criteria for the factors or a formula to determine the placement of a country on the watch list. Furthermore, no particular threshold exists for determining when a country should be upgraded or downgraded on the list.

Some observers speculate that the Special 301 rankings are subject to external influences. The lack of a specific framework for placing countries, aside from the general directives from the Special 301 statute, has raised concerns that foreign policy considerations affect the process. For example, an IIPA representative suggested that USTR placement of countries is influenced by geopolitical reasons.[64] This source cites Russia as an example of a country with high IPR infringement that could be named as a Priority Foreign Country but is not due to unrelated foreign policy considerations. Other observers of U.S. trade policy suggest that pharmaceutical companies have a stronghold on policy direction. Oxfam International, a confederation of poverty-alleviation organizations, contends that the U.S. government's policy on patents "is still largely influenced by the narrow commercial interests of the giant pharmaceutical companies."[65] A USTR official stated that the interests of pharmaceutical companies do not override concerns by other interest groups in evaluating country placement for the Special 301 report. The official emphasized that all industry group submissions are given fair and due consideration.[66]

Section 337

Section 337 of the Tariff Act of 1930 (19 U.S.C. 1337), as amended, prohibits unfair methods of competition or other unfair acts in the importation of products into the United States. It also prohibits the importation of articles that infringe valid U.S. patents, copyrights, processes, trademarks, semiconductor products produced by infringing a protected mask work, or protected design rights. While the statute has been utilized to counter imports of products judged to be produced by unfair competition, monopolistic, or anti-competitive practices, it has become increasingly used for its IPR enforcement functions in recent years. Under the statute, the import or sale of an infringing product is illegal only if a U.S. industry is producing an article covered by the relevant IPR exists or is in the process of being established. However, unlike other trade remedies such as antidumping or countervailing duty actions, no showing of injury due to the import is required.

The U.S. International Trade Commission (ITC) administers section 337 proceedings. USITC must investigate complaints either brought to it or ones commenced under its own initiative. An administrative law judge (ALJ) provides an initial determination (ID) to the ITC which can accept the ID or order a further review of it in whole or in part. If the ITC finds a violation, it may issue two types of remedies: exclusion orders or cease and desist orders. The ITC may issue either a limited or general exclusion order enforced by U.S. Customs. A general exclusion order directs U.S. Customs to keep out all infringing articles regardless of the source. More commonly, a limited exclusion order is employed to exclude infringing articles from the firm subject to the ITC's investigation. Alternatively, the ITC may enforce a cease and desist order to stop the sale of the infringing product in the United States. However, the ITC may consider several public interest criteria and decline to issue a remedy. Also, the President may disapprove a remedial order during a 60 day period for "policy reasons," which has been interpreted to mean national security reasons.[67]

During FY2009, the ITC reported a total of 85 active section 337 investigations and ancillary proceedings, comparable to the FY2008 level. Of the 85 active investigations in FY2009, 29 constituted of new section 337 investigations and 7 were new ancillary proceedings stemming from previously concluded section 337 investigations. The section 337 investigations frequently involved advanced technology areas, such as integrated circuit, computer, telecommunications, and other electronic technologies. Over 60% of the new section 337 investigations that were active in FY2009 involved cases of alleged patent infringement. In FY2009, the ITC issued three general exclusion orders, eight limited exclusion orders, and 23 cease-and-desist orders.[68]

Generalized System of Preferences

The Generalized System of Preferences (GSP) is a program that provides preferential duty-free entry to certain products from designated developing countries. The purpose of the program is to foster economic growth in developing countries by increasing their export markets. The Trade Act of 1974 authorized the GSP for a ten-year time frame, and the program has been renewed from time to time. Most recently, in 2006, Congress extended GSP through December 31, 2010.[69]

Although the GSP is non-reciprocal, it can be used to promote stronger intellectual property protection and enforcement abroad. Under the GSP statute, the President must consider a set of mandatory criteria that a country must fulfill in order to be designated as a GSP beneficiary. Additionally, the President may evaluate a country on the basis of certain discretionary criteria, including the country's provision of IPR protection.[70]

The GSP program undergoes an annual review by the GSP Subcommittee of the Trade Policy Staff Committee (TPSC), which is headed by the USTR. As part of its evaluation, the TPSC addresses concerns about specific country practices (such as intellectual property protection) and makes recommendations to the President. For 2009, the USTR continued to evaluate IPR protection in Lebanon, Russia, and Uzbekistan on the basis of IIPA petitions for ongoing GSP reviews.[71]

U.S. Agency Functions and Funding for IPR

The United States has a complex apparatus for supporting intellectual property rights, with responsibilities cutting across many different federal government agencies. Protection activities include developing IPR policy, informing and advising Congress about IPR-related issues, participating in international trade negotiations to promote IPR, and providing IPR training and technical assistance in other countries. Enforcement activities involve the conduct of criminal investigations in the United States and abroad, interdiction of pirated and counterfeit goods, and monitoring of compliance with trade agreements. Enforcement also involves capacity-building activities to foster stronger IPR law enforcement in other countries.

It is difficult to obtain a complete picture of the magnitude of federal budget devoted to intellectual property laws. Some of these agencies perform their IPR related activities within existing budget parameters, and do not differentiate specific sums devoted to IPR-related activities. What follows is a discussion of the various IPR functions of U.S. agencies.

Department of Commerce (Commerce)

Two agencies within the Department of Commerce, the Patent and Trademark Office (PTO) and the International Trade Administration (ITA), address IPR issues.[72]

United States Patent and Trademark Office (PTO)

The PTO administers the U.S. laws pertaining to patents and trademarks. The agency processes patent and trademark applications, issues patents and registers trademarks, and circulates patent and trademark information. The PTO develops IPR protection and enforcement policy and collaborates with other agencies to develop intellectual property provisions in FTAs and other international agreements. Additionally, the PTO offers training, technical assistance, and trade capacity building programs to assist in promoting strong IPR regimes in foreign countries.[73] The PTO does not have jurisdiction over determining patent and trademark infringements; such determinations and remedies are made at the U.S. federal district court level or through the U.S. International Trade Commission's section 337 proceedings (discussed above).[74] The PTO is fully funded through fees generated from patent and trademark applications. The Consolidated Appropriations Act, 2010 (P.L. 111-117) provided $1.89 billion in budgetary authority to the PTO for FY2010, down from $2.01 billion provided for FY2009 (P.L. 111-8).

International Trade Administration (ITA)

The ITA administers many of the international trade programs of the Department of Commerce, include aspects involving IPR. The ITA monitors foreign countries' progress in implementing intellectual property agreements; reviews Generalized System of Preferences (GSP) petitions submitted by industry and coordinates the Commerce Department's response to these petitions; represents the Commerce Department at the WTO TRIPS Council; meets with trading partners to advance U.S. intellectual property interests abroad; and works with U.S. businesses and industry groups to make sure that IPR-related trade concerns are addressed.[75] For FY2010, the Consolidated Appropriations Act, 2010 (P.L. 111-117) provided the ITA with $456.20 million (including both direct appropriation and anticipated receipts from fees), up from $429.9 million provided in FY2009 (P.L. 111-8).

Department of Justice (DOJ)

The DOJ enforces criminal laws that protect IPR in the United States and internationally through the prosecution of intellectual property cases. The Civil Division's Office of Consumer Litigation specializes in intellectual property cases involving public health and safety. The Federal Bureau of Investigation (FBI) has an intellectual property enforcement program focusing on those intellectual property crimes that have the most bearing on national and economic security, such as trade secret theft, Internet piracy, and counterfeit good trafficking.[76] In addition to enforcement activities, the DOJ also works with Congress to develop laws that increase protection of IPR and provides training and technical assistance programs on IPR enforcement through its Criminal Division. The Consolidated Appropriations Act, 2010 (P.L. 111-117) provided $7.66 billion to the FBI for FY2010, up from the FY2009 level of $7.07 billion (P.L. 111-8).

Department of Homeland Security (DHS)

The DHS, through its Customs and Border Protection (CPB) unit and Immigration and Customs Enforcement (ICE) unit, conducts intellectual property rights enforcement activities. Neither DHS unit has a line item for IPR enforcement. The ICE and the FBI jointly run the National Intellectual Property Rights Coordination Center that coordinates U.S. Government domestic and international law enforcement activities.[77]

Customs and Border Protection (CBP)

Taking the lead in day-to-day IPR enforcement activities at the U.S. border, the CBP is responsible for detecting and seizing counterfeit and pirated goods entering the United States and determining penalties for infringement.[78] CBP has the authority to determine whether or not imports infringe federally registered trademarks and copyrights and to detain or seize such infringing goods. Owners of copyrights and trademarks are able to record information about their rights in the CBP's electronic IPR database. As noted earlier, in contrast to trademarks and copyrights, CBP does not have the jurisdiction to make determinations about patent infringements. However, it is able to block imports determined by the ITC to infringe a U.S. patent by a Section 337 investigation.[79] For FY2010, the Consolidated Appropriations Act, 2010 provided $8.07 billion in budget authority to CBP, up from $7.60 billion in FY2009.

Immigration and Customs Enforcement (ICE)

ICE is charged with investigating violations of U.S. law that are connected with U.S. borders. ICE "identifies, investigates, apprehends, and removes" international criminal groups and other criminals. ICE conducts inquiries into the importation and distribution of counterfeit goods. ICE activities are closely linked with those of CBP. For instance, when CBP identifies and seizes counterfeit goods, the issue is referred to ICE for criminal investigation. Likewise, information obtained from ICE activities that is relevant to identifying and apprehending counterfeit shipments is provided to CBP.[80] For FY2010, the Consolidated Appropriations Act, 2010 provided $5.34 billion in budget authority to ICE, up from $4.93 billion in FY2009.

Food and Drug Administration (FDA)

The FDA, which is an agency of the Department of Health and Human Services (DHHS), is responsible for protecting public health by ensuring the safety and effectiveness of medicines, food, and other products. As part of its activities, the FDA works to protect consumers against counterfeit medicines. To combat the entry of foreign counterfeit drugs into the U.S. drug supply, the FDA works in conjunction with the CBP to conduct border inspections of FDA-regulated products. The FDA also engages in foreign inspections to ensure that foreign manufacturers meet FDA quality and labeling requirements. Funding for preventing counterfeits from entering the United States is part of overall FDA import safety efforts.[81] The enacted FY2010 Agricultural appropriation, P.L. 111-80, contained $2.36 billion in budget authority for the FDA, up from $2.05 billion for FY2009.

Copyright Office

The Copyright Office of the Library of Congress administers U.S. copyright law by registering claims to copyright and related documents, including "assignments or transfers of rights" and maintains information on registrations, recordings, compulsory licenses, and other copyright-related actions. Additionally, the Copyright Office provides legal and technical expertise on national and international copyright issues to the U.S. government. The Copyright Office also works with other federal agencies to provide assistance and advice in negotiations for international intellectual property agreements, as well as technical assistance to foreign countries crafting their own copyright laws.[82] The enacted FY2010 Legislative appropriation, P.L. 111-68, contained $20.9 million in new budget authority (not including authority to spend $33.3 million in receipts) for the Copyright Office, up from $18.3 million in new budget authority in FY2009 (not including authority to spend $33.3 million receipts).

Copyright Office appropriations also specify funding for IPR-related activities in developing countries. As in previous years, the FY2010 appropriations act provided $100,000 to the International Copyright Institute for such activities.

Department of State (State)

State represents U.S. views in both bilateral and multilateral arenas. State works to build international consensus for intellectual property rights enforcement. Information from State's foreign postings informs the USTR Special 301 review. In particular, the Bureau of International Narcotics Control and Law Enforcement (INCLE) works to combat intellectual property piracy, while the Bureau of Energy, Economics and Business Affairs supports stronger international IPR standards to fight global piracy and counterfeiting.[83] As in previous years, the Consolidated Appropriations Act, 2010 (P.L. 111-117) provided $5 million from the INCLE Account for combating copyright piracy (Section 688).

U.S. Agency for International Development (AID)

AID funds training and technical assistance to improve the compliance with the TRIPS Agreement and bilateral trade agreements with the United States. Funding for these projects generally have been undertaken by regional or country missions; there is no separate budgetary line item for IPR enforcement and training.[84]

United States Trade Representative (USTR)

The USTR is the lead trade agency of the United States government. Through its annual Special 301 report, USTR is charged with monitoring the adequacy and effectiveness of IPR protection of our trading partners as well as their compliance with bilateral and multilateral trade agreements, to identify countries not in compliance with such agreements, and to negotiate with those countries better compliance. USTR also advances greater protection and enforcement of IPR in its negotiations of U.S. free trade agreements. Additionally, USTR works to implement the Administration's STOP! Initiative, which draws together the major federal government agencies, private sector groups, and trading partners to take targeted action in fighting piracy and counterfeiting.[85] The FY2010 funding level for USTR was $47.83 million, under the Consolidated Appropriations Act, 2010 (P.L. 111-117), up from the FY2009 funding level of $47.3 million. Explanatory language in H.Rept. 111-149, accompanying P.L. 111-117, encouraged the USTR to continue prioritizing IPR issues with China, Russia, and Canada in bilateral and multilateral trade negotiations.

United States International Trade Commission (ITC)

The ITC is a quasi-judicial federal government agency responsible for investigating and arbitrating complaints of unfair trade practices. The ITC adjudicates allegations of imported products that infringe U.S. patents, trademarks, and copyrights through its section 337 proceedings (see above). The primary remedy employed by the ITC is to order the CBP to stop imports from entering the border. Additionally, the ITC may issue "cease and desist" orders against individuals determined to be IPR violators. Damages for IPR infringement cannot be received through ITC court proceedings; rights-holders seeking damages must file action with the U.S. federal district court.[86] For FY2010, the Consolidated Appropriations Act, 2010 (P.L. 111-117) provided the ITC with $81.86 million in budget authority, up from the FY2009 level of $75.1 million.

Intellectual Property Enforcement Coordinator (IPEC)

In October 2008, Congress created an Intellectual Property Enforcement Coordinator (IPEC), through the Prioritizing Resources and Organization for Intellectual Property Act of 2008 (P.L. 110-403). The IPEC, located in the Executive Office of the President – specifically in the Office of Management and Budget – and subject to Senate confirmation, is charged with coordinating U.S. government agency IPR enforcement actions and with providing assistance to the USTR in conducting trade negotiations relating to IPR enforcement abroad.[87]

Under P.L. 110-403, the IPEC is to chair a Advisory Committee composed of representatives from the Office of Management and Budget, the Departments of Justice, Commerce, State, Homeland Security, Agriculture, the Food and Drug Administration, the Agency for International Development, and the Register of Copyrights.

The IPEC, assisted by its Advisory Committee, also is charged with developing a "Joint Strategic Plan" for combating counterfeiting and piracy. Legislation requires the Joint Strategic Plan to include in its objectives: reducing counterfeiting and infringing goods in the domestic and international supply chain, identifying and addressing barriers to effective enforcement domestically, ensuring that information is shared among the relevant departments and agencies, eliminating domestic and international counterfeiting and infringement networks, strengthening the capacity of foreign countries to protect and enforce IPR, and cooperating with other countries to establish international standards and policies to enforce IPR.

In 2009, President Obama nominated and the Senate confirmed Victoria A. Espinel as the IPEC. In June 2010, IPEC Espinel released the *2010 Joint Strategic Plan on Intellectual Property Enforcement*. The plan identifies 33 "enforcement strategy action items," categorized under six major areas of focus: (1) leading by example; (2) increasing transparency; (3) ensuring efficiency and coordination; (4) enforcing U.S. rights internationally; (5) securing the supply chain; and (6) building a data-driven government.[88]

The House Conference Report (H.Rept. 111-366 to H.R. 3288) provided for a transfer of $176,000 from the White House to the OMB, to reflect the Administration's decision to locate the new IPEC in the OMB rather than the White House.

Issues for Congress

The role of Congress in addressing IPR and trade-related issues stems from the U.S. Constitution, which provides Congress with the power "To promote the Progress of Science and useful Arts, by securing for limited Times to Authors and Inventors the exclusive Right to their respective Writings and Discoveries" and "To regulate Commerce with foreign Nations."[89] While the U.S. Constitution provides Congress with the power to regulate international trade, the authority to negotiate trade agreements has been delegated periodically to the President. However, congressional action is needed to bring the trade agreements into force.

From a policy perspective, congressional consideration of IPR may take place in the context of the National Export Initiative (NEI), an Obama Administration plan introduced in early 2010 to double U.S. exports in five years to create two million U.S. jobs.[90] A report submitted by the President's Export Promotion Cabinet on implementing the NEI discussed the relationship between strengthening IPR regimes internationally and promoting U.S. exports.[91] In December 2010, the President's Export Council sent a letter to President Obama highlighting the importance of addressing inadequate protection and enforcement of IPR as a means for "boosting exports and foreign sales, and promoting the sustained growth of well compensated U.S. jobs." The President's Export Council expressed support for making "efforts to combat weak and ineffective intellectual property regimes abroad an integral and essential part of the National Export Initiative." [92]

U.S. Efforts to Promote IPR through Trade Policy

Since the inclusion of IPR provisions in the TRIPS Agreement, there has been an ongoing debate about the appropriateness of including IPR as a component of U.S. trade policy. Some argue that IPR, which grant legal temporary monopolies to rights-holders for their creations, are actually barriers to trade and have no place in trade liberalization negotiations. Others contend that IPR promote trade through innovation, economic growth, and technology transfer from advanced to developing countries.

In addition to this broader discussion about the role of IPR in trade policy, concerns have been voiced about the trade policy channels used by the United States to promote international IPR protection and enforcement. Some question the appropriateness of using regional and bilateral FTAs for this pursuing stronger IPR, contending that such actions take away from the effectiveness of multilateral IPR promotion efforts. Periodically, Members of Congress have expressed concern over U.S attempts to expand the IPR obligations of foreign countries through trade agreements. In 2002, the Trade Promotion Authority (TPA) legislation was amended to state that the United States recognized the Doha Declaration on the TRIPS Agreement and Public Health in the context of negotiating FTAs. In the 110th Congress, congressional leaders and the Bush Administration agreed to modifications of the patent provisions in the Peru FTA as a result of the May 2007 bipartisan trade agreement. Still, a Government Accountability Office (GAO) report suggests that USTR should offer clearer policy guidance to align FTA negotiating activities with the WTO Doha Declaration.[93] Additionally, there is concern by some that the ratchet of IPR commitments pursued through regional and bilateral FTAs may be too stringent for developing countries and may limit innovation and creativity by stifling the exchange of ideas.

Further expansion of IPR provisions may be affected by the language of any future TPA. In discussions about renewal of TPA, Congress may choose to consider possible reiteration or expansion on its IPR goals related to global health from the 2002 TPA. Congress also may choose to consider whether or not to follow the template provided by the Peru, Panama, and Colombia FTAs in future trade negotiations, such as negotiations on the Trans-Pacific Partnership Agreement.

Effectiveness of the U.S. IPR Organizational Structure

There are concerns on the part of some lawmakers about whether or not the present U.S. IPR organizational structure is doing enough to enforce foreign countries' IPR obligations, as well as concerns about whether or not the structure is capable of doing more.

Prior to the establishment of the Intellectual Property Enforcement Coordinator (IPEC), the U.S. IPR organizational structure was coordinated by the National Intellectual Property Law Enforcement Coordinating Council (NIPLECC). Some Members of Congress were critical of NIPLECC's organizational response to international IPR protection and enforcement. Recent GAO testimony pointed out some of the problems associated with NIPLECC, including an absence of mission, dearth of activities, and poor image among businesses.[94] The FY2007 CJS Committee Report (S.Rept. 109-280) expressed concern about the lack of information on NIPLECC's progress and evidence of success.

In the 110th Congress, several bills were introduced to repeal and replace NIPLECC. The Prioritizing Resources and Organization for Intellectual Property Act of 2008 (P.L. 110-403) was signed by President Bush on October 13, 2008. The act, among other provisions, replaced NIPLECC with an IPEC. Elevating the IPEC's profile by placing it in the EOP, some lawmakers hope, will promote more effective coordination of the organizational structure's response to international IPR protection and enforcement issues. Others argue that the effectiveness of the IPEC will depend on what resources are allocated for its activities.

While protection and enforcement of IPR is a stated trade policy priority for the United States, it is difficult to get a sense of the magnitude of funding and resources devoted toward IPR support. Some agencies do not have a separate budgetary line item for IPR-related activities, and Congress does not always designate specific funds for IPR activities in its appropriations for agencies.[95] Additionally, there is limited information on the economic and other impacts of piracy and counterfeiting on the United States. For example, in its Special 301 Report, USTR uses industry figures that are not independently confirmed. This may complicate the ability of lawmakers to weigh the threat of IPR infringement against the federal resources available for IPR and other government priorities.

Legislation was introduced in the 111th Congress to advance U.S. IPR protection and enforcement efforts as part of U.S. trade policy. The Trade Enforcement Act of 2009 (H.R. 496, S. 1466) would have created new IPR coordinator positions in the Department of the Treasury and the Department of Homeland Security's Customs and Border Protection (CBP) and Immigration and Customs Enforcement (ICE) agencies; increased IPR resources, staff, funding, and training for CBP and ICE; required the development of a strategy for IPR enforcement; and created a Advisory Committee on Import Safety and Intellectual Property Rights Enforcement, among other provisions.

Some lawmakers also support increasing the priority that IPR is given as part of U.S. foreign policy. Foreign relations appropriations legislation for FY2010 (H.R. 2410, H.R. 2475) would have required the Secretary of State to appoint ten intellectual property attachés to serve in U.S. missions overseas and would have directed the Secretary of State to consider assigning such attachés to missions in countries which have been identified under Section 182 of the Trade Act of 1974.

Some may support efforts to promote IPR as a part of U.S. trade, foreign, or other forms of policy. Others may raise concerns about how the promotion of IPR may affect U.S. efforts to advance other policy goals. In addition, while some support efforts to increase resources dedicated to IPR protection and enforcement, others question what implications such increased resources might have for U.S. coordination of IPR protection and enforcement activities.

End Notes

[1] Uniform Trade Secret Act, §1(4).

[2] For information on geographical indications and international trade negotiations, see CRS Report RS21569, *Geographical Indications and WTO Negotiations*, by Charles E. Hanrahan.

[3] Counterfeit goods should be distinguished from generic goods, i.e., in the case of generic forms of pharmaceutical medicines.

[4] WIPO, "Global Economic Slowdown Impacts 2008 International Patent Filings," press release, January 27, 2009, http://www.wipo.int/pressroom/en/articles/2009/article_0002.html.

[5] WIPO, "International Patent Filings Recover in 2010," press release, February 9, 2011, http://www.wipo.int/pressroom/en/articles/2011/article_0004.html.

[6] Stephen E. Siwek, "Engines of Growth: Economic Contributions of the US Intellectual Property Industries," commissioned by NBC Universal, 2005, p. 2.

[7] Arti Rai, Stuart Graham, and Mark Doms, *Patent Reform: Unleashing Innovation, Promoting Economic Growth & Producing High-Paying Jobs*, Department of Commerce, A White Paper from the U.S. Department of Commerce, April 13, 2010.

[8] Nam D. Pham, *The Impact of Innovation and the Role of Intellectual Property Rights on U.S. Productivity, Competitiveness, Jobs, Wages, and Exports*, NDP Consulting Group, April 2010.

[9] Stephen E. Siwek, *Copyright Industries in the U.S. Economy: The 2003-2007 Report*, prepared for the International Intellectual Property Alliance (IIPA), http://www.iipa.com, pp. 3-7.

[10] PhRMA, *Pharmaceutical Industry Profile 2010*, Washington, D.C., March 2010, http://www.phrma.org, p. 50.

[11] Amanda Horan, Christopher Johnson, and Heather Sykes, *Foreign Infringement of Intellectual Property Rights: Implications for Selected U.S. Industries*, U.S. International Trade Commission, Office of Industries Working Paper, October 2005, p. 4.

[12] Jennifer Koncz and Anne Flatness, "U.S. International Services," *Survey of Current Business*, U.S. Bureau of Economic Analysis (BEA), October 2010. This measure of cross-border trade in royalties and license fees by U.S. companies include transactions with both affiliated and unaffiliated foreign companies.

[13] Thomas Rogers and Andrew Zamosszegi, *Fair Use in the U.S. Economy:Economic Contribution of Industries Relying on Fair Use*, Prepared for the Computer & Communications Industry Association (CCIA), 2010. CCIA, "Fair Use Doctrine Vital for All of Us," press release, November 18, 2009, http://www.ccianet.org/index.asp?sid=5&artid=125&evtflg=False. See also CRS Report RL33631, *Copyright Licensing in Music Distribution, Reproduction, and Public Performance*, by Brian T. Yeh.

[14] Ibid., p. 2.

[15] OECD, *The Economic Impact of Counterfeiting and Piracy*, 2007, p. 4, http://www.oecd.org/dataoecd/13/12/38707619.pdf.

[16] Organization for Economic Cooperation and Development (OECD), *The Economic Impact of Counterfeiting and Piracy*, 2007. OECD, *Magnitude of Counterfeiting and Piracy of Tangible Products: An Update*, November 2009.

[17] U.S CBP and U.S. ICE, *Intellectual Property Rights Seizure Statistics: FY2009*, October 2010.

[18] Ibid.

[19] Ibid.

[20] There may be limitations on data estimating the impact of counterfeiting and piracy on the U.S. economy. Some critics point out that many of the estimates for losses associated with IPR infringement are generated by industry groups that may have self-interested motivations and hence, the negative effects may be exaggerated.

[21] The IIPA member associations are: Association of American Publishers (AAP), Business Software Alliance (BSA), Entertainment Software Alliance (ESA), Independent Film & Television Alliance (I.F.T.A.), Motion Picture Association of America (MPAA), National Music Publishers' Association (NMPA), and Recording Industry Association of America (RIAA).

[22] IIPA, *IIPA 2009 "Special 301" USTR Decisions*, issued June 30, 2009.

[23] PhRMA's calculations of damage due to violations of data exclusivity are based on a five-year data protection period; any sales not made by the patent holder within the data exclusivity period were regarded as data exclusivity damages. For damages from patent protection violations, PhRMA used a ten-year patent protection period and considered any sales not made by the patent holder within that period to be damages. For some countries, PhRMA did not report damages because data was not available at the time.

[24] Economic losses in PhRMA's annual Special 301 submission are not reported on calendar-year basis because fourth quarter economic data is not available at the time the report is issued.

[25] PhRMA, *Special 301 Submission for 2007.* See Appendix: Damage Estimate Methodology, p. v.

[26] PhRMA, *Special 301 Submission 2008.*

[27] U.S. Government Accountability Office, *Intellectual Property: Observations on Efforts to Quantify the Economic Effects of Counterfeit and Pirated Goods*, GAO-10-423, April 2010.

[28] Monika Ermert, "Speculation Persists on ACTA as First Official Meeting Concludes," *Intellectual Property Watch*, June 5, 2008. Robin Gross, *IP Justice White Paper on the Proposed Anti-Counterfeiting Trade Agreement (ACTA)*, IP Justice, March 25, 2008, p. 6.

[29] Robert G. Picard, "A Note on Economic Losses Due to Theft, Infringement, and Piracy of Protected Works," *Journal of Media Economics*, 17(3), 207-217, 2004.

[30] U.S. Government Accountability Office, *Intellectual Property: Observations on Efforts to Quantify the Economic Effects of Counterfeit and Pirated Goods*, GAO-10-423, April 2010.

[31] IIPA, "IIPA's 2009 Special 301 Report on Copyright Protection and Enforcement," submitted to the U.S. Trade Representative by IIPA on February 17, 2009, http://www.iipa.com.

[32] Envisional, *Technical Report: An Estimate of Infringing Use of the Internet*, January 2011.

[33] USTR, "United States Files WTO Cases Against China Over Deficiencies in China's Intellectual Property Rights Laws and Market Access Barriers to Copyright-Based Industries," press release, April 9, 2007, http://www.ustr.gov. See also CRS Report RL33536, *China-U.S. Trade Issues*, by Wayne M. Morrison.

[34] WTO, "WTO issues panel report on U.S.-China dispute over intellectual property rights," press release, January 26, 2009. USTR, "United States Wins WTO Dispute Over Deficiencies in China's Intellectual Property Rights Law," press release, January 26, 2009. Daniel Pruzin, "WTO Publishes Final Ruling in U.S. Complaint Against Chinese IPR Enforcement Measures," *International Trade Daily*, January 27, 2009.

[35] For more information on U.S-China IPR and other trade issues, see CRS Report RL33536, *China-U.S. Trade Issues*, by Wayne M. Morrison.

[36] Pascal Lamy, "Trade-Related Aspects of Intellectual Property Rights - Ten Years Later," *Journal of World Trade,* October 2004, p. 925.

[37] "Extension of the Transition Period under Article 66.1 of the TRIPS Agreement for Least-Developed Country Members for Certain Obligations with Respect to Pharmaceutical Products," WTO Document IP/C/25, July 1, 2002.

[38] See CRS Report R40607, *Intellectual Property Rights and Access to Medicines: International Trade Issues*, by Shayerah Ilias.

[39] Declaration on the TRIPS Agreement and Public Health, (WT/MIN(01)/DEC/2), November 14, 2001, available at http://www.wto.org/english/thewto_e/minist_e/min01_e/mindecl_trips_e.htm.

[40] "Implementation of Paragraph 6 of the Doha Declaration on the TRIPS Agreement and Public Health," IP/C/W/405, August 30, 2003, and accompanying Chairman's statement, available at http://www.wto.org/english/news_e/pres03_e/ pr350_e.htm.

[41] "Members accepting amendment of the TRIPS Agreement," http://www.wto.org/english/tratop_e/trips_e/ amendment_e.htm.

[42] "Canada Issues Compulsory License For HIV/AIDS Drug Export To Rwanda, In First Test Of WTO Procedure," *Bridges Weekly Trade News Digest*, September 26, 2007, http://www.ictsd.org/weekly/07-09-26/story2.htm.

[43] OECD, *The Impact of Trade-Related Intellectual Property Rights on Trade and Foreign Direct Investment in Developing Countries*, May 28, 2003, p. 21, http://www.oecd.org.

[44] Keith E. Maskus, *Intellectual Property Rights in the Global Economy*, Institute for International Economics (IIE), Washington, D.C., August 2000.

[45] Commission on Intellectual Property Rights (CIPR), *Integrating Intellectual Property Rights and Development Policy*, September 2002.

[46] These WCT and WPPT frequently are referred to as the WIPO Internet Treaties.

[47] Monika Ermert, "G8 Governments Want ACTA Finalised This Year, SPLT Talks Accelerated ," *Intellectual Property Watch*, July 9, 2008.

[48] "Agreement between the World Intellectual Property Organization and the World Trade Organization," http://www.wto.org/english/tratop_e/trips_e/wtowip_e.htm.

[49] WIPO, *Intellectual Property Handbook*, http://www.wipo.org, p. 359.

[50] P.L. 107-210, Sec. 2102(b)(4).

[51] The May 10, 2007 bipartisan trade agreement is available online at: http://www.ustr.gov/assets/Document_Library/Fact_Sheets/2007/asset_upload_file127_11319.pdf.

[52] For more information, see CRS Report R41107, *The Proposed Anti-Counterfeiting Trade Agreement: Background and Key Issues*, by Shayerah Ilias.

[53] For a more detailed discussion of the differences between the TRIPS Agreement and regional FTAs that are in force, see CRS Report RL33205, *Intellectual Property and the Free Trade Agreements: Innovation Policy Issues*, by John R. Thomas.

[54] "Brand-Name Industry Alarmed at IPR Precedent of FTA Template," *Inside US Trade*, May 18, 2007.

[55] While TRIPS does not directly speak to the rights of generic drug manufacturers in obtaining marketing approval for a generic drug before the expiration of the patented drug, Article 30 of TRIPS permits exceptions of patent rights for activities such as "research, prior user rights, and pre-expiration testing."

[56] For example, under the Peru FTA, if a company files to market a new drug in Peru after making an initial filing in another country, such as the United States, and Peru approves the drug within six months of the filing, the data exclusivity period begins at the time the drug was approved in the country of the initial filing, not Peru.

[57] U.S. Government Accountability Office, *U.S. Trade Policy Guidance on WTO Declaration on Access to Medicines May Need Clarification*, GAO-97-1198, September 2007, p. 19.

[58] CRS Report RL33205, *Intellectual Property and the Free Trade Agreements: Innovation Policy Issues*, by John R. Thomas.

[59] The DMCA (P.L. 105-304) prohibits disabling technological protection measures designed to protect copyright works through activities such as descrambling or decrypting copyrighted workers.

[60] For the Special 301 provisions, see 19 U.S.C. §2242; Trade Act of 1974, as amended, (P.L. 93-618), §182.

[61] The USTR *Special 301 Report 2010* is available on the USTR website, http://www.ustr.gov.

[62] Letter from Ambassador Ron Kirk, U.S. Trade Representative, to The Honorable Benyamin Ben-Eliezer, Ministry of Industry, Trade and Labor, February 18, 2010.

[63] Conversation with USTR official, July 2006.

[64] Telephone conversation with PhRMA representative, July 2006.

[65] Oxfam International, *US bullying on drug patents: One year after Doha*, Briefing Paper 33.

[66] Telephone conversation with USTR official, July 2006.

[67] For more information on the Section 337 investigation and enforcement process, see CRS Report RS22880, *Intellectual Property Rights Protection and Enforcement: Section 337 of the Tariff Act of 1930*, by Shayerah Ilias.

[68] U.S. International Trade Commission, *Year in Review: Fiscal Year 2009*, USITC Publication 4167, p. 14.

[69] For a more thorough discussion of GSP, see CRS Report RL33663, *Generalized System of Preferences: Background and Renewal Debate*, by Vivian C. Jones.

[70] 91 USC 2462(b)(2)

[71] USTR, *GSP: 2009 Annual Review*, http://www.ustr.gov.

[72] General information about the Department of Commerce is available at http://www.doc.gov.

[73] NIPLECC, *Report to the President and Congress on Coordination of Intellectual Property Enforcement and Protection*, January 2008, p. 21.

[74] Conversation with PTO official, November 26, 2007.

[75] NIPLECC, *Report to the President and Congress on Coordination of Intellectual Property Enforcement and Protection*, January 2008, p. 21.

[76] DOJ, *Progress Report of the Department of Justice's Task Force on Intellectual Property*, June 2006, http://www.usdoj.gov/opa/documents/ipreport61906.pdf, pp. 17-24.

[77] Information about the DHS is available at http://www.dhs.gov.

[78] Certain customs-related IPR policy-making resides within the Treasury.

[79] NIPLECC, *Report to the President and Congress on Coordination of Intellectual Property Enforcement and Protection*, January 2008, pp. 15-16. Additional information about CBP is available at http://www.cbp.gov.

[80] Ibid. Also refer to the ICE website, http://www.ice.gov.

[81] Conversation with FDA official, November 26, 2007. Additional information is available on the FDA website, http://www.fda.gov.

[82] NIPLECC, *Report to the President and Congress on Coordination of Intellectual Property Enforcement and Protection*, January 2008, p. 18. Also see Copyright Office website, http://www.copyright.gov.

[83] NIPLECC, *Report to the President and Congress on Coordination of Intellectual Property Enforcement and Protection*, January 2008, pp. 17-18. Additional information about the State Department is available at http://www.state.gov.

[84] Trade Capacity Database and general AID information is accessible at http://www.usaid.gov.

[85] NIPLECC, *Report to the President and Congress on Coordination of Intellectual Property Enforcement and Protection*, January 2008, p. 25. Also see USTR website, http://www.ustr.gov.

[86] U.S. ITC website, http://www.usitc.gov.

[87] In creating the IPEC, P.L. 110-403 repealed the authorities creating the National Intellectual Property Law Enforcement Coordination Council (NIPLECC). Established by Congress in 1999, NIPLECC coordinated U.S. activities to protect and enforce IPR domestically and abroad, drawing together the major federal agencies the help to enforce IPR. The Copyright Office participated in the Council in an advisory role. The U.S. Coordinator for International Intellectual Property Enforcement headed NIPLECC's interagency coordination efforts. NIPLECC, *Report to the President and Congress on Coordination of Intellectual Property Enforcement and Protection*, January 2008, pp. 3-4.

[88] Executive Office of the President, *2010 Joint Strategic Plan on Intellectual Property Enforcement*, June 2010, http://www.whitehouse.gov/sites/default/files/omb/assets/intellectualproperty/intellectualproperty_strategic_plan.pdf.

[89] *U.S. Constitution*, Article 1, Section 8.

[90] "National Export Initiative," Executive Order 13534 of March 11, 2010, 75 *Federal Registrar* 12433, March 16, 2010.

[91] Export Promotion Cabinet, *Report to the President on the National Export Initiative: The Export Promotion Cabinet's Plan for Doubling U.S. Exports in Five Years*, Washington, D.C., September 2010. The President's Export Promotion Cabinet is a high-level body comprised of the Secretaries or Directors of key federal agencies involved in U.S. export promotion efforts.

[92] Letter from Jim McNerney, The President's Export Council, to President Obama, December 9, 2010, http://trade.gov/pec/docs/PEC_IPR_Letter_120910.pdf. The President's Export Council is a private sector national advisory committee on international trade.

[93] U.S. Government Accountability Office, *U.S. Trade Policy Guidance on WTO Declaration on Access to Medicines May Need Clarification,* GAO-07-1198, September 2007.

[94] U.S. Government Accountability Office, *National Enforcement Strategy Needs Stronger Leadership and More Accountability*, GAO-07-710T, April 12, 2007, pp. 8-10.

[95] Liza Porteus Viana, "US Fiscal 2009 Proposed Budget Shows IP Enforcement a Priority," *Intellectual Property Watch*, February 6, 2008.

In: Intellectual Property
Editor: Nicholas D. Melark

ISBN: 978-1-61470-506-2

Chapter 2

INTELLECTUAL PROPERTY RIGHTS AND ACCESS TO MEDICINES: INTERNATIONAL TRADE ISSUES

Shayerah Ilias

SUMMARY

A patent, which is a form of intellectual property right (IPR), is a legal, exclusive right granted for the invention of a new product, process, organism, design, and plant. It allows the right holder to exclude others from making, using, or selling the protected invention for a period of 20 years. Patents constitute the most common method for governments to encourage research and development (R&D) in order to find pharmaceutical treatments and cures for diseases and other illnesses.

IPR protection and enforcement have evolved from an area primarily of national concern to an area of international trade policy. The World Trade Organization (WTO) Agreement on Trade-Related Aspects of Intellectual Property Rights (TRIPS) established minimum standards for IPR protection and enforcement.

The U.S. government considers the protection and enforcement of international IPR standards, including those for patents, to be an important goal of U.S. trade policy for economic, health and safety, and national security reasons. As such, the United States has pursued strong IPR regimes through multilateral, regional, and bilateral free trade agreement (FTA) negotiations and unilateral trade policy tools, namely the Special 301 process and the Generalized System of Preferences (GSP).

IPR provisions in trade policies are among the range of social, economic, and political factors that may affect public health, including the ability of countries to deliver health services to their populations. Patents, through their possible impact on innovation and drug prices, may affect access to existing medicines and the development of new medicines. According to the World Health Organization (WHO), about one-third of the world's population, primarily those residing in poorer parts of Africa and Asia, lacks regular access to essential medicines.

While the United States places priority on promoting a strong international IPR regime, some Members of Congress have expressed concern over how to balance the goals of providing long-term incentives for innovation through patents and addressing the short-term need to provide affordable access to medicines.

This report focuses on the relationship between IPR provisions in international and U.S. trade policy and access to medicines. This issue represents one component of a broader debate about the relationship between trade policy and public health. Possible issues of interest for Congress include incorporating public health concerns into the U.S. trade policy advisory process, developing new U.S. trade policy guidance on public health, considering the implications of the U.S. strategy on IPRs and trade for U.S. access to medicines, and reviewing the range of options utilized for expanding global access to medicines.

INTRODUCTION

This report focuses on the relationship between intellectual property rights (IPRs) provisions pursued through international and U.S. trade policy and access to medicines.[1] Patents, a form of IPR, constitute the most common method by which governments encourage research and development (R&D) in order to find treatments and cures for diseases and other illnesses. A patent is a legal, exclusive right granted for the invention of a new product, process, organism, design, or plant that allows the right holder to exclude others from making, using, or selling the protected invention for a period of 20 years. By granting a temporary, exclusive right to the market for the protected product, a patent enables the right holder to generate profits to recover the costs for investment in R&D and to invest in future innovations. However, some express concerns that patents enable right holders to price drugs at levels that greatly surpass marginal costs of R&D and production, raising questions about the role of patents in affecting access to medicines and public health.

IPR protection and enforcement have evolved from an area primarily of national concern to an area of international trade policy. The World Trade Organization (WTO) Agreement on Trade-Related Aspects of Intellectual Property Rights (TRIPS) established minimum standards for IPR protection and enforcement. Countries have advanced IPR protection and enforcement efforts through multilateral, regional, and bilateral free trade agreements (FTAs) and unilateral trade policies.[2]

Congress makes and shapes U.S. trade policy by passing statutory authorities that authorize trade programs, governing trade policy in a range of issue areas, setting trade negotiating objectives into law, engaging in consultations with the Executive Branch on trade negotiations, and conducting oversight hearings on U.S. trade policy and programs.[3] Within Congress, there has been significant interest in promoting and protecting IPRs through trade policy for economic, health and safety, and national security reasons. IPR-based industries are viewed as an important contributor to U.S. innovation, productivity, economic growth, employment, and international trade. Advocates of a strong international IPR regime claim that counterfeiting and piracy inflict billions of dollars of revenue and trade losses annually on U.S. IPR-based industries. Some policymakers also have expressed concern about the health and safety implications of counterfeit goods, including pharmaceutical drugs. In addition, there is concern that trade in IPR-infringing products may feed into cross-border organized criminal networks.[4]

The Office of the U.S. Trade Representative (USTR) considers the protection and enforcement of international IPR standards to be a high priority for U.S. trade policy. As such, the USTR has pursued strong IPR regimes by participating in multilateral, regional and bilateral FTAs, as well as through unilateral trade policy tools, namely the Special 301 process and the Generalized System of Preferences (GSP).

IPR provisions in trade policies are among the range of social, economic, and political factors that may affect public health. While patents may provide incentives for innovation, their granting of market exclusivities and impact on prices raise questions about the affordability of medicines, particularly for (but not limited to) low-income countries and their populations. Through their possible impact on innovation and drug prices, patents may affect the ability of countries to provide medicines to their populations and for populations in general to access medicines. For some observers, this may represent a conflict between free market and public health policies. While the commercialization of public health may promote innovation and efficiency, the laws of supply and demand may cause some people to be "priced out" of a given market.

According to the World Health Organization (WHO), about one-third of the world's population, primarily residing in poorer parts of Africa and Asia, lacks regular access to essential medicines. [5] Infectious diseases are major contributors of illness, death, and poverty in the developing world. At the end of 2008, an estimated 33.4 million people were living with HIV/AIDS, with about two-thirds of them in Sub-Saharan Africa.[6] Other infectious diseases, such as tuberculosis, malaria, and influenza, present critical global health challenges as well. Over one billion people, primarily among the world's poorest, also are afflicted with neglected tropical diseases, which largely are infectious parasitic diseases prevalent in "impoverished" environments.[7] With the global economic crisis, access to medicines may deteriorate.[8]

In 2000, the United Nations established eight Millennium Development Goals (MDGs), to which the United States is a signatory, in an effort to end poverty by year 2015. One of the U.N. targets is to achieve universal access to treatment for HIV/AIDS by 2010 and to have halted and reversed the spread of HIV/AIDS, malaria, and other major diseases by 2015. While prevention is key to combating infectious diseases, access to treatment is also critical to controlling epidemics. As such, another MDG target is to cooperate with pharmaceutical companies to provide access to affordable essential drugs in developing countries. Access to medicines has improved dramatically over the past couple of decades. For example, of the approximately 9.5 million people in need of treatment for HIV/AIDS in 2008 in low- and middle-income countries, 42% had access, compared to 33% in 2007.[9]

Although access to medicines is an important goal and is the focus of the discussion at hand, some public health professionals caution that "over-access" also can be a problem. Proponents of this view assert that that the availability of medicines due to lower prices may promote misuse, leading to the faster onset of drug resistance and shorter duration of the drug's usefulness.[10]

There is ongoing debate within Congress about the impact that IPR provisions in international and U.S. trade policies may have on access to medicines and public health. At the center of the debate is the question of how to balance providing long-term incentives for innovation through patents and addressing the short-term need to provide affordable access to medicines. The debate over the role of patents and trade policy in affecting access to medicines often has been framed as one in which high-income, developed countries and innovator ("brand name") pharmaceutical companies are pitted against low-income, developing countries and global health advocates. However, the number of stakeholders is more diverse, and includes middle-income, industrializing countries, and generic drug manufacturers. In addition, there is debate within the governments of countries about how to balance advancing economic interests and public health outcomes through trade policy.

The debate over IPRs and access to medicines represents one component of a broader debate over the relationship between international trade policy and global public health. Over time, these two arenas have shown increasing overlap. In some cases, the linkages have been clear. For instance, international trade in goods that contain dangerous pathogens or counterfeit substances presents clear threats to public health. In other cases, as in the debate at hand, the linkages may not be so clear-cutting, or trade issues may only form one component of the public health issue.[11]

BACKGROUND

The global pharmaceutical industry is classified as a high-technology industry by the Organization for Economic Cooperation and Development (OECD). As a high-technology manufacturing industry, the pharmaceutical industry spends a high proportion of its revenues on R&D, which can lead to innovative solutions to treat global health problems.[12]

The pharmaceutical industry is heavily reliant on protection of intellectual property rights, specifically patents. Patents are the most common way for governments to encourage R&D and to foster innovation. A patent is a time-limited, legal, exclusive right granted for the invention of new products, processes, organisms, designs, and plants that allows the right holder to exclude others from making, using, or selling the protected invention for a period of 20 years. A patent does not necessarily provide the right holder with the "right to sell" the protected invention, as the right holder may need to comply with other regulatory laws. For example, pharmaceutical drugs generally also must be reviewed by a regulatory body (in the case of the United States, the Food and Drug Administration, FDA) for other considerations, such as health and safety, before it may be sold to consumers.

Incentives for Innovation

By granting time-limited, exclusive monopolies on the market for a product, patents generate above-market financial returns that are believed to enable pharmaceutical inventors to recoup the costs of R&D and to invest in future innovations. By some estimates, the cost to drug researchers and manufacturers for creating a single new medicine is upwards of $800 million.[13] Pointing to the high costs and uncertainty associated with R&D, supporters of patents argue that they are important for innovation in medicine by allowing right holders to recoup the costs of R&D, earn profits, and invest in future R&D.

Proponents maintain that financial incentives for innovation may be even more critical now with the global economic downturn. Some fear that tighter credit markets may compel pharmaceutical companies to reduce current R&D spending.[14] For example, the World

Intellectual Property Organization (WIPO) reported a drop of 4.5% in international patent filings in 2009.[15]

Others are skeptical of the reportedly high estimates of the costs of R&D in the creation of new medicines. Some critics argue that PhRMA's cost estimate includes both the actual expenditures and the economic opportunity costs of developing new drugs. They also contend that a growing proportion of the financial returns generated from patented drugs is not directed toward new innovations, but rather to commercial marketing and political lobbying activities.[16]

Additionally, pharmaceutical companies often use publicly-funded research to develop drugs for commercialization.[17] For instance, in the United States, the National Institutes of Health (NIH) and the Centers for Disease Control (CDC) provide funding for health-related research. In general, the public sector funds R&D that is focused on basic scientific research. Pharmaceutical companies then build on this research to develop products that are patentable and commercially marketable.

R&D for "Developing Country Diseases"

While patents may provide incentives for innovation, some argue that the economic premise behind patents only holds in situations where markets offer sufficient financial incentives for a return on investment. Many developing countries may be unable to provide a profitable market for treatments against diseases that disproportionately affect their populations. The WHO "Global Strategy and Plan of Action of Public Health, Innovation and Intellectual Property" acknowledges that IPRs serve an important incentive function, but notes, "This incentive alone does not meet the need for the development of new products to fight diseases where the potential paying market is small or uncertain (WHA61.21.6)."

According to a classification system used by the WHO, there are three main types of diseases that vary in the level of market-based incentives they offer for R&D.

- **Type I** diseases ("chronic diseases"), such as cancer, diabetes, and cardiovascular disease, are prevalent in developed countries and increasingly in developing countries. Pharmaceutical companies have a strong financial incentive to invest in treatments for these diseases.
- **Type II** diseases are prevalent in developing countries. Pharmaceutical companies may have incentives to invest in such diseases if there is sufficient demand by high-income countries for research, as in the case of HIV/AIDS. For other Type II diseases, such as malaria and tuberculosis, high-income country demand for treatments is limited and consequently, market-based incentives are not sufficient for pharmaceutical companies to invest in R&D.
- **Type III** diseases, such as dengue fever and African sleeping sickness, are those that have virtually no developed country demand. These diseases (often referred to as "neglected tropical diseases"), largely are concentrated in impoverished areas in developing countries. Pharmaceutical companies have little financial incentive to invest in R&D for these diseases, but may have social motivations.[18]

According to one commonly cited statistic, less than 10% of global expenditures on health research and development is directed toward the major health problems of 90% of the world's population (the so-called "10/90 gap").[19] Some point out that low rates of R&D investment in "developing country diseases" may be one of many factors affecting health conditions in impoverished areas. For instance, some neglected tropical diseases are prevalent due to poverty-related conditions such as unsafe water, poor sanitation, and lack of basic health care infrastructure.[20]

Some of the pharmaceutical needs of developed and developing countries are increasingly converging. For example, many Type I diseases, typically associated with high-income countries ("age" diseases), also now account for a growing share of the disease burden in developing countries as they experience economic growth and development.[21] The WHO estimates that 80% of the burden of chronic diseases is concentrated in low- and middle-income countries.[22] Additionally, increasing outbreaks of infectious diseases, such as the H5N1 "avian influenza" and H1N1 "swine influenza," and growing resistance to highly infectious diseases, such as tuberculosis, may lead to R&D for diseases that affect all populations.

Drug Pricing

Pharmaceutical patents are among the many factors that may affect the price of medicines. Other factors include the level of economic development, taxes, tariffs, efficiency of global supply and distribution chains, government procurement plans, national health policies, and national and industry pricing decisions. These factors also are potentially significant determinants of drug pricing, but are beyond the scope of this paper.[23]

By granting a time-limited monopoly on the sale of a pharmaceutical drug, patents may raise the cost of the drug by delaying the entry of generic competitors into the market. Although the time-limited, exclusive right may serve an incentive function, some public health advocates are critical of the prices charged for patented medicines, arguing that patents enable right holders to price drugs at levels that greatly surpass marginal costs of R&D and production.

Generic medicines—typically defined as copies of a patented drugs, predominantly of drugs whose patents have expired[24]—tend to lower the price of drugs in the global marketplace in a number of ways. In general, generic manufacturers do not have to repeat research and clinical trials conducted by name brand pharmaceutical companies in order to obtain regulatory approval, but rather only need to demonstrate the "bioequivalence" of their product to the patented, branded medicine. In the United States, the Drug Price Competition and Patent Restoration Act of 1984 (the "Hatch-Waxman Act of 1984"), among other provisions, permits the FDA to provide marketing approval for generics on the basis of "bioequivalence" data rather than more costly, clinical data.[25] Without this obligation, generic manufacturers are able to enter the market more quickly once patents have expired and to offer the drugs at lower prices.

By serving as market competitors, generics also encourage innovator pharmaceutical companies to lower the prices of their branded drugs. In addition, the entry of generic drugs into a market may encourage innovator companies to develop newer drugs, thus increasing the supply of medicines.[26]

ACCESS TO ESSENTIAL MEDICINES

The public health landscape has changed dramatically over the past 30 years. The world has witnessed the emergence of the HIV/AIDS pandemic in the 1980s, as well as an increasing resistance to treatments against malaria, tuberculosis, and a host of bacteria over the past couple of decades. While HIV/AIDS is a global pandemic, it disproportionately affects developing countries. In addition, many other communicable and infectious diseases have afflicted the developing world.

Public health outcomes depend on a wide variety of often inter-related social, economic, and political factors, one of which is access to medicines.[27] According to the U.N. Millennium Development Goals, access to medicines is defined as "having medicines continuously available and affordable at public or private health facilities or medicine outlets that are within one hour's walk from the homes of the population."[28]

In discussing access to medicines, many public health advocates focus on "essential medicines." Given that national governments face resource constraints in providing health care, some argue that governments should rationalize their public health policy choices, including the provision of medicines. According to the WHO, essential medicines are

> those that satisfy the priority health care needs of the population. They are selected with due regard to public health relevance, evidence on efficacy and safety, and comparative cost-effectiveness. Essential medicines are intended to be available within the context of functioning health systems at all times in adequate amounts, in the appropriate dosage forms, with assured quality and adequate information, and at a price the individual and the community can afford. The implementation of the concept of essential medicines is intended to be flexible and adaptable to many different situations; exactly which medicines are regarded as essential remains a national responsibility.[29]

For low-income countries and populations, pharmaceutical drug prices may constitute a significant barrier in accessing essential and other medicines. In most parts of the world, health services are offered through a combination of public and private health services. Oftentimes, in developing countries (and in some cases, developed countries such as the United States), consumers bear much of their health care costs directly. In contrast, some countries, such as Thailand, Japan, Turkey, and France, have more publicly-funded pharmaceutical markets, reducing the costs borne by consumers. However, in situations where the government is funding a larger share of health care, higher-priced drugs may add limits to the government's ability to provide public health care.

There is considerable debate on the extent to which patent protection affects access to essential medicines. The complexity is fueled by differing definitions of what is meant by "essential medicines" and "access to medicines." For instance, there often are no agreed-upon units of analysis for evaluating access to essential medicines. Since 1977, the WHO has maintained a Model Essential Medicines List (EML) to assist national governments to select medicines to address their public health needs and to develop national lists.[30] While the WHO EML often is used as a basis for analysis, some global health activists express concern that the EML may not be comprehensive. They argue that the EML may exclude essential medicines based on cost concerns. They contend that patents raise the cost of medicines, and that the EML includes very few medicines currently under patent. However, the EML notes that cost is not a reason to automatically exclude a medicine and points out that multiple criteria are considered in the decision process.

Moreover, some argue that the number of essential medicines under patent is under "constant flux" because patents will expire for existing medicines, new patents will be sought for new medicines, new medicines will be added to the WHO's Model Essential Medicines List, and others will be removed from the EML.

QUANTIFYING ESSENTIAL MEDICINES UNDER PATENTS

Despite data limitations, some studies have attempted to quantify how many essential medicines are patented. According to one study published in 2004, 1.4% of essential medicines were patented in 2003. The study quantified the frequency with which "essential medicines" as defined by the WHO's 13th Model Essential Medicines List (EML) are patented in 65 low- and middle-income countries and examined the data using statistical regression methods. Of the 349 products listed in the WHO EML, the study concluded that 17 essential medicines could be subject to patents in 2003. While the overall patent incidence rate for essential medicines may be low, the study noted that patents were more frequent for antiretroviral medicines (ARVs) for HIV/AIDS treatment. In addition, HIV/AIDS treatment often utilizes combination therapy (use of multiple drugs for a treatment), so that a patent on one medicine can limit access to "fully-generic based therapy."[31]

According to the study, inventors were more likely to seek patents for patentable drugs in larger, developed markets than in developing countries, whose markets may not provide sufficient financial incentives for inventors to incur the costs of seeking patents. The study found that patenting was more prevalent in large, middle-income countries, such as China, South Africa, and Mexico. Pharmaceutical companies also may choose not to seek patents in low-income countries due to social motivations to increase access to drugs in these countries or reputational concerns. In addition, pharmaceutical companies may not have had the option to apply for a patent if the developing country did not recognize patents. The study suggests that views of both health care activities and pharmaceutical companies are exaggerated: "Patents cannot cause essential medicines to be inaccessible in 'many' developing countries because they do not exist 98.6 percent of the time; similarly, patents cannot be a 'global' necessity of pharmaceutical business because companies forgo them 69 percent of the time."[32]

INTERNATIONAL TRADE IN PHARMACEUTICALS

Like many other IPR-sensitive industries, the pharmaceutical industry is heavily involved in international trade. IPR-sensitive products generally rank among the fastest-growing trade commodities. International trade in pharmaceutical products is heavily dominated by the developed world, both in terms of supply and demand.

The global pharmaceutical market is expected to grow by 4-6% in 2010, down from 7% in 2009.[33] The international economic downturn poses uncertainties and may affect international demand for pharmaceuticals. Although demand for pharmaceutical products tends to be more price-inelastic than for other commodities, the global pharmaceutical market is not wholly insulated from factors affecting the global economy. The international economic slowdown may constrain performance in some pharmaceutical markets more so than others. For instance, the pharmaceutical markets of countries in which consumers bear a large degree of the cost of health care may be particularly susceptible to global economic changes.[34] However, emerging market economies are predicted to fuel growth in the pharmaceutical market sales over the next five years. [35]

Supply of Pharmaceuticals

According to the most recent statistics compiled by the National Science Foundation (NSF), total global production in the pharmaceuticals industry was about $319 billion in 2007 (see Table 1). The United States ranked as the largest single-country contributor to global value-added of the pharmaceutical industry, accounting for about one-third (32%) of the world market share. The European Union accounted for another third (31%) of the global share. Other significant contributors to pharmaceutical production were China (9%), Japan (8%), and Korea (3%).[36]

The global pharmaceutical industry is comprised mainly of a small number of multinational corporations "who negotiate with buyers and set prices and volumes for drugs."[37] The top corporations are concentrated in the United States, the United Kingdom, Germany, Switzerland, and France. Industry consolidation among branded companies has become more prevalent as generic companies have made greater inroads into the global pharmaceutical market.

While high-income countries constitute the largest source of pharmaceuticals, developing countries have accounted for a growing share of global production in the pharmaceutical industry. For instance, China's share of total pharmaceutical production in 2007 was three times its share in 1997. Likewise, India's share in 2007 was six-fold greater than a decade ago.

Table 1. Global Production in Pharmaceutical Industry Value in Millions of U.S. Dollars.

Country/Region	1997		2007	
	Value	Share	Value	Share
United States	43,040	29%	101,572	32%
European Union	44,814	30%	99,266	31%
China	4,802	3%	30,059	9%
Japan	27,458	18%	26,559	8%
India	1,719	1%	22,812	7%
Korea	4,168	3%	8,313	3%
Other	23,261	16%	30,228	9%
World	149,262	100%	318,809	100%

Source: National Science Foundation (NSF), analyzed and adapted by CRS.

India and China have become important exporters of generic drugs and active pharmaceutical ingredients. Several industrializing countries—primarily Brazil, China, Cuba, India, among others—also are developing innovative capacity for biomedical research.[38]

Demand for Pharmaceuticals

In terms of demand for pharmaceutical products, the multi-billion dollar global pharmaceutical market is highly polarized. The United States is the world's largest pharmaceutical market, and along with Japan and Europe, account for about 75% of global sales of pharmaceutical products.[39] In total, the thirty wealthiest countries in the OECD account for 80% to 90% of global sales of patented medications.[40] In contrast, the developing world, which comprises over 80% of the world's population, represents about 10% of global pharmaceutical sales.

However, the geographic balance may be shifting toward emerging market economies. A report by IMS Health, a market research firm, identified 17 countries as "pharmerging" markets.[41] These 17 countries are expected to generate the largest amount of pharmaceutical market growth over the next five years. The shift in the global pharmaceutical market may be due to a number of factors, including changes in the global economy, such as growing middle classes in some countries; changes in the health care environment, including greater access to health care; and the growth of the generic drug market.[42]

In the report, IMS Health categorizes the countries into three levels. China, the only country to be in the first tier, is expected to contribute an additional $40 billion in annual pharmaceutical sales by 2013. The second tier is comprised of Brazil, India, and Russia, which are expected to generate between $5 billion to $15 billion each annually in sales over the next five years. Another thirteen countries (Argentina, Egypt, Indonesia, Mexico, Pakistan, Poland, Romania, Thailand, Turkey, Ukraine, and Venezuela) in the third tier are predicted to contribute between $1 billion to $5 billion each in annual sales in the next five years. Collectively, these seventeen countries are expected to contribute about 48% of annual market growth in 2013.[43]

U.S. Trade in Pharmaceutical Products

For the United States, the pharmaceutical industry contributes to U.S. economic growth and employment. After experiencing lower levels of growth in the past few years amid the global and U.S. economic downturn, the U.S. pharmaceutical market is expected to rebound in 2010. Consumer spending on pharmaceuticals is forecasted to grow by 3.3% in 2010. Generic drugs are expected to apply downward pressure on the overall prices for the industry, while making more products available to the public and raising sales. Following a slowdown over the past couple of years, pharmaceutical industrial production is predicted to grow by 7.2% in 2010. [44]

Recent trends in international trade in the U.S. pharmaceutical industry are similar to those of U.S. high technology industries overall.[45] Through the 1980s and early 1990s, the U.S. high technology industries were net exporters. However, since the late 1990s, the United States has become a net importer of pharmaceuticals. [46]

Table 2. U.S. Trade in Pharmaceuticals, 1996-2009 U.S. Billions of Dollars.

Year	Exports	Imports	Trade Balance[a]	Total Trade[b]
2000	10.5	12.2	-1.7	22.7
2001	12.5	15.9	-3.4	28.4
2002	13.1	21.6	-8.5	34.7
2003	15.9	27.8	-11.9	43.7
2004	19.6	31.2	-11.6	50.8
2005	21.7	35.4	-13.7	57.1
2006	25.3	42.2	-16.9	67.5
2007	29.2	48.9	-19.7	78.1
2008	34.2	52.3	-18.1	86.5
2009	40.7	55.6	-14.9	96.3

Source: U.S. International Trade Co mmission, CRS analysis.

Notes: Pharmaceutical data based on the U.S. Harmonized Tariff Schedule (HTS), Chapter 30.

a. The trade balance is exports less imports.

b. Total trade is exports plus imports.

For the U.S. pharmaceutical industry, total trade has grown as both exports and imports of pharmaceuticals have grown. However, imports have grown faster than exports, resulting in a U.S. trade deficit (see Table 2). Some observers question whether this is a signal of a decline in the U.S. pharmaceutical industry's competitiveness or simply an indication of the growing role of other countries in the global pharmaceutical industry. Also, these data do not reflect which pharmaceutical products traded by the United States are high-technology and which are low-technology.

The WTO Agreement on Trade-Related Aspects of Intellectual Property Rights

Historically, intellectual property rights have been a matter of U.S. national concern, but over time, have evolved into a cornerstone of international trade agreements. At the center of the present international IPR system is the World Trade Organization (WTO) Agreement on Trade-Related Aspects of Intellectual Property Rights ("TRIPS Agreement"). The conclusion of the Uruguay Round (1986-1994) of the General Agreement on Tariffs and Trade (GATT) resulted in the creation of the WTO, an international organization established in 1995 as the successor to the GATT. The Uruguay Round also culminated in numerous WTO agreements on trade in goods, services, investment and other non-tariff barriers to trade, one of which was the TRIPS Agreement.

The TRIPS Agreement sets minimum standards of protection and enforcement for patents, copyrights, trademarks and other forms of intellectual property. [47] The agreement is based on three core commitments of the WTO: minimum standards, national treatment, and most-favored-nation treatment. Adherence to the TRIPS Agreement is a prerequisite for WTO membership, and provisions of the agreement can be enforced through the WTO's Dispute Settlement Understanding Mechanism (DSM).

Efforts by the United States, European countries, and the IPR business community in the late 1980s were important in elevating IPR as a trade issue on the agenda of the Uruguay Round of the GATT. They argued that the prevailing international IPR regime, largely administered through "unenforceable" international treaties, was ineffective. U.S. industry criticized the lack of consistency in the promotion, protection, and enforcement of IPR across countries.[48] Others contended that IPR protection and enforcement should not be viewed as a trade issue. Among those who held this view, some may have agreed that the movement of counterfeit and pirated goods across national borders could be a trade issue, but may have questioned the inclusion of a wider-ranging set of IPR issues on the Uruguay Round agenda.

Among the debates about the implications of the TRIPS Agreement, one of the most controversial is its impact on public health. Prior to the TRIPS Agreement, developing country governments regulated public health with little involvement of international IPR regimes. This is because developing countries either did not have IPR systems in place or excluded pharmaceutical products from patents. Proponents of the TRIPS Agreement, mainly developed countries, argued that IPR protection and enforcement contribute to economic growth and development by promoting trade, investment, and technology transfer. Developed countries also asserted that patent protection is critical to public health because patents provide financial incentives for R&D to find pharmaceutical solutions for diseases.

In contrast, critics of the TRIPS, including many developing countries and civil society organizations, asserted that developed countries, which are the major producers of intellectual property, would be the prime beneficiaries of the TRIPS Agreement. Some also held the view that the TRIPS Agreement would raise the costs of IPR-sensitive goods, such as public health goods, constrain the ability of governments to provide health services to their populations, and hinder innovation and economic development for low-income countries. In addition, many developing countries preferred to discuss IPR issues under the auspices of the World Intellectual Property Organization (WIPO) instead of the WTO. WIPO is a United Nations agency that administers all international IPR treaties with the exception of TRIPS.[49]

Ultimately, developing countries acceded to the TRIPS Agreement, after being granted delayed compliance periods and after negotiating goals on other issues in the Uruguay Round such as textiles and clothing. They also favored the prospect of operating under a rules-based trading system. [50] Nevertheless, many stakeholders continue to be critical of the TRIPS Agreement. They argue that the IPR regime's architecture is biased toward IP right holders. They also contend that, in negotiations, high-income countries had greater bargaining power than lower-income countries, which are often dependent on developed countries economically. In addition, some argue that the interests of such groups as IP users, consumers, small- and medium-sized manufacturers, and public health advocates were not sufficiently represented in the TRIPS Agreement negotiations.

Doha Declaration on Public Health

In agreeing to launch the Doha Round of the WTO trade negotiations, trade ministers adopted a "Declaration on the TRIPS Agreement and Public Health" (the "Doha Declaration") on November 14, 2001. The Declaration sought to alleviate developing country dissatisfaction with aspects of the TRIPS regime, confirming that the "TRIPS Agreement does not and should not prevent members from taking measures to protect public health." The

Declaration committed member states to interpret and implement the agreement to support public health and to promote access to medicines for all.

Public Health Debates Surrounding the WTO TRIPS Agreement and the Doha Declaration

The provisions in the TRIPS Agreement and the Doha Declaration that affect pharmaceuticals continue to be the subject of ongoing debate. Issues of concern include the transitional implementation of the TRIPS Agreement, compulsory licensing provisions, parallel importing, and trade in counterfeit pharmaceuticals.

Transitional Implementation of the TRIPS Agreement

In many ways, the TRIPS Agreement was modeled on the IPR standards of developed countries. Many developing countries would have to devote more resources, to develop more technical expertise and capacity, and to make more significant changes to their laws and enforcement practices to become compliant with the TRIPS Agreement than developed countries. The Doha Declaration acknowledged the burden differential by allowing developing countries to delay implementation of the TRIPS Agreement until 2005, and allowing least developed countries (LDCs) to delay implementation until 2016. The WTO does not designate countries by level of development, and under the Doha Declaration, countries are able to self-identify themselves as developing countries.

The TRIPS Agreement does not apply to inventions that already were in the public domain during the time that the Agreement became effective. As such, pharmaceutical inventions that were open to generic competition prior to the implementation of TRIPS do not receive patent exclusivity under TRIPS. Some public health advocates express concerns about how full implementation of the TRIPS Agreement will affect international trade in generic medicines.[51] For example, in the case of HIV/AIDS treatment, most first-line (initial treatments) ARV treatments are off-patent, available through lower-priced generic suppliers, or are offered at significantly discounted prices by innovator pharmaceutical companies. However, second- and third-line (newer products, often developed due to increasing resistance to initial treatments) ARVs tend to be more recent innovations that are patentable under the TRIPS Agreement. In addition, observers point out that new pharmaceutical solutions for infectious diseases, such as malaria and tuberculosis, and noncommunicable diseases such as coronary disease, cancer, diabetes, and asthma may be subject to patents.[52]

Critics of the TRIPS Agreement maintain that implementation of the agreement will affect countries with strong domestic generic drug industries. For example, in 2005, India began implementing its national patent law as part of its TRIPS Agreement requirements. Accordingly, India has started offering patents (including for the larger number of "mailbox" patent applications that were held during the transitional period) for pharmaceutical products. Some question how this provision of patents may affect India's generic supplies of future pharmaceuticals for second-line and third-line ARVS, as well as for new treatments of other diseases.

Some public health advocates express concern that full implementation of the TRIPS Agreement will affect the ability of countries to take advantage of generic goods from countries that serve as generic suppliers. For instance, the ability of Brazil and Thailand to provide HIV/AIDS treatments and other medicines to their nationals largely has been a result of access to India's low-priced generic supplies. [53] Others argue that full implementation of the TRIPS Agreement may not greatly change access to medicines, given that a multitude of other social, political, and economic factors affect access to medicines.

Others also point out that while many WTO signatories have been amenable to changing their laws to increase IPR protection, enforcement of these IPR laws has sometimes been weak or inconsistent.

Compulsory Licensing

Compulsory licenses are issued by governments to authorize the use or production of a patented item by a domestic party other than a patent holder (without the permission of the right holder). They are authorized by Article 31 of TRIPS, which places certain limitations on their use, scope, and duration in an attempt to balance promotion of pharmaceutical innovation and access to new medicines. A government can only issue a compulsory license under certain conditions intended to protect the right of the patent holder. The government must have "made efforts to obtain authorization from the right holder on reasonable commercial terms and conditions." This requirement to first seek authorization can be waived in a time of "national emergency," "other circumstances of extreme urgency," "public non-commercial use," or to address anti-competitive practices (Article 31(b)). If a compulsory license is issued, then "the right holder shall be paid adequate remuneration in the circumstances of each case, taking into account the economic value of the authorization" (Article 31(h)). The TRIPS Agreement also predominantly restricts production authorized by compulsory licenses to the domestic market (Article 31(f)).

Some public health advocates view compulsory licenses as an important mechanism for national governments to provide access to medicines at affordable prices. Supporters of strong IPR regimes argue that, while compulsory licensing may increase short-term access to medicines in developing countries, their widespread use may harm long-term access to medicines. Pharmaceutical companies may opt not to offer their products in countries that consistently break or threaten to break patents in the future. In addition, pharmaceutical companies may not be as willing to invest in finding cures for diseases prevalent in developing countries if their profits are undermined. Others contend that because developing country markets are small, issuing compulsory licenses in these markets does not markedly affect pharmaceutical industry profits or research directions.[54]

National Emergencies

Part of the controversy surrounding compulsory licenses centers on the definition of a "national emergency" under Article 31(b) of the TRIPS Agreement. According to the Doha Declaration, each WTO member country has the right to grant compulsory licenses and to determine the grounds upon which such licenses are issued, including defining what constitutes a national emergency or other cases of extreme urgency. The Doha Declaration cites crises related to HIV/AIDS, tuberculosis, malaria, and other epidemics as situations of potential national emergency or extreme urgency.

CASE STUDY: COMPULSORY LICENSES FOR ANTI-INFLUENZA MEDICINES

In response to recent concerns about the H1N1 "swine flu" outbreak in Mexico, the Mexican government issued a compulsory license for Tamiflu, the leading, brand name anti-influenza drug produced through efforts by the Swiss pharmaceutical company Roche and American pharmaceutical company Gilead. Mexico signed a deal with Cipla, an Indian generic pharmaceutical company, for the manufacture and export of a generic version of Tamiflu to Mexico. The generic version would be sold at a lower price. Roche, which holds the marketing license for Tamiflu, has opposed the decision, arguing that it "has confirmed its willingness to provide the Mexican government with Tamiflu in significant quantities in a timely manner and therefore sees no rationale for compulsory licensing."[55]

Limited Use of Compulsory Licenses By Low- and Middle-Income Countries

Low-income countries have issued compulsory licenses for pharmaceutical drugs under patents on a limited basis. Some speculate that the "underuse" of Article 31 of the TRIPS Agreement is due to the prospect of foreign trade sanctions and/or the threat of corporate litigation. While national governments and multinational companies have expressed support for the Doha Declaration, they reportedly often have opposed the "practical implementation" of compulsory licensing provisions under Article 31 of the TRIPS Agreement.[56] Others suggest that low-income countries may not issue compulsory licenses due to a dearth in administrative or legal resources. Some also suggest that low-income countries may be concerned that issuing compulsory licenses may raise concerns about their business environment and deter foreign investment.

CASE STUDY: BRAZIL'S ISSUANCE OF COMPULSORY LICENSES FOR HIV/AIDS DRUGS

Brazil, a middle-income country, threatened to issue a compulsory license for an HIV/AIDS drug in 2001 following unsuccessful price negotiations with the Swiss pharmaceutical company Roche, citing the HIV/AIDS crisis as a national emergency. Brazil has a national healthcare program that offers free treatment to the entire HIV/AIDS population in Brazil. To that end, Brazil began domestically producing HIV/AIDS drugs, but Efavirenz, a drug produced by the Roche, constituted nearly 30% of the government's spending on HIV/AIDS at that time. Roche eventually conceded to dramatic price reductions, reportedly out of concerns that if Brazil issued a compulsory license, the company would lose out on a significant market.[57]

In contrast, middle-income countries such as Brazil and Thailand, have threatened to issue compulsory licenses for pharmaceutical products in order to negotiate price reductions.

Some assert that compulsory license threats may be a viable option limited to countries with sufficient manufacturing capacity and a sizeable market that can affect pharmaceutical companies' profits.

Utility of Compulsory Licenses

During the Doha Round of the WTO, the requirement under Article 31(f) of the TRIPS Agreement that compulsory licenses must be issued predominantly for the domestic market became a focal point of negotiations. In effect, Article 31(f) conveys the right of compulsory licensing only to countries with the capability to manufacture a given product and precludes countries without domestic manufacturing capability to take advantage of the flexibility. The Doha Declaration acknowledged that "WTO members with insufficient or no manufacturing capacities in the pharmaceutical sector could face difficulties in making effective use of compulsory licensing under the TRIPS Agreement." As such, the Declaration ("Paragraph 6") directed the WTO members to formulate a solution to address the use of compulsory licensing by countries with insufficient or inadequate manufacturing capability.

Prior to the WTO Cancun Ministerial in August 2003, WTO members agreed on a decision to waive the domestic market provision of the TRIPS article on compulsory licensing (Article 31(f)) for exports of pharmaceutical products for "HIV/AIDS, malaria, tuberculosis and other epidemics" to LDCs and countries with insufficient manufacturing capacity. This decision was incorporated as an amendment to the TRIPS agreement at the Hong Kong Ministerial in December 2005. The amendment must be ratified by two-thirds of the 153 WTO member states. Until then, the 2003 waiver continues in force. To date, 54 countries/regions (the United States, Switzerland, El Salvador, South Korea, Norway, India, the Philippines, Israel, Japan, Australia, Singapore, Hong Kong, China, the 27 countries of the European Union, Mauritius, Egypt, Mexico, Jordan, Brazil, Morocco, Albania, Macau-China, Canada, Bahrain, Colombia, Zambia, Pakistan, and the Former Yugoslav Republic of Macedonia) have ratified the amendment. The deadline for ratification has been extended to December 31, 2011.

The system established by the WTO allows LDCs and countries without sufficient manufacturing capacity to issue a compulsory license to a company in a country that can produce such a good. After a matching compulsory license is issued by the producer country, the drug can be manufactured and exported subject to various notification requirements, quantity and safeguard restrictions. Under the safeguard provisions, the drugs issued must be specially marketed or packaged with identifiable characteristics, such as distinguishable colors or shapes "provided that such distinction is feasible and does not have a significant impact on price." It also declared that importing countries should take measures "within their means" to prevent trade diversion.

While the TRIPS Agreement waiver arguably represents a lowering of IPR standards, its supporters assert that the waiver effectively balances the need to promote innovation and protect IPRs with the need for countries with insufficient manufacturing capacity to access medicines through trade. For some public health advocates, the extensive safeguard provisions raise concerns about whether or not manufacturing companies will have sufficient financial incentives to develop such drugs. Moreover, developing countries may not have the resources to protect against the illegitimate export of such drugs to other countries. Some observers argue that the requirements may pose extreme burdens on developing countries that are politically unstable.[58] Some commentators also criticize the case-by-case, country-by-country nature of the notification requirements, which must be fulfilled for every request for parallel importing under a compulsory license. While several exporting countries have established laws and procedures for implementing this system, only Rwanda has availed itself to use the WTO system to import HIV/AIDS medicines from a generic manufacturer in Canada.[59]

An ongoing issue is the extent to "middle-income" countries, such as Brazil, Thailand, India, and China, can or should take advantage of TRIPS Agreement waiver.[60] Developing countries range from the poorest, least-developed, and low-income countries to industrializing, middle-income countries. Some supporters of a strong IPR regime argue that a hard line should be drawn between low-income and middle-income countries. Others hold that international trade policies on innovation should acknowledge the unique needs and capacities of middle-income countries. Some observers have expressed concern that compulsory licensing may be used as an "industrial policy" tool. Countries may issue compulsory licenses for pharmaceuticals in order to develop their domestic pharmaceutical industries.

Parallel Importation

Parallel ("grey market") imports are products marketed by the right holder or with the right holder's permission in one country and imported into another country without the approval of the patent owner. Supporters of parallel trade of pharmaceuticals argue that the practice enables public health providers to take advantage of international differences in the prices of patented drugs. For some countries, importing drugs may be a more cost-effective way of accessing lower-priced medicines than manufacturing them directly.[61] Others contend that parallel importing policies avoid addressing "root" problems in countries' national drug pricing strategies or manufacturing capacity. Some pharmaceutical companies that oppose parallel importation of pharmaceuticals allege that the practice prevents them from offering tiered-pricing for medicines within and among countries. For instance, some pharmaceutical companies may opt to charge lower prices for drugs in least developed countries compared to other countries. In addition, pharmaceutical companies express concern that, in the process, such drugs may be diverted to higher-income markets. Some also express concern about the impact of parallel importing on the supply of medicines in exporting countries.

In the United States, there has been an ongoing debate on parallel importing of pharmaceuticals. U.S. innovator pharmaceutical industries have tended to oppose U.S. imports of generic medicines. In order to increase U.S. access to more affordably-priced medicines, the 111th Congress introduced several bills that would allow Americans to import prescription drugs from foreign countries for personal use. Although debated, no such provisions were included in the final health care legislation (P.L. 111-148, P.L. 111-152). If such provisions were passed, Canada likely would be a leading source of parallel imports of prescription drugs.

Some U.S. consumers and other groups support parallel importation on the basis that it allow Americans to access less expensive drugs. They argue that allowing such importation would reduce drug prices. Prescription drug costs in Canada and the United States may differ due to factors such as government price controls, purchasing power, and negotiating ability. Although "grey market" importation of pharmaceuticals is currently prohibited in the United

States, Americans are able to do so through Internet pharmacies that enable such transactions. Prosecution of these individuals has been limited. While parallel importation may exert pressure on the price of drugs, some consumers contend that it does not address broader issues in the pricing of drugs in the United States.

Pharmaceutical drug companies have raised concerns that allowing such importation may lead to health and safety threats based on counterfeiting concerns. Canada has expressed concerns that parallel importation has led to shortages of drugs. Because some drug companies reportedly restrict the supply of their products to Canada, the Canadian government has threatened to clamp down on the export of drugs to the United States.[62]

Debates about parallel trade raise a question of at what point of sale is the patent right exhausted. The TRIPS Agreement does not address the issue of IPR exhaustion.[63] The Doha Declaration further says that the TRIPS Agreement implies that WTO members can chose their own IPR exhaustion regime.

Patent Exhaustion Regimes

National exhaustion: Some countries, such as the United States and Switzerland, have a national exhaustion regime, meaning that the first sale of a patented good in the country exhausts the patent right in that country and the buyer of the patented good may resell the product without violating the patent right. Conversely, if the first sale of the patented good takes place in a foreign country, the patent may not be exhausted in the home country. As such, importing the patented good from the foreign country into the home country without the permission of the right holder may violate the patent.

Regional exhaustion: In contrast, the European Union subscribes to a regional exhaustion regime. Thus, the first sale of a patented product anywhere in the European Union allows parallel importation within the European Union. However, without the permission of the right holder, parallel importation with a country outside of the European Union is banned without a first sale.

International exhaustion: At the other end of the spectrum, some countries, such as China, subscribe to an international exhaustion regime, in which the first sale of a good internationally exhausts the patent right. Thus, a buyer of the patented good may resell the product anywhere in the world without violating the patent right. In this situation, parallel importing of a good after the first sale does not violate the patent.

Trade in Counterfeit Pharmaceuticals

In the international supply and distribution of pharmaceuticals, there are concerns about the quality of medicines traded. There is broad-based concern about trade in counterfeit pharmaceuticals, which are manufactured and/or sold with the intent to deceive consumers about their origin, legitimacy, and effectiveness. Both brand name and generic medicines can be vulnerable to counterfeiting. Examples of counterfeit drugs include those that are mislabeled, have no or incorrect active pharmaceutical ingredients (APIs), or have correct APIs but in incorrect quantities.

It is difficult to estimate the extent to which counterfeiting occurs. The very nature of IPR infringement—secretive and illicit—makes it difficult to track production and trade in counterfeit goods. Data compiled on counterfeiting comes from many different streams, including national regulatory authorities, enforcement agencies, pharmaceutical companies, non-government organizations, and other groups across geographic regions. These various groups may use different methods to gather their data, which can complicate efforts to compile and compare statistics.[64] In addition, in some cases, companies may be reluctant to release information about IPR infringement problems that they face with their products out of concern that such public information may affect the marketing of their products.[65]

According to previous estimates by the WHO, many countries in Africa, Asia, and Latin America have areas where 10% to 30% of medicines sold are counterfeit. In contrast, in many developed countries, which tend to have stronger regulatory systems, the prevalence of counterfeit drugs is significantly lower. By some estimates, in developed countries, counterfeit medicines constitute less than 1% of market value. In over half of cases in which medicine is purchased over the Internet from unauthorized sites that do not disclose their physical address, the medicines have been found to be counterfeit. [66]

Generic medicines are distinguished from counterfeit medicines in that they are legitimately produced, generally copies of off-patent drugs, and their sale or distribution is not intended to deceive consumers about their origin, authenticity, or effectiveness.[67] While generic medicines are legitimately produced, some innovator pharmaceutical companies and public health advocates express concerns that some generic medicines may be sub-standard.

CASE STUDY: SEIZURE OF GENERIC MEDICINE SHIPMENTS IN TRANSIT FROM INDIA TO BRAZIL

In December 2008, Dutch customs authorities temporarily stopped a shipment of generic high-blood pressure medicines in transit from India to Brazil, reportedly based on concerns that the generic ingredients in the drugs were counterfeit. Previously, Dutch customs authorities temporarily halted shipments of generic medicines manufactured in India and in transit to Colombia and Peru via the Netherlands. Critics, including some non-governmental organizations, asserted that seizures of legitimate generic medicines in transit posit risks to public health by placing trade in generic medicines in peril. They claimed that the actions of the Dutch customs officials and European Union rules are designed to "disrupt the supply of legitimate generic medicines to developing countries" and that such actions set dangerous precedents. EU officials countered that the GATT permits customs officials to stop and inspect transit shipments.[68] Supporters of the seizures also may contend that such actions could help combat global trade flows of counterfeit goods. During the week of May 14, 2010, Brazil and India filed requests for WTO consultations with the European Union and the Netherlands as an initial step toward a dispute settlement case over repeated seizures in the EU of generic medicines in transit from India to Brazil.[69]

Some industrialized countries have begun to detain shipments of generic medicines for inspection due to concerns that the drugs are counterfeit. On the one hand, increased IPR seizures may limit instances of counterfeit drugs, thus mitigating health and safety risks. On the other hand, confusion between counterfeit and legitimate generic goods may result in increased incidences of seizures of legitimate generics in transit and delay delivery of medicines. Some nongovernmental organizations (NGOs) also assert that industrialized countries are using this strategy to discourage generic drug production and have urged the WTO and the WHO to take action to address this issue.

U.S. Trade Policies on Intellectual Property Rights

The U.S. government has placed significant priority on pursuing stronger international IPR protection and enforcement through U.S. trade policy. In addition to participating in multilateral trade policy negotiations regarding IPRs, the United States seeks stronger international IPR protection and enforcement through regional and bilateral free trade agreements (FTAs) and unilateral trade policy tools.

Free Trade Agreements

In pursuing IPR provisions in regional and bilateral FTAs, USTR is guided by three main goals: (1) to promote strong IPR protection and enforcement in FTAs; (2) to secure market access opportunities for U.S. businesses that rely on IPR protection; and (3) to respect the Doha Declaration on the TRIPS Agreement and Public Health.[70] Currently, the United States has two regional FTAs and nine bilateral FTAs in force. Three FTAs (Panama, Colombia, and Korea) have been negotiated and are pending congressional approval.

In negotiating FTAs, the USTR frequently has sought levels of protection that exceed the minimum standards of the TRIPS Agreement (the so-called "TRIPS-plus" provisions). For pharmaceutical-related IPR provisions in FTAs, the USTR generally has pursued requirements on data exclusivity, patent term extensions, and patent linkage. In some cases, the USTR also has sought provisions to limit the issuance of compulsory licenses and parallel importing, particularly when negotiating FTAs with middle-income countries.

TRIPS-Plus Provisions in U.S. FTAs

While the specific IPR provisions vary across FTAs, there are a number of typical "TRIPS-plus" provisions that the United States has pursued.

Data exclusivity: In general, data exclusivity requirements stipulate that "a generic company cannot obtain market approval based on the safety and efficacy of the innovator company for a period of at least five years from the data marketing approval was granted to the innovator." Consequently, this provision gives the patent holder five years "of effective marketing exclusivity, unless the generic firm produces its own safety and efficacy data with new drug trials."

Patent term extensions: Patent terms may be extended beyond 20 years in order to compensate for "unreasonable delays" in granting patent licenses or market approval.

Patent linkage: The FTAs may prohibit a country's drug regulatory authority from approving a generic drug for marketing while the brand-name drug is still under patent.

Compulsory licensing: The FTAs may limit the grounds on which to issue compulsory licenses. This is largely restricted to national emergencies, such as anti-competitive remedies and for public non-commercial use. Some question whether or not this restricts the ability of countries to issue compulsory licenses to protect public health in cases that are serious but may not be viewed as national emergencies. Prohibiting compulsory licenses for nonnational emergencies may disallow compulsory licenses to promote generic competition on medicines.

Parallel importing: In some FTAs, patent holders can contractually prevent parallel importation.

The USTR asserts that strong IPR provisions ultimately promote access to medicines for developing countries by encouraging innovation. However, the adoption of "TRIPS-plus" provisions in FTAs has garnered much criticism from public health advocates and developing countries. Some critics contend that the FTAs and unilateral U.S. trade actions (discussed below) are eroding developing countries' abilities to exercise their legal rights to issue compulsory licenses and engage in parallel importing under the TRIPS Agreement. Public health advocates also express concerns that these TRIPS-plus standards run contrary to the spirit of the Doha Declaration. Under this viewpoint, these standards "limit national strategies to provide affordable medicines and limit market access for generic medicines, irrespective of the country's level of development or disease burden."[71]

In addition, some argue that U.S. rigidity regarding IPRs may take away from potential U.S. gains in other areas of trade negotiation. For, FTA negotiations between the United States and Thailand, initiated in 2003, reportedly have been hampered by U.S. concerns about deficiencies in Thailand's IPR regime and Thailand's concern about the impact that raising IPRs may have on public health in Thailand, including the government's ability to provide generic versions of HIV/AIDS medicines to its population.

Because U.S. trade partners have expressed reservations about the stringent IPR standards pursued by the United States, some question why countries would want to enter into FTAs with the United States. Some argue that for low-income and middle-income countries, "Securing favorable market access for exports has usually outweighed public-health priorities—even when benefits are likely to be short lived and eroded as tariffs decrease."[72]

In response to concerns that U.S. trade negotiations may affect public health in developing countries, among other concerns (including environmental issues and labor rights), there has been somewhat of a shift in U.S. trade policy regarding pharmaceutical IPRs. A May 10, 2007 bipartisan trade deal between former President George W. Bush and congressional leaders yielded changes to the provisions in the U.S. FTA template, which is the basic text with which the United States begins FTA negotiations.[73] The deal made optional the previously mandatory requirements for patent linkage and patent term extensions.

In addition, the deal includes provisions that may shorten the period of data exclusivity used for providing marketing approval. The bipartisan trade deal scaled down IPR provisions for pharmaceutical patents in U.S. FTAs with Peru, Panama, and Colombia. The Obama Administration is reviewing U.S. trade policy, including IPRs and pharmaceuticals.

Unilateral Trade Policy

Domestic trade policy tools also are available for U.S. efforts to advance international patent protection and enforcement. Such trade policy tools are often effective in influencing developing countries' decisions because the United States is a significant market for some trade partners. However, the use of these tools has been criticized by various interest groups.

Special 301

The most prominent of these tools is the USTR "Special 301" Report. Pursuant to Section 182 of the Trade Act of 1974, as amended (P.L. 93-618), the USTR identifies countries with inadequate IPR protection and enforcement regimes in its yearly Special 301 Report. USTR country identifications under Special 301 consider all forms of IPR and take into account a host of factors, including the level and scope of the country's IPR infringement; the impact of infringement on the U.S. economy; the strength of the country's IPR laws and enforcement of IPR laws; the progress made by the country in improving IPR protection and enforcement; and the sincerity of the country's commitment to multilateral and bilateral trade agreements. The USTR can identify a country as denying sufficient intellectual property protection even if the country is complying with its commitments under the TRIPS Agreement.

The USTR identifies countries through a three-tier system, depending on the severity of the country's IPR violations. If a country is named as a "Priority Foreign Country," the USTR must launch an investigation into that country's IPR practices, and the country is subjected potentially to trade sanctions, including the suspension of trade concessions or the imposition of import restrictions or duties.[74] "Priority Watch List" countries are those whose acts, policies, and practices warrant concern, but do not meet all of the criteria for identification as a Priority Foreign Country. "Watch List" countries have intellectual property protection inadequacies that are less severe than those on the Priority Watch List, but still warrant U.S. attention. Countries identified for "Section 306" are monitored for compliance with bilateral intellectual property agreements used to resolve investigations under Section 301. Oftentimes, USTR identification of countries on the Special 301 list prompts countries to take actions to change their IPR practices.

The USTR also launches out-of-cycle reviews (OCRs) to monitor certain countries' progress on intellectual property issues. These reviews are conducted on countries that USTR considers to require further review and may result in status changes for the following year's Special 301 report.

CASE STUDY: THAILAND'S ISSUANCE OF COMPULSORY LICENSES FOR MEDICINES

Thailand has a national health care program that includes HIV/AIDS treatment. As more patients have become resistant to the first-line ARVs, they have required treatment with newer, more expensive ARVs. In response to the rising cost of medicines, in 2006, Thailand issued compulsory licenses for two ARVs for HIV/AIDS, as well as a heart medication. Prior to issuing the compulsory licenses, the Thai government reportedly engaged in negotiations with pharmaceutical companies to lower the prices of medicines.

In 2007, the USTR identified Thailand as a Priority Watch List country in its Special 301 report, citing "a weakening of respect for patents" and a "lack of transparency and due process" in the issuance of compulsory licenses. Although the USTR did not specifically mention Thailand's issuance of compulsory licenses for HIV/AIDS drugs, several Members of Congress interpreted USTR's decision as retaliation for Thailand's recent actions. Members argued that Thailand's actions were consistent with the WTO TRIPS Agreement. They pointed out that no prior consultation with patent holders is required in cases of extreme urgency or public non-commercial use and that Thailand entered into pharmaceutical consultations, even though it was under no obligation to do so. Members also expressed concern that the USTR decision would be viewed as a warning by the public health community and would deter other countries from pursuing similar actions.[75] Since 2007, Thailand has remained on the Priority Watch List.[76] In response to U.S. pressure, Thailand reportedly decided not to continue its compulsory licensing policy and to promote access to medicines in other ways.[77] In the 2010 Special 301 report, the USTR stated that it would conduct an out-of-cycle review on Thailand this year.

CASE STUDY: SOUTH AFRICA AND ACCESS TO HIV/AIDS DRUGS

During the 1990s, South Africa considered issuing compulsory licenses for HIV/AIDS drugs. The United States strongly opposed these measures, on the grounds that they would hurt pharmaceutical innovation. Subsequently, the United States refused South Africa's request for additional GSP concessions and also placed South Africa on its Special 301 Watch List. In addition, South Africa was faced with corporate litigation. Ultimately, due to international pressure, the United States dropped its opposition and the pharmaceutical companies dropped its lawsuit against South Africa.[79]

Generalized System of Preferences

Another domestic policy tool used to protect intellectual property rights is the Generalized System of Preferences (GSP). The United States may consider a developing country's IPR policies and practices as a basis for granting preferential duty-free entry to certain products from the country, and can suspend GSP benefits if IPR protection is lacking. For 2008, the USTR was scheduled to continue evaluating IPR protection in Russia, Lebanon, and Uzbekistan on the basis of petitions by the International Intellectual Property Alliance (IIPA) for ongoing GSP reviews.[78] The citation of a country on the USTR Special 301 watch lists may be grounds for withdrawing GSP benefits from that country. Because it is trade preferences that are being withdrawn, countries are unable to raise the removal of trade concessions as a WTO violation.

U.S. Trade Policy and Support for Public Health

The USTR holds the view that its pursuit of a strong international IPR regime advances U.S. economic interests while at the same time supports public health. However, the U.S. government does not necessarily view trade policy as the primary policy tool to promote public health. According to a recent GAO report, "Trade and IP efforts are only one small part of the larger U.S. government effort to increase access to medicines."[80]

U.S. government efforts directed at increasing access to medicines may be promoted through foreign, health, education, and other policy areas. There are a number of U.S. government initiatives specifically designed to increase developing countries' access to medicines. For instance, the U.S. Department of State "primarily makes an effort to balance IP rights and access to medicines through public health initiatives it coordinates with other agencies or administers itself ... ."[81]

The United States has advocated for greater availability of certain generic drugs in certain areas of the world. One example of this is through PEPFAR, the U.S. President's Emergency Plan for AIDS Relief.[82] This initiative "supports the increased availability of safe, effective, low-cost, and generic antiretroviral drugs (ARVs) in the developing world ... " To meet the need for such ARVs, the FDA introduced an expedited "tentative approval" process through which ARVs produced by any manufacturer, including generic manufacturers, internationally could be reviewed quickly for quality standards and approved for purchase under PEPFAR.[83]

Issues for Congressional Consideration

Possible issues of interest for Congress include incorporating public health input into the U.S. trade policy advisory process, developing new U.S. trade policy guidance on public health, considering the implications of the U.S. strategy on IPRs and trade for U.S. access to medicines, and reviewing the range of options utilized for expanding global access to medicines.

Public Health Representation in U.S. Trade Policy Process

Some observers of the U.S. trade policy process assert that the protection of intellectual property has been given more emphasis than the protection of public health. Advocates of public health maintain that the United States has a legal and moral imperative to ensure that public health is safeguarded through trade policy. They point out that the United States is a signatory to the United Nation's International Covenant on Economic, Social and Cultural Rights. Among the human rights agreed upon in the covenant, Article 12.1 provides "the right of everyone to the enjoyment of the highest attainable standard of physical and mental health." Many human rights organizations view access to medicines as a critical component of the fundamental human right to health. Other observers of the U.S. trade policy process assert that protection of IPRs contributes to the protection of public health, and that U.S. trade policy is one of multiple policy arenas that support public health.

USTR Advisory Committee

Some proponents of greater public health representation in the U.S. trade policy process often direct their attention to the USTR Advisory Committee structure, the central mechanism through which the USTR consults with the private sector and civil society organizations regarding the U.S. trade policy agenda and negotiations. Critics argue that private sector interests are granted greater representation in the advisory system than public health or other civil society interests. They argue that this "privileged access to government policy makers" allows commercial interests to influence the formulation of U.S. trade negotiating positions, which in turn have affected the WTO's agenda.[84]

According to a recent Government Accountability Office (GAO) report, for the review period of the report (November 2006 through November 2007), there were 16 Industry Trade Advisory Committees (ITACs), two of which each had a single public health representative. These committees are the Intellectual Property Committee and the Chemicals, Pharmaceuticals, Health Science Products and Services Committee, which were composed of 20 and 33 members, respectively, during the review period. Defenders of the current advisory system argue that public health representation is included in the ITACs most relevant to public health. Furthermore, according to officials from the USTR, it was "not necessary to have two public health representatives on one committee representing the same view, and they said they did not find any other viable candidates with additional perspectives beyond the individuals selected."[85]

Some lawmakers have urged the USTR to reform the formal trade advisory committee system. Among the suggestions put forth are creating a new advisory committee that addresses public health issues, including issues pertaining to developing countries, or a committee focusing on trade and development.[86] In the 111th Congress, H.R. 2293 (Van Hollen) was introduced and referred to the House Ways and Means Committee on May 6, 2009, to ensure that public health views are represented and accommodated in developing U.S. trade policy. Specifically, the bill would require the creation of a Public Health Advisory Committee on Trade, whose membership would be restricted to individuals with expertise in various trade and public health issues, including issues in access to affordable pharmaceuticals. Membership would exclude individuals who represent commercial interests in health services or regulations. This committee would be located in the second tier of the Trade Advisory Committee System. In addition, the bill would require non-governmental public health officials to be appointed to the Advisory Committee for Trade Policy and Negotiations, a first-tier committee.

In the 110th Congress, Representative Van Hollen also introduced legislation to reform the trade advisory system (H.R. 3204) that differed from H.R. 2293 in certain ways. Both pieces of legislation include provisions for creating a Public Health Advisory Committee on Trade. However, H.R. 3204 also would have required that each ITAC must have at least one representative of labor, consumer interest, and public health. This provision was not included in H.R. 2293 in the 111th Congress.

While many public health advocates applaud legislation to increase public health representation on advisory trade committees, some caution against creating a trade advisory committee that focuses solely on health issues as this may insulate trade policy discussions from public health concerns. For instance, critics express concern that the USTR may limit consultations with the proposed health committee to a narrow set of technical issues and not on the broader implications of trade policy for public health. Among industry advocates, some may be critical of legislation that would dilute industry representation on the ITACs. They may contend that the ITACs were created as a vehicle for the USTR to consult specifically with industry.

Other channels for input on FTA negotiations include the "USTR's formal public hearings and the Federal Register comments." While the public health input through these alternate mechanisms may be higher, some question the relative weight of such input compared to that received through the ITACs.[87]

Special 301

For some observers of the U.S. trade policy process, another area of concern is the USTR Special 301 report. USTR identification of countries also involves gathering information and analysis based on the USTR's annual trade barriers report, as well as consultations with a wide variety of sources, including government agencies, industry groups, other private sector representatives, congressional leaders, and foreign governments. Some observers express concern that U.S. industry interests, such as those of PhRMA, heavily influence USTR's country identifications and that there is limited input from public health advocates, generic drug manufacturers, and other groups. Although the Special 301 Report is regarded by some as an effective form of U.S. political pressure on trading partners, others express concern that disproportionate representation of industry interests may limit the legitimacy of the Special 301 trade policy tool.[88]

U.S. Trade Policy Guidance

In 2002, Congress granted Trade Promotion Authority (TPA) to then President Bush. The TPA included a commitment to ensure that U.S international trade agreements respected public health. Should Congress decide to renew Trade Promotion Authority (TPA) for President Obama, Members may choose to consider what, if any, public health mandate should the TPA include.

Another issue that Congress may choose to consider is the extent to which the May 10, 2007 bipartisan trade deal between then President Bush and congressional leaders will serve as a template for the IPR provisions in future FTAs. Some also question whether or not this FTA template will be used for all future FTAs, or if will it be used according to the income status of a country. For instance, the template's scale-down in patent requirements was incorporated into the recently negotiated FTAs with Peru, Panama, and Colombia, which are considered low-income countries. They were not incorporated into the FTA with South Korea, which is considered to be a middle-income country. Some also question whether or not the May 10, 2007 bipartisan trade deal's changes to FTA patent provisions will be applied to existing FTAs.[89]

Some stakeholders encourage Congress to revisit the IPR provisions in the May 10, 2007, bipartisan trade deal. Among those stakeholders, some innovator pharmaceutical industry representatives hope that the Administration will decided to reverse the previous scale-down in patent provisions. For instance, the National Association of Manufacturers (NAM) believes that the pharmaceutical industry was unfairly singled out in the trade deal. However, others express concern that revisiting the deal may lead to re-evaluation of previously resolved issues. Global health advocates and generic pharmaceutical companies likely would resist changes to the IPR portions and could encourage further weakening of patent provisions in an effort to increase access to medicines.[90]

The Trade Reform, Accountability, Development and Employment (TRADE) Act of 2009 (H.R. 3012, Michaud) and its companion bill (S. 2021, Brown), introduced in the 111th Congress, would require a review of the economic, environmental, national security, health, safety, and other impacts of certain U.S. free trade agreements and renegotiation of those agreements based on the review. The bills also would require that the implementing bills of new trade agreements would not be expedited unless they met certain standards in fourteen different areas. With respect to IPR, under the bills, terms related to patents in the trade agreements could not limit the flexibilities and rights established in the WTO Doha Declaration on the TRIPS Agreement and Public Health, either overtly or in application. The United States-Peru FTA, which incorporates the provisions of the May 10, 2007, bipartisan trade deal, largely reflects the IPR and public health provisions called for in H.R. 3012 and S. 2021.

Implications of U.S. Strategy on IPR and Trade for U.S. Access to Medicines

Given that the United States is a primary producer of patents, some argue that a strong international IPR regime is economically beneficial to the United States. However, some observers question whether continually seeking higher standards of IPR will always be in the U.S. interest. Situations may arise in which the United States may wish to issue compulsory licenses to address global health or security threats. For instance, when the anthrax scare occurred in 2001, the United States and Canada considered issuing compulsory licenses for Cipro, a drug produced by the German company Bayer, so that their populations could access the drug at affordable prices. Some viewed U.S. and Canadian action as hypocritical, considering that these two countries had pledged to "opt out" of using the TRIPS Agreement flexibilities and had pressured other countries to do the same. Some observers saw the incident as a cautionary example of how limiting flexibilities in patent regimes may be detrimental to U.S. interests. Another example is the H5N1 "avian influenza" crisis of 2005. The United States threatened to issue a compulsory license for the production of Tamiflu, the anti-viral drug produced by the Swiss company Roche. The United States was concerned that Roche lacked the production capacity to meet global demand for the medication. Roche ultimately agreed to ramp up production for Tamiflu by sublicensing the patent to other manufacturers.[91]

Higher vaccine and drug prices associated with IPR protection and enforcement may reduce incentives for developing countries to share virus samples with the WHO in order to find cures for diseases. For instance, during the H5N1 "avian influenza" pandemic, Indonesia limited sharing H5N1 virus samples with WHO researchers. Indonesia expressed concerns that the vaccines would be patented and then offered for purchase at marked-up prices unaffordable for Indonesia and other developing countries. In March 2007, Indonesia began sharing virus samples again under the condition that an international agreement would be negotiated for more equitable, affordable sharing of vaccines.[92]

As China, India, and other industrializing countries continue to develop, a larger proportion of global patents may originate from these countries. Although the United States continued to rank as the leading source of applications under WIPO's Patent Cooperation Treaty (PCT) in 2009, U.S. patent filings fell by 11.4% from the previous year. In contrast, the growth rate in patent filings stood at 29.4% for China.[93] These shifts in the concentration of patents and the pharmaceutical marketplace may have implications for the cost of medicines for the United States and other developed countries. [94]

Non-Patent Options for Expanding Access to Medicines

Some public health advocates argue that the public should play a greater role in the provision of pharmaceutical solutions for diseases. Some suggest that U.S. strategies to address public health needs through trade policy should expand beyond patenting and compulsory licensing. The WHO Global Strategy on Public Health, Innovation and Intellectual Property calls for an exploration of a range of incentive mechanisms. In addition to patents, other methods of incentivizing the private sector to target R&D toward addressing public health needs of developing countries may include advance market commitments, patent pools, and innovation prizes. While such mechanisms may direct pharmaceutical R&D toward meeting the needs of developing countries, they may require governments to bear a greater share of the risks associated with R&D.[95]

End Notes

[1] This report builds on CRS Report RL33750, *The WTO, Intellectual Property Rights, and the Access to Medicines Controversy*, by Ian F. Fergusson.

[2] For an overview on IPRs and international trade issues in general, see CRS Report RL34292, *Intellectual Property Rights and International Trade*, by Shayerah Ilias and Ian F. Fergusson.

[3] CRS Report RL33944, *Trade Primer: Qs and As on Trade Concepts, Performance, and Policy*, coordinated by Raymond J. Ahearn.

[4] Office of the U.S. Trade Representative (USTR), *Special 301 Report 2010*, April 30, 2010, p. 5.

[5] The World Health Organization (WHO) defines essential medicines as "those that satisfy the priority health care needs of the population. They are selected with due regard to public health relevance, evidence on efficacy and safety, and comparative cost-effectiveness."

[6] WHO, *Online Q&A: HIV/AIDS*, November 2009, http://www.who.int/features/qa/71/en/index.html/

[7] WHO, *Neglected Tropical Diseases: Frequently Asked Questions*, updated March 25, 2009, http://www.who.int/neglected_diseases/en/.

[8] United Nations, *Keeping the promise: a forward-looking review to promote an agreed action agenda to achieve the Millennium Development Goals by 2015: Report of the Secretary-General*, A/64/665, February 12, 2010, p. 27, http://www.un.org/ga/search/view_doc.asp?symbol=A/64/665.

[9] WHO, "More than four million HIV-positive people now receiving life-saving treatment," press release, September 30, 2009, http://www.who.int/mediacentre/news/releases/2009/universal_coverage_hiv_20090930/en/index.html.

[10] Ramanan Laxminarayan, Mead Over, and David L. Smith, "Will a Global Subsidy of Artemisinin-Based Combination Treatment (ACT) for Malaria Delay the Emergence of Resistance and Save Lives?", World Bank, Policy Research Working Paper No. 3670, Washington, D.C., 2005. Cited by Carsten Fink, "Intellectual Property and Public Health: An Overview of the Debate with a Focus on U.S. Policy," Working Paper Number 146, June 2008.

[11] David P. Fidler, Nick Drager, and Kelley Lee, "Managing the Pursuit of Health and Wealth: The Key Challenges," *The Lancet*, vol. 373 (January 24, 2009), pp. 328-329.

[12] National Science Foundation (NSF), "*Science and Engineering Indicators 2008*, "Industry, Technology, and the Marketplace," NSB 08-01; NSB 08-01A, Arlington, VA, January 2008, p. 16.

[13] Pharmaceutical Researchers and Manufacturers of America (PhRMA), *Pharmaceutical Industry Profile 2010*, Washington, DC, March 2010, p. 29, http://www.phrma.org/sites/phrma.org/files/attachments/Profile_2010_FINAL.pdf.

[14] IHS Global Insight, Drugs: *Industry Analysis*, January 2009.

[15] World Intellectual Property Organization (WIPO), "*International Patent Filings Dip in 2009 amid Global Economic Downturn,*" press release, February 8, 2010, http://www.wipo.int/pressroom/en/articles/2010/article_0003.html.

[16] Public Citizen, "Tufts Drug Study Sample Is Skewed; True Figure of R&D Costs Likely Is 75 Percent Lower," press release, December 4, 2001, http://www.citizen.org/pressroom/pressroomredirect.cfm?ID=954.

[17] Carsten Fink, *Intellectual Property and Public Health: An Overview of the Debate with a Focus on U.S. Policy*, Center for Global Development, Working Paper Number 146, June 2008, p. 22.

[18] WHO, *Public Health, Innovation and Intellectual Property Rights: Report of the Commission on Intellectual Property Rights, Innovation and Public Health*, 2006, p. 16.

[19] Ricki Lewis, *Fighting the 10/90 Gap,* Medecins San Frontiers (MSF), May 13, 2002.

[20] Phillip Stevens, *Diseases of Poverty and the 10/90 Gap, International Policy Network*, November 2004.

[21] Ibid, pp. 5-7.

[22] WHO, *Preventing Chronic Disease: A Global Investment: WHO Global Report*, 2005.

[23] Commission on Social Determinants of Health, *Closing the Gap in a Generation: Health Equity Through Actions on the Social Determinants of Health*, WHO, Final Report of the Commission on Social Determinants of Health, Geneva, 2008.

[24] World Trade Organization (WTO) glossary.

[25] CRS Report RL30756, *Patent Law and Its Application to the Pharmaceutical Industry: An Examination of the Drug Price Competition and Patent Term Restoration Act of 1984 ("The Hatch-Waxman Act"),* by Wendy H. Schacht and John R. Thomas.

[26] GAO, *U.S. Trade Policy Guidance on WTO Declaration on Access to Medicines May Need Clarification*, GAO-07-1198, September 2007, p. 7.

[27] Commission on Social Determinants of Health, *Closing the Gap in a Generation: Health Equity Through Actions on the Social Determinants of Health, WHO, Final Report of the Commission on Social Determinants of Health*, Geneva, 2008.

[28] United Nations, *Delivering on the Global Partnership for Achieving the Millennium Development Goals*, MDG Task Force Report, 2008, p. 35.

[29] WHO, http://www.who.int/topics/essential_medicines/en/, accessed April 6, 2009.

[30] WHO, *WHO Model List of Essential Medicines*, 15th List, March 2007, http://www.who.int/medicines/publications/essentialmedicines/en/.

[31] Amir Attaran, "How Do Patents and Economic Policies Affect Access to Essential Medicines in Developing Countries," *Health Affairs,* vol. 23, no. 3 (May/June 2004).

[32] Ibid., p. 159.

[33] "IMS Forecasts Global Pharmaceutical Market Growth of 5-8% Annually through 2014; Maintains Expectations of 4-6% Growth in 2010," *AIDS Weekly*, May 3, 2010, p. 181.

[34] Gary Gatyas and Clive Savage, "IMS Health Forecasts 4.5-5.5 Percent Growth for Global Pharmaceutical Market in 2009, Exceeding $820 Billion," *Business Wire*, October 29, 2008.

[35] "IMS Forecasts Global Pharmaceutical Market Growth of 5-8% Annually through 2014; Maintains Expectations of 4-6% Growth in 2010," *AIDS Weekly*, May 3, 2010, p. 181.

[36] National Science Foundation (NSF), "*Science and Engineering Indicators 2010*, "Industry, Technology, and the Marketplace," NSB 10-01, Arlington, VA, 2010.

[37] IHS Global Insight, *Drugs: Industry Analysis*, January 2009.

[38] WHO, *Public Health, Innovation and Intellectual Property Rights: Report of the Commission on Intellectual Property Rights, Innovation and Public Health*, Switzerland, 2006, p. 26.

[39] Richard D. Smith, Carlos Correa, and Cecilia Oh, "Trade, TRIPS, and Pharmaceuticals," *The Lancet*, vol. 373 (February 21, 2009).

[40] Kevin Outterson, "Patent Buy-Outs for Global Disease Innovations for Low- and Middle-Income Countries," *American Journal of Law & Medicine*, vol. 32 (2006), p. 160.

[41] Previously IMS Health had identified seven countries as "pharmerging": China, Brazil, Mexico, India, Russia, South Korea, and Turkey.

[42] "IMS Announces 17 Countries Now Rank as High-Growth 'Pharmerging' Markets; Forecast to Contribute Nearly Half of Industry Growth by 2013," *Biotech Business Week*, March 29, 2010, p. 4072. Angie Drakulich, "Seventeen, Not Seven, Markets Now Hold "Pharmerging" Title," Pharmaceutical Technology, vol. 34, no. 4 (April 2010), p. 25.

[43] Ibid.

[44] Gary Gatyas and Clive Savage, "IMS Health Forecasts 4.5-5.5 Percent Growth for Global Pharmaceutical Market in 2009, Exceeding $820 Billion," *Business Wire*, October 29, 2008. T.J. Dufour, "Drugs: Overview: Forecast Highlights," Global Insight, March 31, 2010.

[45] U.S. classification of technology industries differs from that of the OECD. While the OECD classifies technologies as "high-technology," "medium-technology," and "low-technology."

[46] NSF, "*Science and Engineering Indicators 2008*, "Industry, Technology, and the Marketplace," NSB 08-01; NSB 08-01A, Arlington, VA, January 2008.

[47] The North American Free Trade Agreement (NAFTA) signed in 1993 by the United States, Canada, and Mexico was the first international trade agreement to include minimum standards for IPR protection and enforcement. In many respects, the NAFTA served as a framework for the TRIPS Agreement.

[48] Keith E. Maskus, *Intellectual Property Rights in the Global Economy* (Institute for International Economics, 2000).

[49] Frederick M. Abbott and Jerome H. Reichman, "The Doha Round's Public Health Legacy: Strategies for the Production and Diffusion of Patented Medicines Under the Amended TRIPS Provisions," *Journal of International Economic Law*, vol. 10, no. 4, p. 925.

[50] Keith E. Maskus, *Intellectual Property Rights in the Global Economy* (Institute for International Economics, 2000).

[51] Carsten Fink, *Intellectual Property and Public Health: An Overview of the Debate with a Focus on U.S. Policy*, Center for Global Development, Working Paper Number 146, June 2008.

[52] Frederick M. Abbott, "The WTO Medicines Decision: World Pharmaceutical Trade and the Protection of Public Health," *The American Journal of International Law*, vol. 99, no. 2 (April 2005), p. 320.

[53] Lisa Forman, "Trading Health for Profit: The Impact of Bilateral and Regional Free Trade Agreements on Domestic Intellectual Property Rules on Pharmaceuticals," *in The Power of Pills*, ed. Jillian Clare Coehn, Patricia Illingworth, and Udo Schüklenk (Ann Arbor: Pluto Press, 2006), p. 191.

[54] Martin Foreman, Patents, *Pills and Public Health: Can TRIPS Deliver?,* The Panos Institute, London, 2002, pp. 28-29.

[55] Khomba Singh and Sushmi Dey, "Local drug cos may chip in to treat swine flu," The Economic Times, April 28, 2009. Andrew Jack, "Indian drug company set to sell cheap copy of Tamiflu," *The Financial Times*, May 14, 2009.

[56] Ellen F.m.'t Hoen, LL.M., *The Global Politics of Pharmaceutical Monopoly Power: Drug patents, Access, Innovation and the Application of the WTO Doha Declaration on TRIPS and Public Health* (AMB Publishers, 2009), p. 3.

[57] Jillian Clare Cohen, "Expanding Drug Access in Brazil: Lessons for Latin America and Canada," *Canadian Journal of Public Health*, vol. 97, no. 6 (Nov/Dec 2006).

[58] Pooja Van Dyck, "Importing Western Style, Exporting Tragedy: Changes in Indian Patent Law and Their Impact on AIDS Treatment in Africa," *Northwestern Journal of Technology and Intellectual Property*, vol. 6 (2007-2008), p. 146.

[59] Daniel Pruzin, "Canadian Firm to Begin Exporting Generic Medicines Under WTO Deal," *International Trade Daily*, September 9, 2008.

[60] The World Bank classifies countries as high-, middle-, and low-income countries.

[61] Lisa Forman, "Trading Health for Profit: The Impact of Bilateral and Regional Free Trade Agreements on Domestic Intellectual Property Rules on Pharmaceuticals," *in The Power of Pills*, ed. Jillian Clare Coehn, Patricia Illingworth, and Udo Schüklenk (Ann Arbor: Pluto Press, 2006), p. 191.

[62] Alex Wayne, "Obama Wants to Permit Imports of Prescription Drugs," *CQ Today*, February 26, 2009.

[63] The TRIPS Agreements states that none of its provisions, aside from those concerning non-discrimination (i.e. national treatment and most-favored nation), can be applied to address the issue of exhaustion of IPRs in a WTO dispute.

[64] WHO, *Medicines: Counterfeit Medicines*, Fact Sheet, January 2010, http://www.who.int/mediacentre/factsheets/fs275/en/.

[65] Kevin Outterson and Ryan Smith, "Counterfeit Drugs: The Good, the Bad, and the Ugly," *Albany Law Journal of Science and Technology*, vol. 525 (2006).

[66] WHO, Medicines: Counterfeit Medicines, Fact Sheet, January 2010, http://www.who.int/mediacentre/factsheets/fs275/en/.

[67] WTO glossary.

[68] Daniel Pruzin, "Group Urges WHO, WTO to Prevent Seizure of Legitimate Generic Medicine Shipments," *International Trade Daily*, February 23, 2009.

[69] Catherine Saez, "Drug Access Waiver Debate Looms For June TRIPS Council Meeting ," *Intellectual Property Watch*, May 31, 2010.

[70] U.S. Government Accountability Office (GAO), *U.S. Trade Policy Guidance on WTO Declaration on Access to Medicines May Need Clarification*, GAO-07-1198, September 2007, pp. 27-28.

[71] Lisa Forman, "Trading Health for Profit: The Impact of Bilateral and Regional Free Trade Agreements on Domestic Intellectual Property Rules on Pharmaceuticals," *in The Power of Pills*, ed. Jillian Clare Coehn, Patricia Illingworth, and Udo Schüklenk (Ann Arbor: Pluto Press, 2006), p. 190. Jamie Strawbridge, "NGOs Press USTR To Extend May 10 Deal On IPR To All Trade Pacts," *Inside U.S. Trade*, May 22, 2009.

[72] Kelley Lee, Devi Sridhar, and Mayur Patel, "Bridging the Divide: Global Governance of Trade and Health," *Lancet*, vol. 373 (January 22, 2009), p. 418.

[73] The text of the May 10, 2007, Bipartisan Trade Deal is available on the USTR website at http://www.ustr.gov/assets/ Document_Library/Fact_Sheets/2007/asset_upload_file127_11319.pdf.

[74] Among other factors, the imposition of trade sanctions depends on whether or not the country is a WTO member. If the country is a WTO member, then the United States must use the WTO Dispute Settlement Mechanism to resolve the issue.

[75] Letter from Henry A. Waxman, Member of Congress, et al. to Ambassador Susan C. Schwab, USTR, June 20, 2007.

[76] USTR, *USTR Special 301 Report 2008*, pp. 36-37.

[77] "Thailand: Government not to extend compulsory licensing policy," *BBC Monitoring Asia Pacific*, May 2, 2009.

[78] USTR, *GSP: 2008 Annual Review*, http://www.ustr.gov.

[79] Anna Lanoska, "The Global Politics of Intellectual Property Rights and Pharmaceutical Drug Policies in Developing Countries," *International Political Science Review*, vol. 24, no. 2 (April 2003).

[80] U.S. Government Accountability Office, *U.S. Trade Policy Guidance on WTO Declaration on Access to Medicines May Need Clarification*, GAO-07-1198, September 2007, p. 53.

[81] Ibid., p. 53.

[82] For more information on PEPFAR, see CRS Report RL34569, *PEPFAR Reauthorization: Key Policy Debates and Changes to U.S. International HIV/AIDS, Tuberculosis, and Malaria Programs and Funding*, by Kellie Moss.

[83] The United States President's Emergency Plan for AIDS Relief, "Increasing the Availability of Safe, Effective, Low-Cost Generic Medications," press release, January 2009, http://www.pepfar.gov/press/108120.htm.

[84] Kelley Lee, Devi Sridhar, and Mayur Patel, "Bridging the Divide: Global Governance of Trade and Health," *Lancet*, vol. 373 (January 22, 2009), p. 418.

[85] GAO, *U.S. Trade Policy Guidance on WTO Declaration on Access to Medicines May Need Clarification*, GAO-07-1198, September 2007.

[86] "Ways and Means Democrats Urge U.S. Trade Representative Schwab to Strike balance Between Patent, Public Health Issues in Upcoming Trade Negotiations," *U.S. Fed News*, June 6, 2008.

[87] GAO *U.S. Trade Policy Guidance on WTO Declaration on Access to Medicines May Need Clarification*, GAO-07-1198, September 2007, pp. 56-57.

[88] Richard D. Smith, Carlos Correa, and Cecilia Oh, "Trade, TRIPS, and Pharmaceuticals," *The Lancet*, vol. 373 (February 21, 2009). Oxfam International, *US Bullying on Drug Patents: One Year After Doha*, Briefing Paper 33.

[89] Jamie Strawbridge, "NGOs Press USTR To Extend May 10 Deal On IPR To All Trade Pacts*," Inside U.S. Trade*, May 22, 2009.

[90] Erik Wasson, "Drug Firms Eye Revisit of IPR Template for Future Trade Deals*," Inside U.S. Trade*, March 6, 2009.

[91] For an in-depth analysis, see CRS Report RL33159, *Influenza Antiviral Drugs and Patent Law Issues*, by Brian T. Yeh.

[92] Tim Wilson, "Spread the Flu Virus to Stop It," *The Asian Wall Street Journal*, May 1, 2009.

[93] WIPO, "International Patent Filings Dip in 2009 amid Global Economic Downturn," press release, February 8, 2010, http://www.wipo.int/pressroom/en/articles/2010/article_0003.html.

[94] NSF, "*Science and Engineering Indicators 2008*, "Industry, Technology, and the Marketplace," NSB 08-01; NSB 08-01A, Arlington, VA, January 2008, pp. 20-21.

[95] Carsten Fink, *Intellectual Property and Public Health: An Overview of the Debate with a Focus on U.S. Policy*, Center for Global Development, Working Paper Number 146, June 2008, pp. 22-23.

In: Intellectual Property
Editor: Nicholas D. Melark

ISBN: 978-1-61470-506-2

Chapter 3

THE ROLE OF TRADE SECRETS IN INNOVATION POLICY

John R. Thomas

SUMMARY

Many businesses have developed proprietary information that provides a competitive advantage because it is not known to others. As the United States continues its shift to a knowledge- and service-based economy, the strength and competitiveness of domestic firms increasingly depends upon their know-how and intangible assets. Trade secrets are the form of intellectual property that protects this sort of confidential information.

Trade secret law protects secret, valuable business information from misappropriation by others. Subject matter ranging from marketing data to manufacturing know-how may be protected under the trade secret laws. Trade secret status is not limited to a fixed number of years, but endures so long as the information is valuable and maintained as a secret. A trade secret is misappropriated when it has been obtained through the abuse of a confidential relationship or improper means of acquisition.

A number of competing innovation policy concerns help shape the particular doctrines that comprise trade secret law. The availability of legal protection for trade secrets potentially promotes innovation, encourages firms to invest in employee development, and confirms standards of commercial ethics and morality. On the other hand, trade secret protection involves the suppression of information, which may hinder competition and the proper functioning of the marketplace. An overly robust trade secret law also could restrain employee mobility and promote investment in costly, but socially inefficient security measures.

Trade secrets are primarily a matter of state law. In 1996, Congress enacted the Economic Espionage Act (EEA), a statute that criminalizes both "economic espionage" and the "theft of trade secrets." The EEA provides for substantial fines and imprisonment penalties, as well as criminal forfeiture of property and court orders preserving the confidentiality of trade secrets. Some commentators believe that few prosecutions have occurred under the EEA since its enactment and have deemed the legislation ineffective.

Patents and trade secrets provide different intellectual property options for many new inventions. Inventors typically must choose (1) to maintain an invention as a trade secret, (2) to obtain a patent on the invention, or (3) allow the invention to enter the public domain. As a result, federal legislation or other developments that are perceived to alter the effectiveness of the patent system may make the trade secret more or less attractive to industry.

Some commentators have encouraged Congress to supplement the EEA, which is a criminal statute, with civil federal trade secret legislation. They believe that this step would improve uniformity within the system. However, others believe that no compelling case has been made to federalize trade secret law. Other observers assert that the EEA should be amended to involve a private cause of action for economic espionage and trade secret misappropriation.

INTRODUCTION

In recent years the Congress has shown considerable interest in promoting the strength and international competitiveness of U.S. industry. Several recent legislative proposals have concerned the intellectual property laws, a widely recognized mechanism for promoting innovation. In particular, several bills introduced in the 111th Congress address the topic of trade secrets. For example, both the Electronic Device Recycling R&D Act[1] and the Motor Vehicle Owners Right to Repair Act of 2009[2] would allow firms to maintain confidential information as trade secrets. On the other hand, one recently enacted law arguably reduces the value of information that firms had retained as trade secrets. The Patient Protection and Affordable Care Act effectively allows manufacturers of follow-on biologics to rely upon the confidential clinical data generated by the product's sponsors in order to sell competing products.[3] In view of congressional interest in this form of intellectual property, an overview of trade secret law appears appropriate.

The term "trade secret" generally refers to secret, commercially valuable information, including such subject matter as confidential formulae, techniques for manufacturing a product, and customer lists.[4] Trade secret protection is largely a matter of state law.[5] Under those laws, misappropriation of a trade secret may be enjoined by a court and the defendant may also be liable for compensatory and punitive damages.[6] One notable federal statute, the Economic Espionage Act of 1996,[7] makes the theft or misappropriation of a trade secret a federal crime under certain circumstances.

Trade secrets play a role in U.S. innovation policy. Trade secrets may establish incentives to innovate because they provide a mechanism for firms to capture the benefits of their inventions.[8] Yet trade secrets also have proven controversial because they suppress, rather than disclose, particular innovations to the public.[9] They also may have a significant impact upon the mobility of highly trained employees between firms.[10] Further, because innovators often face a mutually exclusive choice between patenting their inventions or maintaining them as trade secrets,[11] alterations to one of these regimes may alter the perceived attractiveness of the other.[12]

This report provides an overview of the law and policy of trade secrets. It discusses the role of trade secrets in U.S. innovation policy. It then reviews the sources of trade secret law and the substantive rules that they provide. The report then provides a more detailed review of existing federal legislation that pertains to trade secrets. In its next section, the report then discusses the relationship between patent law and trade secret law. The report closes with an identification of congressional issues and options within this field.

TRADE SECRETS AND INNOVATION POLICY

Many businesses have developed proprietary information that provides a competitive advantage because it is not known to others.[13] This category may include "high-tech" information such as chemical formulae, manufacturing techniques, product design, and technical data. But it may also include relatively "low-tech" information such as customer lists, business leads, marketing strategies, pricing schedules, and sales techniques.[14] Potentially of additional competitive value is "negative know-how": previously attempted, but flawed techniques or "blind alleys" that did not achieve their intended results.[15]

As the United States continues its shift to a knowledge- and service-based economy, the economic strength and competitiveness of firms increasingly depend upon their know-how and intangible assets. Leonard I. Nakamura, Assistant Vice President and Economist of the Federal Reserve Bank of Philadelphia, explains that in the U.S economy over the past half-century, "mass production and tangible investment have become less important, while new products . . . and intangible investment have become more important."[16] One recent estimate placed the value of trade secrets owned by U.S. publicly traded companies at five trillion dollars.[17]

Another way of measuring the increasing importance of intangible assets is by considering the value of the Standard & Poor's 500. The "S&P 500" consists of the marketplace value of 500 large publicly held companies.[18] In 1975, 16.8% of the total value of the S&P 500 reportedly consisted of intangible assets. In 2005, intangible assets reportedly constituted 79.7% of the total value of these firms.[19] According to attorney R. Mark Halligan, "the vast bulk of intangible assets are trade secret assets."[20]

Yet the rise of computer technology, the ubiquity of cell phones and the Internet, and our transition to the Information Age have increased the difficulty that firms encounter in maintaining the confidentiality of their proprietary information. Years ago, the theft of trade secrets may have involved the taking of laboratory notebooks, memoranda, or other papers from a competitor's office despite the presence of security personnel or surveillance cameras. Today, a trade secret misappropriator can download proprietary information from company computers, or take photographs of confidential documents using a cell phone camera, within moments. As attorney Victoria A. Cundiff concisely states: "The digital world is no friend to trade secrets."[21]

As U.S. firms become increasingly immersed in global competition, some observers believe that foreign firms and even foreign governments have devoted significant resources towards industrial espionage.[22] According to the Office of the National Counterintelligence Executive, "[t]he United States remains the prime target for foreign economic collection and industrial espionage by virtue of its global technological leadership and innovation."[23] These efforts have been linked not just to the economic competitiveness of the United States, but also to its national security.[24]

The legal concept of trade secrets addresses these circumstances. Principles of trade secret law guard against the misappropriation of information that is not generally known. In view of the increasing prominence of information, it is unsurprising that Michael Risch, a member of the law faculty of the West Virginia University College of Law, asserts that trade secrets are "arguably the most important and most heavily litigated intellectual property right."[25]

Framing the trade secret law requires a balancing of competing interests. A robust trade secret law that provides strong protection to proprietary commercial information potentially holds many advantages. It may allow firms to capture the benefits of the costs and time it takes to develop the information, without having to share the benefits of that information with others. Trade secret law therefore may be seen as providing incentives to innovate.[26]

Trade secret law may also encourage firms to invest in human capital. A firm is more likely to invest in employee development if it has some confidence that employee cannot immediately use his knowledge in the service of a competitor.[27] Firms may also establish a trade secret easily through self-help measures. Commercially valuable information is protected once a firm makes reasonable efforts to maintain it in confidence. There is no need for formal government involvement, in contrast to patents.[28]

Trade secret law also confirms and regulates standards of commercial ethics and morality.[29] The misappropriation doctrine applies only against wrongdoers—those who have breached a duty of confidence, engaged in espionage, or otherwise acted in bad faith.[30] Trade secret law thus recognizes that even within a marketplace based open free competition, certain kinds of competitive behavior step beyond our social norms and should be discouraged.[31]

On the other hand, trade secret laws potentially have negative aspects. First, although trade secret law may promote advancement, it might facilitate a particular kind of innovation—the development of information that is itself amenable to being kept secret.[32] In addition, the protection of trade secrets necessarily requires firms to conceal their new developments. But as Judge Goldberg observed 40 years ago, "for our industrial competition to remain healthy there must be breathing room for observing a competing industrialist."[33] Thus, while some degree of information protection may be needed to promote innovation, some amount of information sharing may be essential for competition and proper functioning of the market.[34]

As well, firms must expend resources to maintain information as a trade secret. Employees must sign confidentiality agreements, locks and safes must be installed, and electronic protection measures must be in place on computer systems. These measures entail time and expense.[35] Employers also may be encouraged to limit access to valuable information to select employees. Disclosing valuable trade secrets on a "need to know" basis to one's employees may restrict employee development and ultimately hinder the operation of the firm.[36]

Trade secret law may negatively impact employee mobility. Individuals who are unable to take their knowledge from job to job may be limited in their ability to change employers.[37] As explained by Alan L. Durham, a member of the law faculty of the University of Alabama, an overly robust view of trade secret law potentially may "limit individual freedom, weaken employee bargaining power, and harm society through diminished competition."[38]

The various rules that together comprise the discipline of trade secret law may be fashioned in an effort to maximize the potential advantages of trade secrets while minimizing their disadvantages. This report next provides a more detailed review of the doctrines that regulate the acquisition and enforcement of trade secrets.

AN OVERVIEW OF TRADE SECRET LAW

Basic Principles

While it has been written that an "exact definition of a trade secret is not possible,"[39] a trade secret generally consists of secret, commercially valuable information.[40] As explained by Henry Perritt, Jr., a member of the faculty of the Chicago-Kent College of Law, "trade secret subject matter includes any of the major functions of business enterprise: production and operations, engineering and research and development, marketing, finance, purchasing, and management."[41] Specific examples of trade secret subject matter include customer lists, manufacturing processes, marketing strategies, pricing information, product design, recipes, and sales techniques.[42] One court has described trade secrets as follows:

> A trade secret is really just a piece of information (such as a customer list, or a method of production, or a secret formula for a soft drink) that the holder tries to keep secret by executing confidentiality agreements with employees and others and by hiding the information from outsiders by means of fences, safes, encryption, and other means of concealment, so that the only way the secret can be unmasked is by a breach of contract or a tort.[43]

Whether information qualifies as a "trade secret" is a question of fact that may be determined by a jury. Among the factors in assessing whether certain subject matter is a trade secret are:

- the extent to which the information is known outside of the company;
- the extent to which it is known by employees and others involved in the company;
- the extent of measures taken by the company to guard the secrecy of the information;
- the value of the information to the company and to its competitors;
- the amount of effort or money expended by the company in developing the information; and
- the ease or difficulty with which the information could be properly acquired or duplicated by others.[44]

The law protects trade secrets from misappropriation by others. Misappropriation is a tort that may occur in several distinct ways. One is when an individual acquires the trade secret through improper means, such as theft, bribery, misrepresentation, or espionage.[45] Another is when the individual uses or discloses the trade secret through a breach of confidence. For example, an employee might switch jobs, and then disclose his previous employer's trade secrets in violation of a confidentiality agreement.[46]

Finally, a trade secret may be misappropriated if it is used or disclosed with knowledge that the trade secret had been acquired improperly or through mistake. A person who uses information that he knows to have been stolen by another is therefore also guilty of misappropriation.[47] Misappropriation of a trade secret may be enjoined by a court and the defendant may also be liable for compensatory and punitive damages.[48]

Conversely, it is not a violation of trade secret law for another firm to discover the subject matter of a trade secret independently.[49] "Reverse engineering" is also considered to be an appropriate means for one firm to acquire the subject matter of another's trade secret.[50] A firm that discerns the subject matter of the trade secret by inspecting products available to the public also has not engaged in misappropriation.[51]

Trade secret protection may extend indefinitely. So long as information is not generally known to the public, confers an economic benefit to its holder, and is subject to reasonable efforts to maintain its secrecy, it may be considered a trade secret.[52] However, the trade secret status of information may be lost if the information is accidentally or intentionally disclosed by an employee.[53] Once a trade secret has been exposed to the public, its protected character is lost and cannot later be retrieved.[54] However, disclosures of trade secrets to third parties for certain limited reasons do not waive trade secret protections, so long as the trade secret owner took reasonable measures to maintain its secrecy before and during disclosure, such as requiring non-disclosure or confidentiality agreements from each recipient of confidential information.[55]

Sources of Law

The discipline of trade secrets was traditionally developed through state common law. State courts developed the essential principles of trade secret law through their decisions, which were then observed as precedent in subsequent litigation. In 1939, the American Law Institute (ALI), a group of lawyers, judges, and legal scholars, published a treatise titled the "Restatement of Torts." The Restatement of Torts included two sections dealing with the law of trade secrets. Section 757 explained the subject matter of trade secrets, while Section 758 spelled out the elements of a trade secret misappropriation cause of action. Although this treatment was succinct, many commentators believe that these definitions proved influential in the courts.[56]

Trade secrets were not addressed in the Second Restatement of Torts published in 1978. The ALI at that time concluded that trade secret law had grown "no more dependent on Tort law than it is on many other general fields of law and upon broad statutory developments,"[57] and opted not to house trade secrets there. The ALI addressed this gap in its 1993 Restatement (Third) of Unfair Competition, which deals with trade secrets in sections 39–45.

In addition, the National Conference of Commissioners on Uniform State Law (NCCUSL) issued the Uniform Trade Secrets Act (UTSA) in 1979. The NCCUSL consists of a group of academics, attorneys, and judges who draft statutes addressing a variety of issues, and then propose that each state enact them.[58] The NCCUSL lacks direct legislative authority itself. Its uniform acts become law only to the extent that state legislatures adopt them.

The UTSA has arguably proven successful, as it has reportedly been enacted in 46 states, the District of Columbia, and the Virgin Islands.[59] The four states that have reportedly not enacted the UTSA are Massachusetts, New Jersey, New York, and Texas. These states do recognize trade secrets, but provide protection through a distinct statute or the common law. As attorney David S. Almeling reports, those four states represent 22% of the U.S. Gross Domestic Product.[60]

It should be appreciated that many jurisdictions have enacted the UTSA after making some changes to the original text of the proposed legislation. Opinions vary on how significant these modifications have been. While some commentators view state-by-state variations as "generally minor,"[61] others have opined that "they include fundamental differences about what constitutes a trade secret, what is required to misappropriate it, and what remedies are available."[62]

THE ECONOMIC ESPIONAGE ACT

As noted previously, trade secrets have traditionally been the subject of state law. Prior to 1996, arguably the most significant federal legislation on point was the Trade Secrets Act.[63] Although broadly titled, this 1948 statute is actually of narrow application. It forbids federal government employees and government contractors from making an unauthorized disclosure of confidential government information, including trade secrets. The sanctions for violating this criminal offense are removal from office or employment, and a fine and/or imprisonment of not more than one year. The law does not apply to state or local government actors or to private sector employees.

In 1996, motivated by concerns over growing international and domestic economic espionage against U.S. firms, Congress enacted new legislation pertaining to trade secrets. The Economic Espionage Act (EEA) criminalizes both "economic espionage" and the "theft of trade secrets." The "economic espionage" provision punishes those who knowingly misappropriate, or attempt or conspire to misappropriate, trade secrets with the intent or knowledge that the offense will benefit a foreign government, instrumentality or agent.[64] The "theft of trade secrets" prohibition is of more general application. The principal elements of an EEA claim for theft of trade secrets are: (1) the intentional and/or knowing theft, appropriation, destruction, alteration, or duplication of (2) a trade secret placed in interstate commerce (3) with intent to convert the trade secret and (4) intent or knowledge that such action will injure the owner.[65]

The EEA provides for substantial fines and imprisonment penalties. For economic espionage, the maximum penalties increase to $500,000 for individuals and imprisonment of 15 years, or $10 million for corporations.[66] Theft of trade secrets is punishable by a fine of up to $250,000 for individuals as well as imprisonment of up to 10 years. Organizations can be fined up to $5 million.[67] The EEA also provides for criminal forfeiture of property and court orders preserving the confidentiality of trade secrets.[68]

The EEA has been subject to critical commentary. Attorney R. Mark Halligan expressed the view that the legislation was "ineffective" and observed, in 2008, that there had been fewer than 60 prosecutions in keeping with its provisions.[69] Susan W. Brenner, a member of the law faculty of the University of Dayton, and security expert Anthony C. Crescenzi opine that the "paucity" of prosecutions under the EEA are due to a number of factors, including the complexity of the cases, the desire of the Department of Justice only to bring cases it can win, the diplomatic repercussions of bringing such a case, and the unwelcome possibility of additional disclosure of trade secrets during the litigation.[70] Brenner and Crescenzi conclude that the "individual and combined effect of the systemic factors discussed above is to erode the EEA's effectiveness as a weapon against economic espionage."[71]

TRADE SECRETS AND PATENTS

Trade secrets and patents form two distinct fields within the U.S. intellectual property system. In one sense, trade secrecy serves as the chief alternative to the patent system. Most inventors must choose one of three options: (1) maintain a technology as a trade secret, (2) seek patent protection, (3) or decline to seek intellectual property protection at all and allow the technology to enter the public domain.[72] In view of the close relationship between trade secrets and patents, this report next provides an overview of the patent system and its interaction with trade secret law.

Introduction to the Patent System

An inventor may seek the grant of a patent by preparing and submitting an application to the U.S. Patent and Trademark Office, or USPTO.[73] USPTO officials known as examiners then determine whether the invention disclosed in the application merits the award of a patent.[74] The USPTO examiner will consider a number of legal requirements, including whether the submitted application fully explains and distinctly claims the invention. In particular, the application must enable persons skilled in the art to make and use the invention without undue experimentation. In addition, the application must provide the "best mode," or preferred way, that the applicant knows to practice the invention.[75]

The examiner will also determine whether the invention itself fulfills certain substantive standards set by the patent statute. To be patentable, an invention must meet four primary requirements. First, the invention must fall within at least one category of patentable subject matter.[76] According to the Patent Act, an invention which is a "process, machine, manufacture, or composition of matter" is eligible for patenting. Second, the invention must be useful, a requirement that is satisfied if the invention is operable and provides a tangible benefit.[77] Third, the invention must be novel, or different, from subject matter disclosed by an earlier patent, publication, or other state-of-the-art knowledge.[78] Finally, an invention is not patentable if "the subject matter as a whole would have been obvious at the time the invention was made to a person having ordinary skill in the art to which said subject matter pertains."[79] This requirement of "nonobviousness" prevents the issuance of patents claiming subject matter that a skilled artisan would have been able to implement in view of the knowledge of the state of the art. If the USPTO allows the patent to issue, its owner obtains the right to exclude others from making, using, selling, offering to sell, or importing into the United States the patented invention.[80]

Trade Secrets and Patents Compared

Inventors who do not wish to dedicate their technologies to the public domain must, as a general matter, choose between trade secret and patent protection. A number of factors inform this decision. One is whether the inventor will practically be able to keep the technology secret. A knowledgeable observer may readily be able to inspect a motor, machine, or other mechanical technology in order to learn its design, for example. On the other hand, the composition of a chemical compound may be much more difficult to discern.[81]

The costs associated with acquiring and maintaining patents are another factor. In this respect, it should be appreciated that a U.S. patent provides rights only with the United States. However, virtually anyone in the world may review a U.S. patent to learn of its contents. As a result, U.S. inventors may need to obtain patents in many foreign countries in order to secure meaningful protection.

In addition, the process of acquiring a patent may take many years.[82] A USPTO examiner in 2009 would not review a patent application until, on average, 25.8 months after it was filed.[83] The "first action pendency" during 2000 was 13.6 months.[84] Many observers believe that if current conditions continue, the backlog and delay are likely to grow at the USPTO in coming years.[85] These delays may prove too lengthy for innovators in fast-moving industries, suggesting that trade secret protection is the more appropriate choice.

Also, trade secrets may potentially extend indefinitely, so long as the requirements for trade secret protection are maintained. In contrast, patents expire after a set period of time, normally 20 years after the date they were filed. On the other hand, trade secret protection may be lost through a competitor's reverse engineering or independent discovery. As explained by Dan Burk, a member of the faculty of the University of California, Irvine School of Law, "the inventor's choice is an election between twenty years of certain patent protection or perpetual, but less certain, trade secret protection."[86]

It should also be appreciated that when an inventor obtains a patent on an invention, the USPTO publishes that patent in a formal document. That publication destroys the trade secret status of any previously confidential information disclosed within it.[87] In addition, the USPTO publishes many, but not all, pending patent applications "promptly after the expiration of a period of 18 months" after they are filed.[88] This measure also destroys the trade secret status of information contained within the published application, even if the USPTO subsequently rejects the application and no patent ever issues on that invention.[89]

Potential Policy Conflicts

The trade secret and patent systems are sometimes viewed as acting in conflicting ways. Trade secret protection is predicated upon the maintenance of the protected information in confidence. In contrast, each patented invention is the subject of a formal document, the patent instrument, which provides a complete description of the invention. As a result, while the patent system appears to promote the public disclosure of new technologies, the trade secret discourages disclosure.[90] As described previously, it could be argued that trade secret law encourages the development of technologies that are capable of being kept secret.[91]

However, some commentators believe that patents and trade secrets generally act in a complementary manner.[92] Mark Lemley, a member of the faculty of the Stanford Law School, has explained that trade secret law provides valuable incentives to innovate in areas where the patent law does not reach, such as customer lists and business plans.[93] Lemley further explains that although the law requires that reasonable efforts must be made to maintain secrecy, absent trade secret law, firms might need to engage in even more physical and contractual measures to prevent disclosure. As a result, a society without trade secret law might potentially have more, rather than less secrecy.[94]

In any event, patent law doctrine may be viewed as disfavoring trade secret holders. Well-established patent law provides that an inventor who makes a secret, commercial use of an invention for more than one year prior to filing a patent application at the USPTO forfeits his own right to a patent.[95] This policy is based principally upon the desire to maintain the integrity of the statutorily prescribed patent term. The patent law grants patents a term of twenty years, commencing from the date a patent application is filed.[96] If the trade secret holder could make commercial use of an invention for many years before choosing to file a patent application, he could disrupt this regime by delaying the expiration date of his patent.

On the other hand, settled patent law principles established that prior secret uses would not defeat the patents of later inventors.[97] If an earlier inventor made secret commercial use of an invention, and another person independently invented the same technology later and obtained patent protection, then the trade secret holder could face liability for patent infringement. This policy is based upon the reasoning that once issued, published patent instruments fully inform the public about the invention, while trade secrets do not. As between a subsequent inventor who patented the invention, and thus had disclosed the invention to the public, and an earlier trade secret holder who had not, the law favored the patent holder.[98]

An example may clarify this rather complex legal situation. Suppose that Inventor X develops and makes commercial use of a new manufacturing process. Inventor X chooses not to obtain patent protection, yet maintains that process as a trade secret. Many years later, Inventor Y independently develops the same manufacturing process and promptly files a patent application claiming that invention. In such circumstances, Inventor X's earlier, trade secret use does not prevent Inventor Y from procuring a patent. Furthermore, if the USPTO approves the patent application, then Inventor X faces infringement liability should Inventor Y file suit against him.[99]

The First Inventor Defense

Congress modified the usual rules governing the relationship between trade secrets and patents when it established the "first inventor defense" in the American Inventors Protection Act of 1999.[100] That statute in part provided an infringement defense for an earlier inventor of a "method of doing or conducting business" that was later patented by another. By limiting this defense to patented methods of doing business, Congress responded to the 1998 Federal Circuit opinion in *State Street Bank and Trust Co. v. Signature Financial Group*.[101] That judicial opinion recognized that business methods could be subject to patenting, potentially exposing individuals who had maintained business methods as trade secrets to liability for patent infringement.

Again, an example may aid understanding of the first inventor defense. Suppose that Inventor X develops and exploits commercially a new method of doing business. Inventor X maintains his business method as a trade secret. Many years later, Inventor Y independently develops the same business method and promptly files a patent application claiming that invention. Even following the enactment of the American Inventors Protection Act, Inventor X's earlier, trade secret use would not prevent Inventor Y from procuring a patent. However, should the USPTO approve Inventor Y's patent application, and should Inventor Y sue Inventor X for patent infringement, then Inventor X may potentially claim the benefit of the first inventor defense. If successful, Inventor X would enjoy a complete defense to infringement of Inventor Y's patent.

At the time this report was published, no reported judicial opinion considers the first inventor defense. The most prominent judicial treatment of the first inventor defense arguably occurred in the 2010 Supreme Court opinion in *Bilski v. Kappos*.[102] There, a plurality of the Supreme Court concluded that the American Inventors Protection Act evidenced the congressional intent that business methods were appropriately patented. The concurring opinion of Justice Stevens expressed a distinct view, stating that "that the 1999 Congress would never have enacted §273 if it had foreseen that this Court would rely on the provision as a basis for concluding that business methods are patentable."[103]

Legislation before the 111th Congress would modify the first inventor defense. Both H.R. 1260 and S. 515, each titled the Patent Reform Act of 2009, would expand the first inventor defense as it was established in 1999. The defense currently applies to "the person who performed the acts necessary to establish the defense...." Both bills would also allow "any other entity that controls, is controlled by, or is under common control" with that person to claim entitlement to the first inventor defense.[104] A third bill titled the Patent Reform Act of 2009, S. 610, does not address the first inventor defense.

Congressional Issues and Options

A variety of options are available for Congress with respect to trade secrets. If the current situation is deemed appropriate, then no action need be taken. Alternatively, Congress may wish to consider the adoption of a federal trade secret law. Several commentators believe that this step would promote the uniformity of trade secret law throughout the United States.[105] As attorney David S. Almeling asserts:

> Trade secrets stand alone as the only major type of intellectual property governed primarily by state law. Trademarks, copyrights, and patents are each governed primarily by federal statutes. Trade secrets, by contrast, are governed by fifty state statutes and common laws. The result is that trade secret law differs from state to state. It is time to eliminate these differences—and the significant problems they cause—by enacting a Federal Trade Secrets Act ("FTSA").[106]

According to Alemeling, general federal trade secret legislation would establish greater uniformity in substantive and procedural law than is possible in a state-based regime.

Other commentators have further suggested that the current state-based trade secrets system places the United States in violation of its obligations under two international agreements: the North American Free Trade Agreement (NAFTA) and the World Trade Organization Agreement on Trade-Related Aspects of Intellectual Property (TRIPS Agreement).[107] Both NAFTA and the TRIPS Agreement require member states to provide certain levels of trade secret protection. Because the portions of NAFTA and the TRIPS Agreement concerning trade secrets were modeled after the Uniform Trade Secrets Act (UTSA), those states that have adopted the UTSA without restrictive modifications likely comply with these international standards. But some states have not adopted the UTSA, and some states that have done so have arguably included more restrictive standards. Some commentators have asserted that these states place the United States in violation of NAFTA and the TRIPS Agreement. However, others have observed that any shortcomings of U.S. law on this point have yet to be challenged under either international agreement.[108]

Still other observers assert that no compelling case has been made to federalize trade secret law. Some believe that this step might create additional burdens and costs upon the federal judiciary.[109] Others cite federalism concerns, believing that the states possess a strong interest in regulating local economies in view of their own, local norms.[110] In addition, variation between the laws of the different states does not necessarily compel federalization of the field. For example, meaningful distinctions between the states exist in other areas of law, including such fundamental disciplines as contract law. Yet these disciplines remain subject to state law.[111]

A second possibility for Congress is to amend the Economic Espionage Act. Varying commentators have described the EEA as "seldom enforced,"[112] "futile,"[113] and of "limited" value as a deterrent.[114] Reforms have been proposed to address these perceived deficiencies. Attorney R. Mark Halligan has asserted that the EEA, which is currently limited to criminal prosecution, should include a civil cause of action. According to Halligan, enacting a federal civil cause of action to protect trade secrets would deter the theft of trade secrets and act to the advantage of U.S. firms domestically and abroad.[115] Halligan does not propose wholly federalizing trade secret law—under his proposal, trade secret law would remain primarily a matter of state law. Still, some of the concerns voiced in that context, including burdening the federal judiciary and decreasing state sovereignty, could potentially arise here as well.

In addition, Congress may wish to remain apprised of the potential effect of current patent reform efforts upon trade secrets.[116] As this report has discussed, trade secrets and patents act in complementary ways to protect innovation in the United States.[117] Further, to some degree the two forms of intellectual property act as imperfect substitutes for each other. As a result, legislative reforms that are perceived to make patents more effective may reduce industrial reliance upon trade secrets. Conversely, amendments to the Patent Act that are believed to reduce the effectiveness of patents may increase the willingness of firms to retain information as trade secrets.[118]

CONCLUDING OBSERVATIONS

Trade secrets form a significant component of the intellectual property system of the United States. The importance of trade secrets will likely increase as U.S. industry continues to participate within a knowledge-based, global economy with increasingly sophisticated competitors. Because trade secrets are currently a matter of state law, congressional influence over the system has thus far been indirect: Through the enactment of a criminal statute, the Economic Espionage Act, and through amendment to the patent law. Whether further intervention is required in the U.S. trade secret system remains a matter of congressional judgment.

ACKNOWLEDGMENTS

This report was funded in part by a grant from the John D. and Catherine T. MacArthur Foundation.

End Notes

[1] H.R. 1580, § 3(f)(1).
[2] H.R. 2057, § 3(d)(1).
[3] P.L. 111-148, § 7002.
[4] *See* Uniform Trade Secret Act, § 1.
[5] *See* Michael Traynor and Katy Hutchinson, "Some Open Questions About Intellectual Property Remedies," 14 *Lewis & Clark Law Review* (2010), 453.
[6] *See* Shubha Ghosh, "Open Borders, Intellectual Property & Federal Criminal Trade Secret Law," 9 *John Marshall Review of Intellectual Property Law* (Fall 2009), 24.
[7] 104th Congress, P.L. 104-294 (Oct. 11, 1996).
[8] *See* Michael Risch, "Trade Secret Law and Information Development Incentives," in *The Law and Theory of Trade Secrecy: A Handbook of Contemporary Research* (Rochelle C. Dreyfuss, Katherine J. Strandburg, eds., Edward Elgar Publishing, 2010).
[9] *See* Michael P. Simpson, "The Future of Innovation: Trade Secrets, Property Rights, and Protectionism—An Age-Old Tale," 70 *Brooklyn Law Review* (2005), 1121.
[10] *See* Charles Tait Graves, "Trade Secrets as Property: Theory and Consequences," 15 *Journal of Intellectual Property Law* (2007), 39.
[11] *See* Daniel C. Munson, "The Patent-Trade Secret Decision: An Industrial Perspective," 78 *Journal of the Patent and Trademark Office Society* (1996), 689.
[12] *See* Douglas Lichtman, "How the Law Responds to Self-Help," 1 *Journal of Law, Economics & Policy* (Winter 2005), 215 (observing that trade secret law acts "as both a complement to and competitor for patent law.").
[13] *See* Kurt M. Saunders, "The Law and Ethics of Trade Secrets: A Case Study," 42 *California Western Law Review* (2006), 209.
[14] Milton Babirak, *Secrets of the Uniform Trade Secret Act*, D.C. BAR CLE PROGRAM (Nov. 9, 2005).
[15] Charles Tait Graves, "The Law of Negative Knowledge: A Critique," 15 *Texas Intellectual Property Law Journal* (2007), 387.
[16] Leonard I . Nakamura, *Intangible Assets and National Income Accounting: Measuring a Scientific Revolution*, Working Paper No. 09-11, Federal Reserve Bank of Philadelphia, at 3.
[17] *See* Elizabeth A. Rowe, "Contributory Negligence, Technology, and Trade Secrets," 17 *George Mason Law Review* (2009), 1.
[18] *See* http://www.standardandpoors.com.
[19] James E. Malackowski, "The Intellectual Property Marketplace: Past, Present and Future, 5 *The John Marshall Journal of Intellectual Property Law* (2006), 605.
[20] R. Mark Halligan, "Protection of U.S. Trade Secret Assets: Critical Amendments to the Economic Espionage Act of 1996," 7 *John Marshall Review of Intellectual Property Law* (2008), 656.
[21] Victoria A. Cundiff, "Reasonable Measures to Protect Trade Secrets in a Digital Environment," 49 *IDEA: The Intellectual Property Law Review* (2009), 359.
[22] Susan W. Brenner and Anthony C. Crescenzi, "State-Sponsored Crime: The Futility of the Economic Espionage Act," 28 *Houston Journal of International Law* (2006), 389.
[23] Office of the National Counterintelligence Executive, *Annual Report to Congress on Foreign Economic Collection and Industrial Espionage* (2007), 1.
[24] Aaron J. Burstein, "Trade Secrecy as an Instrument of National Security? Rethinking the Foundations of Economic Espionage," 41 *Arizona State Law Journal* (2009), 933.
[25] Michael Risch, "Why Do We Have Trade Secrets?," 11 *Marquette Intellectual Property Law Review* (2007), 1.
[26] Oren Bar-Gill, "Law and the Boundaries of Technology-Intensive Firms," 157 *University of Pennsylvania Law Review* (2009), 1649.
[27] Miles J. Feldman, "Toward a Clearer Standard of Protectable Information: Trade Secrets and the Employment Relationship," 9 *High Technology Law Journal* (1994), 151.
[28] Lemley, *supra,* at 313.
[29] *See* Elizabeth A. Rowe, "A Sociological Approach to Misappropriation," 58 *University of Kansas Law Review* (2009), 1.

[30] *See* Rebecca S. Eisenberg, "Proprietary Rights and the Norms of Science in Biotechnology Research," 97 *Yale Law Journal* (1987), 177.
[31] *See* James Grimmelmann, "The Ethical Visions of Copyright Law," 77 *Fordham Law Review* (2009), 2005.
[32] Michael P. Simpson, "The Future of Innovation: Trade Secrets, Property Rights, and Protectionism—An Age-Old Tale," 70 *Brooklyn Law Review* (2005), 1121.
[33] E.I. duPont deNemours & Co. v. Christopher, 431 F.2d 1012 (5th Cir. 1970).
[34] Michael J. Garrison and John T. Wendt, "The Evolving Law of Employee Noncompete Agreements: Recent Trends and an Alternative Policy Approach," 45 *American Business Law Journal* (2008), 107.
[35] *See* Douglas Lichtman, "How the Law Responds to Self-Help," 1 *Journal of Law, Economics & Policy* (2005), 215.
[36] *See* Bruce Fallick *et al.*, "Job-Hopping in Silicon Valley: Some Evidence Concerning the Microfoundations of a High-Technology Cluster," 88 *The Review of Economics and Statistics* (2006), 472.
[37] *See* Bruce Alan Kugler, "Limiting Trade Secret Protection," 22 *Valparaiso University Law Review* (1988), 725.
[38] Alan L. Durham, "Natural Laws and Inevitable Infringement," 93 *Minnesota Law Review* (2009), 933.
[39] Restatement (First) of Torts § 757, comment b.
[40] Uniform Trade Secrets Act § 1(4).
[41] Henry H. Perritt, Jr., *Trade Secrets: A Practitioner's Guide* § 3:9 (2d ed. 2006).
[42] *See* Babirak, *supra.*
[43] ConFold Pac. v. Polaris Indus., 433 F.3d 952, 959 (7th Cir. 2006) (citations omitted).
[44] Restatement (First) of Torts § 757, comment b.
[45] Restatement (Third) of Unfair Competition § 40 (1994).
[46] *See* Jennifer Brockett, "Protecting Intellectual Property During Layoffs," 32 *Los Angeles Lawyer* (April 2009).
[47] Restatement (Third) of Unfair Competition § 40 (1994).
[48] Restatement (Third) of Unfair Competition §§ 44, 45 (1994).
[49] Restatement (Third) of Unfair Competition § 43 (1994).
[50] *See* Kristin L. Black, "Crimes of Fashion: Is Imitation Truly the Sincerest Form of Flattery?," 19 *Kansas Journal of Law and Public Policy* (2010), 515.
[51] Restatement (Third) of Unfair Competition § 43 (1994).
[52] Perritt, *supra* , at § 2:2.
[53] *See* Religious Tech. Ctr. v. Netcom On-Line Communication Servs., 923 F. Supp. 1231, 1256 (N.D. Cal. 1995).
[54] In re Remington Arms Co., 952 F.2d 1029, 1033 (8th Cir. 1991).
[55] 1 Roger Milgrim, *Milgrim on Trade Secrets* § 1.04.
[56] *See* Katarzyna A. Czapracka, "Antitrust and Trade Secrets: The U.S. and EU Approach," 24 *Santa Clara Computer High Technology Law Journal* (2008), 207.
[57] ALI, Restatements of Torts (Second), Introduction (1979).
[58] For further information about the organization, see http://www.nccusl.org.
[59] *See* David S. Almeling, "A Statistical Analysis of Trade Secret Litigation in Federal Courts," 45 *Gonzaga Law Review* (2009-10), 291.
[60] David S. Almeling, "Four Reasons to Enact a Federal Trade Secrets Act," 19 *Fordham Intellectual Property, Media & Entertainment Law Journal* (2009), 769 (hereinafter Almeling, *Four Reasons*).
[61] Babirak, *supra,* at 3.
[62] Almeling, *Four Reasons*, *supra,* at 774.
[63] June 25, 1948, c. 645, 62 Stat. 79 (codified at 18 U.S.C. § 1905).
[64] 18 U.S.C. § 1831.
[65] 18 U.S.C. § 1832.
[66] 18 U.S.C. § 1831.
[67] 18 U.S.C. § 1832.
[68] 18 U.S.C. §§ 1834, 1835.
[69] *See* Halligan, *supra.*
[70] Susan W. Brenner and Anthony C. Crescenzi, "State-Sponsored Crime: The Futility of the Economic Espionage Act," 28 *Houston Journal of International Law* (2006), 389.
[71] *Id.* at 439.
[72] *See generally* John S. Paniaguas and Craig William Mandell, "A Practitoner's Guide to Protecting Technology Assets," 20 *DePaul Journal of Art, Technology & Intellectual Property Law* (2010), 279.
[73] 35 U.S.C. § 111.
[74] 35 U.S.C. § 131.
[75] 35 U.S.C. § 112.
[76] 35 U.S.C. § 101.
[77] *Id.*
[78] 35 U.S.C. § 102.
[79] 35 U.S.C. § 103.
[80] 35 U.S.C. § 271.

[81] *See* Daniel C. Munson, "The Patent-Trade Secret Decision: An Industrial Perspective," 78 *Journal of the Patent and Trademark Office Society* (1996), 689.

[82] *See* CRS Report R41261, *Deferred Examination of Patent Applications: Implications for Innovation Policy*, by John R. Thomas.

[83] USPTO, Performance and Accountability Report Fiscal Year 2009 (available at http://www.uspto.gov/web/offices/ com/annual/2009/mda_02_02.html).

[84] USPTO, 2003 Performance and Accountability Report (available at http://www.uspto.gov/about/stratplan/ar/2003/ 040201_patentperform.jsp).

[85] *See, e.g.*, Jon Dudas et al., "Let the PTO Pay Its Own Way," 198 New Jersey Law Journal no. 12 (Dec. 21, 2009), 975; Steven Andersen, "Out of Balance," Inside Counsel (Nov. 1, 2009).

[86] Dan L. Burk, "Legal Constraint of Genetic Use Restriction Technologies," 6 *Minnesota Journal of Law, Science, and Technology* (2004), 335.

[87] *See* BondPro Corp. v. Siemens Power Generation, Inc., 463 F.3d 703, 706 (7th Cir. 2006).

[88] 35 U.S.C. § 122(b)(1).

[89] *See* BondPro v. Siemens, *supra.*

[90] Michael P. Simpson, "The Future of Innovation: Trade Secrets, Property Rights, and Protectionism—An Age-Old Tale," 70 *Brooklyn Law Review* (2005), 1121.

[91] *Id.*

[92] *See, e.g.,* Karl F. Jorda, "Patent and Trade Secret Complementariness: An Unexpected Synergy," 48 *Washburn Law Journal* (2008), 1; Jonathan D. Carpenter, "Intellectual Property: The Overlap Between Utility Patents, Plant Patents, the PVPA, and Trade Secrets and the Limitations on that Overlap," 81 *North Dakota Law Review* (2005), 171.

[93] Mark A. Lemley, "The Surprising Virtues of Treating Trade Secrets as IP Rights," 61 *Stanford Law Review* (2008), 131.

[94] *Id.*

[95] 35 U.S.C. § 102(b). *See* Metallizing Engineering Co. v. Kenyon Bearing & Auto Parts, 153 F.2d 516 (2d Cir. 1946).

[96] 35 U.S.C. § 154.

[97] Sharon K. Sandeen, "*Kewanee* Revisited: Returning to First Principles of Intellectual Property Law to Determine the Issue of Federal Preemption," 12 *Marquette Intellectual Property Law Review* (2008), 299.

[98] W.L. Gore & Associates v. Garlock, Inc., 721 F.2d 1540 (Fed. Cir. 1983).

[99] *See* Roger E. Schechter and John R. Thomas, *Intellectual Property: The Law of Copyrights, Patents and Trademarks* (Thomson-West 2003), § 16.2.2.

[100] The American Inventors Protection Act of 1999, P.L. 106-113, was part of the Intellectual Property and Communications Omnibus Reform Act of 1999, attached by reference to the Consolidated Appropriations Act for Fiscal Year 2000. President Clinton signed this bill on November 29, 1999.

[101] 149 F.3d 1368 (Fed. Cir. 1998).

[102] ___ U.S. ___, 2010 WL 2555192 (2010).

[103] 2010 WL 2555192 at *29.

[104] H.R. 1260 at § 5(c); S. 515 at § 4(c).

[105] *See, e.g.,* Marina Lao, "Federalizing Trade Secrets Law in an Information Economy," 59 *Ohio State Law Journal* 1633 (1998); Rebel J. Pace, "The Case for a Federal Trade Secrets Act," 8 *Harvard Journal of Law & Technology* (1995), 427.

[106] *See* Almeling, *supra.*

[107] *See, e.g.,* Marina Lao, "Federalizing Trade Secrets Law in an Information Economy," 59 *Ohio State Law Journal* 1633 (1998); Rebel J. Pace, "The Case for a Federal Trade Secrets Act," 8 *Harvard Journal of Law & Technology* (1995), 427.

[108] *See* Almeling, *supra.*

[109] *See, e.g.,* American Intellectual Property Law Association, *Report of the AIPLA Trade Secrets Committee* (2007) (available at http://www.aipla.org).

[110] *Id.*

[111] *See generally* Llewellyn Joseph Gibbons, "Stop Mucking Up Copyright Law: A Proposal for a Federal Common Law of Copyright," 35 *Rutgers Law Journal* (2004), 959.

[112] Burstein, *supra.*

[113] Brenner & Crescenzi, *supra.*

[114] Mark E.A. Danielson, "Economic Espionage: A Framework for a Workable Solution," 10 *Minnesota Journal of Law, Science & Technology* (2009), 503.

[115] Halligan, *supra.*

[116] *See* CRS Report R40481, *Patent Reform in the 111th Congress: Innovation Issues*, by Wendy H. Schacht and John R. Thomas.

[117] *See also* Scott W. Cummings, "The Role of Trade Secrets in Today's Nanotechnology Patent Environment," 5 *Nanotechnology Law & Business* (2008), 41.

[118] *See* Christopher A. Cotropia and Mark A. Lemley, "Copying in Patent Law," 87 *North Carolina Law Review* (2009), 1421 (providing a skeptical discussion of this point).

In: Intellectual Property
Editor: Nicholas D. Melark

ISBN: 978-1-61470-506-2

Chapter 4

INTELLECTUAL PROPERTY: AGENCIES PROGRESS IN IMPLEMENTING RECENT LEGISLATION, BUT ENHANCEMENTS COULD IMPROVE FUTURE PLANS

United States Government Accountability Office

WHY GAO DID THIS STUDY

Intellectual property (IP) plays a significant role in the U.S. economy. Enforcing IP laws involves many U.S. agencies, making coordination essential. Under the Prioritizing Resources and Organization for Intellectual Property Act of 2008 (PRO-IP Act), Congress required the U.S. Attorney General, through the Department of Justice (DOJ), to devote additional resources and undertake other specific IP efforts. The PRO-IP Act also created the position of the Intellectual Property Enforcement Coordinator (IPEC) to enhance interagency coordination. The act mandates that GAO provide Congress with a report on the efforts of DOJ and the IPEC.

This status report addresses DOJ and Office of the IPEC's efforts to implement the act. The report also compares the 2010 Joint Strategic Plan on Intellectual Property Enforcement to the content called for in the PRO-IP Act. GAO examined relevant documents, interviewed agency staff and officials, and compared agency actions and the 2010 strategic plan with the PRO-IP Act.

WHAT GAO RECOMMENDS

GAO recommends that the IPEC, in consultation with the Interagency Intellectual Property Enforcement Advisory Committee, take steps to ensure that future joint strategic plans identify implementing departments and agencies for all priorities and related action items and establish resource estimates to carry out the plan's priorities.

WHAT GAO FOUND

Officials from DOJ and its Federal Bureau of Investigation (FBI) report that they have taken many actions called for in the PRO-IP Act. For example, the act calls for two assistant U.S. attorneys to be assigned to each Computer Hacking and Intellectual Property Crime (CHIP) Unit. DOJ has assigned 97 Assistant U.S. Attorneys to work with CHIP units, with all 25 CHIP units having two or more attorneys assigned. FBI officials also report creating agent positions in accordance with the act, adding 31 agent positions to IP enforcement in fiscal year 2009 and an additional 20 IP positions for 2010. However, FBI officials observed the increase in IP dedicated agent positions has not correspondingly increased agent-hour charges for IP investigations, noting delays in funding, hiring, training and deploying IP-dedicated agents.

Office of the IPEC staff report that they have taken steps to implement the PRO-IP Act. The office, located within the Office of Management and Budget, was recently established following the confirmation of the IPEC on December 4, 2009. The office includes the IPEC, an assistant, and four detailees from other federal agencies. Office of the IPEC staff report that the IPEC chaired the first meeting of the Interagency Intellectual Property Enforcement Advisory Committee on February 2, 2010. Moreover, the IPEC coordinated with other federal entities to deliver the 2010 Joint Strategic Plan on Intellectual Property Enforcement to Congress and the public on June 22, 2010, less than 7 months after the IPEC's confirmation. The purpose of the plan is to develop an interagency strategy to combat infringement of IP rights.

In general, the joint strategic plan addressed each content requirement listed in the PRO-IP Act, but two enhancements could help to improve future plans: identifying implementing entities for all action items related to the plan's priorities and establishing resource estimates. In accordance with the act, the plan includes analyses of the economic, health, and safety threats posed by violations of IP rights. The plan also provides a description of the priorities that will carry out the plan's objectives and the means to be employed to achieve these priorities. While the act calls for the plan to identify implementing departments and agencies for all priorities, it did not do so for about one third of the action items aligned to the priorities. In addition, the plan did not include estimates of the resources needed to fulfill the plan's priorities because data collection and analysis are still in progress.

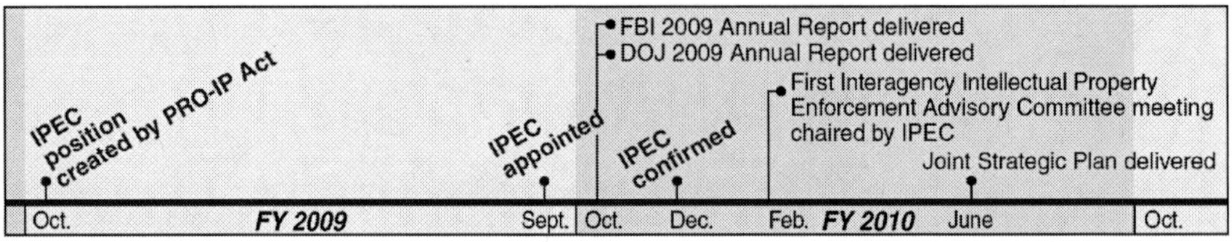

Source: GAO analysis.

Timeline of Key IPEC and DOJ Efforts Related to the PRO-IP Act.

ABBREVIATIONS

BJA	Bureau of Justice Assistance
CCIPS	Computer Crime and Intellectual Property Section
CHIP	Computer Hacking and Intellectual Property
DOJ	Department of Justice
FBI	Federal Bureau of Investigation
IP	intellectual property
IPEC	Intellectual Property Enforcement Coordinator
NIPLECC	National Intellectual Property Law Enforcement Coordination Council
OMB	Office of Management and Budget
PRO-IP Act	Prioritizing Resources and Organization for Intellectual Property Act of 2008
STOP	Strategy for Targeting Organized Piracy
USTR	U.S. Trade Representative

October 13, 2010

The Honorable Patrick J. Leahy
Chairman
The Honorable Jeff Sessions
Ranking Member
Committee on the Judiciary
United States Senate

The Honorable John Conyers, Jr.
Chairman
The Honorable Lamar S. Smith
Ranking Member
Committee on the Judiciary
House of Representatives

Intellectual property (IP) plays a significant role in the U.S. economy, and the United States is an acknowledged leader in its creation. IP is a category of legal rights that grants owners certain exclusive rights to intangible assets or products of the human intellect, such as inventions; literary and artistic works; and symbols, names, images, and design. The federal government grants IP protection through patents, copyrights, and trademarks, and takes enforcement actions that range from seizing IP-infringing goods to prosecuting alleged criminals. IP protection and enforcement efforts cut across a wide range of U.S. agencies, making coordination essential.

Under the Prioritizing Resources and Organization for Intellectual Property Act of 2008[1] (PRO-IP Act), Congress created the position of the Intellectual Property Enforcement Coordinator (IPEC) to serve within the Executive Office of the President. The act outlines the IPEC's duties and includes specific efforts to enhance interagency coordination, such as the development of a comprehensive joint strategic plan. The PRO-IP Act also required the U.S. Attorney General, through the Department of Justice (DOJ) and its Federal Bureau of Investigation (FBI), to devote additional resources to IP enforcement and to undertake other specific IP enforcement related efforts.

The PRO-IP Act mandates that GAO provide Congress with a report on the efforts, activities, and actions of the U.S. Attorney General and the IPEC in achieving the goals and purposes of the act no later than 2 years after its enactment. Because the IPEC was not confirmed until December 2009 and some agencies have only recently undertaken required efforts, we agreed to provide a status report on efforts to implement the act. Specifically, this report addresses efforts undertaken by DOJ and the Office of the IPEC to implement requirements outlined in the act.[2] In addition, this report compares the 2010 Joint Strategic Plan on Intellectual Property Enforcement to content called for in the act.

To determine the status of the implementation of the requirements of the PRO-IP Act that are assigned to the IPEC, DOJ, and the FBI, we examined the act to identify the requirements assigned to each entity and met with staff from the Office of the IPEC and officials from DOJ and the FBI to discuss their implementation efforts. We requested that these entities provide us with a written description of the status of their efforts and describe any challenges they face relating to each requirement under the act. Because of time limitations, we did not independently verify all agency statements, but attributed these statements accordingly. We compared each entity's efforts to those called for in the act to determine the status of its implementation, and then met with agency staff and officials to clarify our observations. To compare the 2010 Joint Strategic Plan on Intellectual Property Enforcement to the content requirements detailed in the PRO-IP Act, we evaluated content from the plan against each content requirement from Title III, Section 303 (e) and (f) to determine whether each content requirement was addressed.

We conducted this performance audit from July 2010 to October 2010 in accordance with generally accepted government auditing standards. Those standards require that we plan and perform the audit to obtain sufficient, appropriate evidence to provide a reasonable basis for our findings and conclusions based on our audit objectives. We believe that the evidence obtained provides a reasonable basis for our findings and conclusions based on our audit objectives. For additional details regarding our scope and methodology, see appendix I.

BACKGROUND

The economic value of goods protected by copyrights, patents, and trademarks makes them attractive targets for criminal networks.[3] Criminal violations of IP rights have potential negative effects for U.S. innovation and investment, on the value and reputation of individual companies, and for consumers who are put at risk by substandard or dangerous products. Industry groups suggest that counterfeiting and piracy are on the rise and that a broader range of products—from auto parts to razor blades, medicines to infant formula—are subject to counterfeit production. The illicit nature of counterfeiting and piracy makes it extremely difficult to estimate the economic impact of IP infringements, but research for specific industries suggests that the problem is sizeable.[4]

Eight key federal agencies, as well as entities within them, undertake a wide range of activities in protecting IP rights. The agencies are the Departments of Commerce, State, Justice, Health and Human Services, and Homeland Security; the U.S. Trade Representative (USTR); the U.S. Copyright Office; and the U.S. International Trade Commission. In many cases, IP-related efforts represent a small part of the agencies' much broader missions.

DOJ's U.S. attorneys' offices, Criminal Division, and the FBI investigate and prosecute federal IP crimes. DOJ established the Computer Hacking and Intellectual Property (CHIP) program, which consists of specially-trained assistant U.S. attorneys to pursue IP cases. Each of the 93 U.S. attorneys offices throughout the country have assistant U.S. attorneys designated as CHIP coordinators, who are available to work on IP cases. In addition, DOJ has created CHIP units in 25 U.S. attorney's offices with histories of large IP case loads. DOJ's Computer Crime and Intellectual Property Section (CCIPS)—based in Washington, D.C.—consists of prosecutors devoted to enforcing computer crime and IP laws. CCIPS attorneys prosecute cases, assist prosecutors and other investigative agents in the field, and help develop and implement an overall criminal enforcement strategy. The FBI's Cyber Division oversees the bureau's IP enforcement efforts, though not all of its IP investigations are cyber-related.[5] FBI IP investigations are primarily conducted in 21 of the FBI's 56 field offices and the FBI's IP Rights Unit located at the National Intellectual Property Rights Coordination Center.[6]

Over the years, Congress and the administration have created interagency mechanisms to coordinate federal IP law enforcement efforts. In 1999, Congress created an interagency mechanism, called the National Intellectual Property Law Enforcement Coordination Council (NIPLECC), to coordinate U.S. law enforcement efforts to protect and enforce IP rights in the United States and abroad.[7] Officials from seven federal entities were members of NIPLECC.[8] In October 2004, the President launched a separate initiative—the Strategy for Targeting Organized Piracy (STOP)—which included for the most part the same agencies as NIPLECC and was intended to target cross-border trade in tangible goods and strengthen U.S. government and industry IP enforcement actions. Congress later passed legislation in December 2004 to enhance NIPLECC's mandate and created the position of the Coordinator for International Intellectual Property Enforcement, located within the Department of Commerce, to head NIPLECC.[9] In November 2006 we reported that NIPLECC continued to face persistent difficulties, creating doubts about its ability to carry out its mandate.[10] We also noted that while STOP had brought attention and energy to IP efforts within the U.S. government because of its executive office status, STOP had limited usefulness as a tool to prioritize, guide, implement, and monitor the combined efforts of multiple agencies. GAO has conducted a variety of assignments related to IP protection and enforcement over the last several years. A list of GAO reports and testimonies on IP protection since 2004 is included at the end of this report.

The PRO-IP Act enacted several changes intended to address weaknesses in prior coordinating structures. For example, the PRO-IP Act specifically required the new interagency advisory committee to prepare a joint strategic plan that addresses key elements of an effective national strategic plan, building in mechanisms for accountability and oversight. Also, the PRO-IP Act required the IPEC to submit the joint strategic plan to committees of Congress every third year after the development of the first strategic plan. In addition, the PRO-IP Act places leadership in the Executive Office of the President, within the Office of Management and Budget (OMB)—a status similar to that of STOP. The PRO-IP Act also repealed NIPLECC upon confirmation of the IPEC by the Senate.

DOJ and FBI Officials Report Taking Actions Called for by the PRO-IP Act

Officials from DOJ and the FBI report that they have taken actions called for in the PRO-IP Act. For example, consistent with efforts authorized by the act, DOJ officials reported that in fiscal 2009 the department awarded 10 grants, totaling approximately $2 million, to fund IP enforcement efforts. In addition, they reported that DOJ has assigned 97 assistant U.S. attorneys to work with CHIP units and that all CHIP units have two or more attorneys assigned as of August 2010. FBI officials also reported that they have created agent positions dedicated to investigating IP crimes, with 31 agent positions funded in fiscal year 2009 and an additional 20 agent positions funded in fiscal year 2010. FBI officials explained that delays in receiving funding for new agent positions and the time needed to hire, train, and deploy agents has meant that new agent positions have not immediately increased agent time spent on investigation. FBI officials also reported that IP-dedicated agents are sometimes used for other investigations but officials reported that they are monitoring IP staff usage and will take corrective action, if needed. DOJ officials reported that the U.S. Attorney General's Organized Crime Council Action Plan emphasizes IP crimes as part of an integrated approach to dealing with the multiple areas affected by organized crime. Finally, both DOJ and FBI officials have submitted reports to Congress on actions taken under the PRO-IP Act.

DOJ Awarded IP Grants to State and Local Law Enforcement Agencies

DOJ officials report that they have used the Intellectual Property Enforcement, Training, and Technical Assistance Program to fund eligible state and local IP efforts consistent with authority provided in the PRO-IP Act. For fiscal year 2009, the Office of Justice Programs' Bureau of Justice Assistance (BJA) awarded 10 grants—totaling $2,005,692—to support IP efforts. DOJ funded these fiscal year 2009 grants from the Economic, HighTech, and Cyber Crime Prevention funds.[11] BJA awarded eight of these grants to state and local agencies to directly assist with IP prevention and enforcement efforts. For example, BJA awarded the city of Los Angeles $199,995 to support the city's anti-piracy unit. DOJ officials noted that it awarded grants to two national organizations to jointly develop and deliver an IP curriculum for presentation to federal, state, local, and tribal law enforcement and prosecutors at 10 regional locations. For information on recipients and grant amounts see table 1 below.

> "The Office of Justice Programs of the Department of Justice may make grants to eligible State or local law enforcement entities, including law enforcement agencies of municipal governments and public educational institutions, for training, prevention, enforcement, and prosecution of intellectual property theft and infringement crimes..."
>
> Source: Section 401(b), P.L. 110-403.

Table 1. Fiscal Year 2009, BJA Intellectual Property Enforcement, Training, and Technical Assistance Program Grants.

Agency receiving grant	Description	Award amount
Virginia Office of the Attorney General	Support IP training and enforcement	$17,575
Bronx County District Attorney, NY	Target stores selling counterfeit goods	43,718
North Carolina Department of the Secretary of State	Purchase equipment to develop IP leads	44,485
Chesterfield County Police Department, VA	Investigate IP crimes connections	199,919
City of Los Angeles Police Department, CA	Support anti-piracy unit	199,995
Los Angeles County Sheriff's Department, CA	Enhance IP law enforcement	200,000
Mississippi Attorney General's Office	Enhance IP law enforcement	200,000
New York City Mayors Office	Hire additional IP investigators	200,000
National White Collar Crime Center (NW3C)	Partnership to develop IP curriculum	450,000
National Association of Attorneys General, D.C.	Partnership to develop IP curriculum	450,000
Total funding for 10 grantees		**$2,005,692**

Source: GAO analysis of BJA grant award announcement.

DOJ officials reported that BJA is currently reviewing applications from state and local law enforcement entities for $4 million in fiscal year 2010 funds[12] under the Intellectual Property Enforcement, Training, and Technical Assistance Program. DOJ intended to award all of these grants by September 30, 2010.

DOJ officials reported several challenges hampering their efforts to aid state and local law enforcement entities with their IP efforts. First, officials cited the lack of knowledge among state and local law enforcement and prosecutors about the importance of IP protection. Officials noted a broad misperception of IP as a "victimless" crime. Officials state that when cases cross jurisdictional lines, this lack of knowledge can lead partner police agencies not to take IP investigations as seriously as warranted. Further, this lack of knowledge can result in reluctance on the part of some prosecutors to file felony charges against suspects. Finally officials cited limited resources, competing priorities, and collateral duties that sometimes impede support for IP efforts at state and local levels.

FBI and DOJ Increased IP Staffing and Training

FBI officials reported increasing the number of FBI agents dedicated to investigating IP crimes in support of DOJ's CCIPS. FBI officials noted that their fiscal year 2009 appropriation[13] provided funding for at least five full-time FBI agents dedicated to working with DOJ's CCIPS. In consultation with CCIPS, FBI officials at headquarters created the

Intellectual Property Rights Unit, locating it at the National Intellectual Property Rights Center in Virginia. As of May 2010, this FBI unit was staffed by six agents, consisting of three unit agents dedicated solely to investigating criminal IP crimes, two supervisory agents guiding unit agents and field office IP programs, and a supervisory agent unit chief. The three unit agents focus on investigating complex, multi-district cases, as well as on working cases with partner agencies. The Intellectual Property Rights Unit is also supported by two management program analysts, one staff operations specialist, and intelligence analyst support from the FBI Cyber Intelligence section. FBI officials also noted that the bureau had recently dedicated FBI agents in the field to IP enforcement and these agents also support CCIPS.

> "Subject to the availability of appropriations to carry out this subsection, the Attorney General, in consultation with the Director of the Federal Bureau of Investigation, shall, with respect to crimes related to theft of intellectual property... ensure that there are at least 10 additional operational agents of the Federal Bureau of Investigation designated to support the Computer Crime and Intellectual Property Section [CCIPS] of the Criminal Division of the Department of Justice in the investigation and coordination of intellectual property crimes..."
>
> Source: 402(a)(1), P.L. 110-403.

> "Sub ject to the availability of appropriations to carry out this subsection, the Attorney General, in consultation with the Director of the Federal Bureau of Investigation, shall, with respect to crimes related to theft of intellectual property… ensure that any Computer Hacking and Intellectual Property Crime [CHIP] Unit in the Department of Justice is supported by at least 1 agent of the Federal Bureau of Investigation (in addition to any agent supporting such unit as of the date of the enactment of this Act) to support such unit for the purpose of investigating or prosecuting intellectual property crimes..."
>
> Source: 402(a)(2), P.L. 110-403.

All 25 CHIP units, according to FBI officials, are supported by at least one FBI agent. FBI officials reported that prior to fiscal 2009, although FBI agents worked IP cases, it did not have agents dedicated to IP enforcement and that the size of the FBI's IP enforcement effort was small relative to other efforts. FBI officials noted that fiscal year 2009 funding allowed it to create 31 IP-dedicated agent positions, and fiscal year 2010 funding allowed it to create an additional 20 IP-dedicated agent positions.[14] The increase in IP-dedicated agents resulted in 22 of 25 CHIP units having at least one assigned agent dedicated to IP investigations in fiscal year 2010. Specifically, 11 of the 22 CHIP units were each assigned one IP-dedicated agent and the remaining 11 CHIP units were assigned two to six IP-dedicated agents. FBI officials reported that they appointed a special agent to act as an IP coordinator for each of the 3 remaining CHIP units to directly support those units.

Although the FBI has added agents dedicated to IP enforcement, FBI officials reported that the number of "agent years" charged to IP investigations has not correspondingly increased. According to FBI officials, field IP investigations totaled 20.5 agent years in fiscal year 2008 even though there were no IP-dedicated agents in fiscal year 2008. Although the FBI had 46 dedicated IP field agent positions in August 2010, FBI officials reported for the first 10.5 months of fiscal year 2010 (through August 14, 2010), field agents charged only 26.2 agent years to IP investigations. However, FBI officials noted at the end of August 2010, there were 37 IP-dedicated field agents actively charging time to IP investigations.[15]

FBI officials noted several factors that contributed to the number of "agent years" charged to IP investigations not increasing correspondingly with the increase in IP-dedicated agent positions. First, FBI officials noted that delays in funding, hiring, training, and deploying new agent positions reduces the time available for new agents to perform IP investigations. FBI officials explained that the bureau received a fiscal year 2009 supplemental appropriation in March 2009, which provided for 31 agent positions, including 26 field agent positions to work solely on IP investigations. FBI officials cited a 6 to 9 month lag in filling some of these positions including time to hire, train, and deploy agents to field offices. Similarly, FBI officials noted that the FBI received fiscal year 2010 funding for 20 additional IP-dedicated agent positions in December 2010, and again time for hiring, training, and deploying agents reduced the time available for IP investigations. Second, FBI officials acknowledged that although they have increased the number of agents dedicated to IP, field office supervisory agents sometimes use these agents for other non-IP related investigations. FBI officials reported that they are monitoring FBI field office usage of IP-dedicated agent time. Those offices found to have underutilized IP-dedicated staff at the end of fiscal year 2010 will be required to implement a strategy to improve IP staff utilization.

"Subject to the availability of appropriations to carry out this subsection, the Attorney General, in consultation with the Director of the Federal Bureau of Investigation, shall, with respect to crimes related to theft of intellectual property… ensure that all Computer Hacking and Intellectual Property Crime Units located at an office of a United States Attorney are assigned at least 2 Assistant United States Attorneys responsible for investigating and prosecuting computer hacking or intellectual property crimes…"

Source: Section 402(a)(3), P.L. 110-403.

DOJ officials reported that as of August 2010, there are two or more assistant U.S. attorneys assigned to all 25 CHIP units. Overall, DOJ assigned 97 assistant U.S. attorneys to work with the various CHIP units and is in the process of hiring and placing an additional 15 assistant U.S. attorneys. However, DOJ officials also noted that ordinary job turnover at individual offices occasionally makes it difficult to maintain two assistant U.S. attorneys at each CHIP unit.

"Subject to the availability of appropriations to carry out this subsection, the Attorney General, in consultation with the Director of the Federal Bureau of Investigation, shall, with respect to crimes related to theft of intellectual property… ensure the implementation of a regular and comprehen-sive training program..."

Source: Section 402(a)(4), P.L. 110-403.

FBI officials reported that the bureau's annual IP rights conference, scheduled every September, has become a comprehensive IP rights training program for IP-dedicated agents and others. For example, in 2009 the FBI conducted a 3-day training session for IP-dedicated agents as well as other field agents and intelligence analysts. Training topics included statutory authorities, DOJ enforcement efforts, major case initiatives, case studies, intelligence analysis for IP rights cases, federal partner efforts, and industry subject matter expert presentations.

FBI officials reported that the annual IP rights training for 2010 will include both a basic training course for newly placed agents and an advanced course for experienced agents. The three agents acting as IP coordinators will also receive this annual training to ensure adequate support for CHIP units.

FBI officials also noted that currently all new agents receive an overview of the laws governing IP violations during new agents training at the FBI academy. According to these officials, the FBI is in the process of developing an expanded IP curriculum for new agents. In addition, all agents on a cyber career track receive additional IP specialized training during the 2-week post new agents training program. This training consists of an IP rights program overview, PRO-IP Act overview, case initiation and investigative techniques, guidance regarding the importance of interagency partnerships, and the benefits of industry coordination efforts.

DOJ's Plans Address Relationship between Organized Crime and IP Offenses

DOJ officials reported that the department has incorporated IP concerns into the U.S. Attorney General's Law Enforcement Strategy for Combating Organized Crime. The strategy establishes an investigation and prosecution framework and includes marshalling information and intelligence, and prioritizing and targeting organized crime threats.

> "Subject to the availability of appropriations to carry out this subsection...the Attorney General, through the United States Attorneys' Offices, the Computer Crime and Intellectual Property section, and the Organized Crime Racketeering section of the Department of Justice, and in consultation with the Federal Bureau of Investigation and other Federal law enforcement agencies, such as the Department of Homeland Security, shall create and implement a comprehensive, long range plan to investigate and prosecute international organized crime syndicates engaging in or supporting crimes relating to the theft of intellectual property."
>
> Source: Section 402(b), P.L. 110-403.

In addition, DOJ officials reported that the U.S. Attorney General's Organized Crime Council[16] Action Plan addresses the relationship between organized crime and IP offenses. The council identifies specific goals in its annual action plan, and has identified IP crimes as a priority since 2008. The 2010 action plan emphasizes IP crimes as part of an integrated approach to dealing with the multiple areas affected by organized crime and identifies the IP-specific goals for understanding criminal organizations engaged in IP violations and coordinating the substantial efforts law enforcement is making in both areas. The plan calls on DOJ to work with investigative agencies to focus efforts on known counterfeit product distribution networks with the goal of tracing the source of products back to countries where the goods are produced. The plan also calls for sharing information and cross-training to allow personnel to identify IP violations that involve organized crime.

The first annual DOJ PRO-IP report[17] detailed several approaches the department intended to deploy to integrate IP enforcement with the departments' overall international organized crime strategy. The plan calls for CCIPS to coordinate with the Organized Crime and Racketeering Section and other federal agencies through the International Organized Crime Intelligence Operations Center to develop and implement a mechanism to address intelligence gaps as they relate to IP, among other items. The plan further noted that the CCIPS' Intellectual Property Rights Unit has detailed a senior attorney to provide legal advice and guidance and coordinate IP cases involving the judicial process and other prosecutorial activities. It also called for the CCIPS and other relevant participating federal agencies to contribute critical IP-related intelligence and case information.

DOJ officials noted that the department expects to see an increase in the number of IP cases developed from traditional organized crime investigations. Further, DOJ officials expected an increase in awareness of U.S. business and Department of State personnel about the role of organized criminal enterprises in IP offenses. Officials noted that integrating IP investigations with traditional organized crime investigations requires coordination between DOJ components that have not traditionally interacted on specific cases. Officials observe that close coordination between the work of investigators and prosecutors handling organized crime and IP crimes creates a much better position for those involved to identify connections between organized crimes and IP crimes.

DOJ and FBI Provide Annual IP Reports

> "...annually...the Attorney General shall submit a report to Congress on actions a t ken to carry out this title. The initial report required under this subsection shall be submitted by May 1, 2009. All subsequent annual reports shall be submitted by May 1st of each fiscal year thereafter. The report required under this subsection may be submitted as part of the annual performance report of the Department of Justice..."
>
> Source: Section 404(a), P.L. 110-403.

DOJ officials reported that the department submitted its report on actions taken to carry out Title IV of the PRO-IP Act to Congress on October 13, 2009. DOJ officials noted that the act provided two options for submitting the report—DOJ can submit the report by May 1 or as part of its annual performance report, which is filed annually in October. They further noted that there is no method to gather statistical data for the report outside the current fiscal year structure. DOJ officials reported that the department provided its first report in October 2009 (and separate from its annual performance report) and intends to submit the fiscal year 2010 report in early October 2010.

> "The first report required to be submitted by the Attorney General under subsection (a) shall include a summary of the efforts, activities, and resources the Department of Justice has allocated in the 5 years prior to the date of enactment of this Act, as well as the 1-year period following such date of enactment, to the enforcement, investigation, and prosecution of intellectual property crimes..."
>
> Source: Section 404(b), P.L. 110-403.

DOJ officials reported that the department's first report contained information on ongoing activities as well as historical data about the enforcement, investigation, and prosecution of IP crimes. Officials noted that the historical information largely duplicated information previously reported to Congress in the department's annual performance report and in reports from the National Intellectual Property Law Enforcement Coordination Council.

> "... annually...the Director of the Federal Bureau of Investigation shall submit a report to Congress on actions taken to carry out this title. The initial report required under this subsection shall be submitted by May 1, 2009. All subsequent annual reports shall be submitted by May 1st of each fiscal year thereafter. The report required under this subsection may be submitted as part of the annual performance report of the Department of Justice..."
>
> Source: Section 404(c), P.L. 110-403.

Separately, FBI officials reported that the bureau submitted its first required report on actions taken under Title IV of the PRO-IP Act in October 2009. Like DOJ, FBI officials noted that its October 2009 report was in line with the timing of DOJ's annual performance report.

> "The first report required to be submitted by the Director of the Federal Bureau of Investigation under subsection (c) shall include a summary of the efforts, activities, and resources the Federal Bureau of Investigation has allocated in the 5 years prior to the date of enactment of this Act, as well as the 1-year period following such date of enactment to the enforcement, investigation, and prosecution of intellectual property crimes..."
>
> Source: 404(d), P.L. 110-403.

The October 2009 FBI report included a presentation of the number of different types of investigative accomplishments from fiscal year 2004 through fiscal year 2009. The report also presented discussions of PRO-IP Act funding, training for PRO-IP Act special agents, and efforts and activities in support of the FBI's IP rights program. FBI officials reported that they intend to submit their next annual report in October 2010.

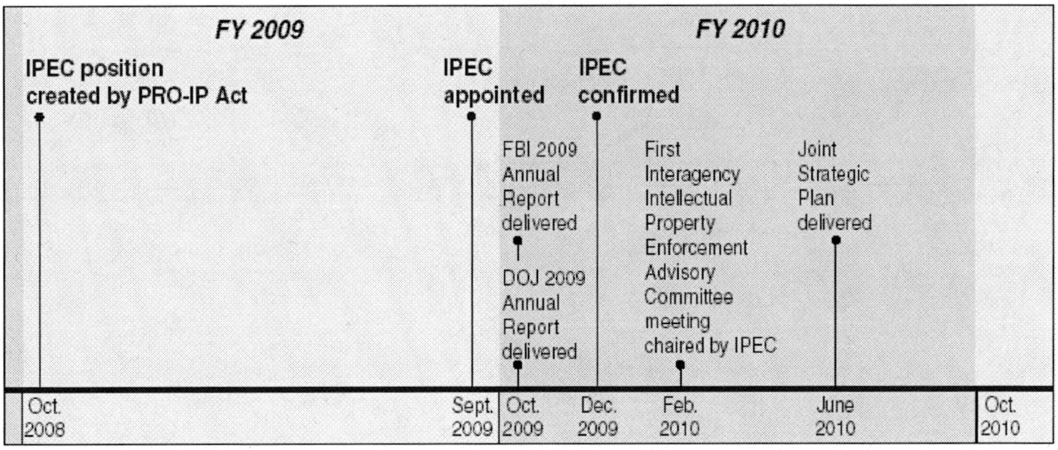

Source: GAO analysis.

Figure 1. Timeline of Key IPEC and DOJ Efforts Related to the PRO-IP Act.

OFFICE OF THE IPEC STAFF REPORT TAKING STEPS TO IMPLEMENT THE PRO-IP ACT

Office of the IPEC staff reported that the IPEC and the Interagency Intellectual Property Enforcement Advisory Committee have taken steps to implement the PRO-IP Act. For example, the Office of the IPEC was established following the appointment and confirmation of the IPEC. The office consists of the IPEC and four temporarily detailed employees with expertise in IP enforcement. In addition, staff reported that the IPEC has begun to carry out its duties required by the PRO-IP Act, such as facilitating the issuance of IP policy guidance and establishing and chairing the Interagency Intellectual Property Enforcement Advisory Committee. Moreover, the IPEC led members of the advisory committee in developing a joint strategic plan required by the PRO-IP Act. Because the IPEC was not confirmed until December 4, 2009, the 2010 joint strategic plan was delivered to Congress and the public on June 22, 2010, rather than October 13, 2009, as called for by the act.

Office of the IPEC Established

On October 13, 2008, the PRO-IP Act created the position of the IPEC, placing it within OMB, in the Executive Office of the President (see figure2). The President nominated Victoria A. Espinel as the first IPEC on September 25, 2009, and the Senate confirmed Espinel on December 4, 2009. The Office of the IPEC has a relatively small but experienced staff. In addition to the IPEC, the office includes one assistant who is a permanent employee and four employees temporarily detailed from the U.S. Patent and Trademark Office; Department of Homeland Security's Office of Policy; DOJ's Civil Rights Division; and DOJ's U.S. Attorney's Office for the Central District of California, Cyber, and Intellectual Property Crimes Section. Staff reported that the attorney detailed from the U.S. Patent and Trademark Office has experience handling all aspects of IP litigation. They also reported that the staff member detailed from the Department of Homeland Security has significant trade and IP related experience. In addition, both staff detailed from DOJ have criminal prosecutor experience, and one has experience as a CHIP unit attorney.

> "The President shall appoint, by and with the advice and consent of the Senate, an Intellectual Property Enforcement Coordinator (in this title referred to as the 'IPEC') to serve within the Executive Office of the President…"
>
> Source: Section 301(a), P.L. 110-403.

IPEC Facilitating Issuance of IP Policy Guidance

Staff from the Office of the IPEC reported that the IPEC has begun to facilitate the issuance of policy guidance by coordinating discussions on IP enforcement policy issues. For example, the Office of the IPEC worked with the departments and agencies involved in the development of the 2010 Joint Strategic Plan on Intellectual Property Enforcement to resolve IP enforcement policy issues and to incorporate the administration's position on these issues into the plan. Staff reported that these discussions resulted in developing administration policies, which were reflected in several areas of the joint strategic plan, including the action item titled *Facilitating Cooperation to Reduce Intellectual Property Infringement Occurring Over the Internet*. The IPEC has also provided guidance in public statements on a variety of IP enforcement issues.

> "The IPEC shall…facilitate the issuance of policy guidance to departments and agencies on basic issues of policy and interpretation, to the extent necessary to assure the coordination of intellectual property enforcement policy and consistency with other law..."
>
> Source: Section 301(b)(1)(D), P.L. 110-403.

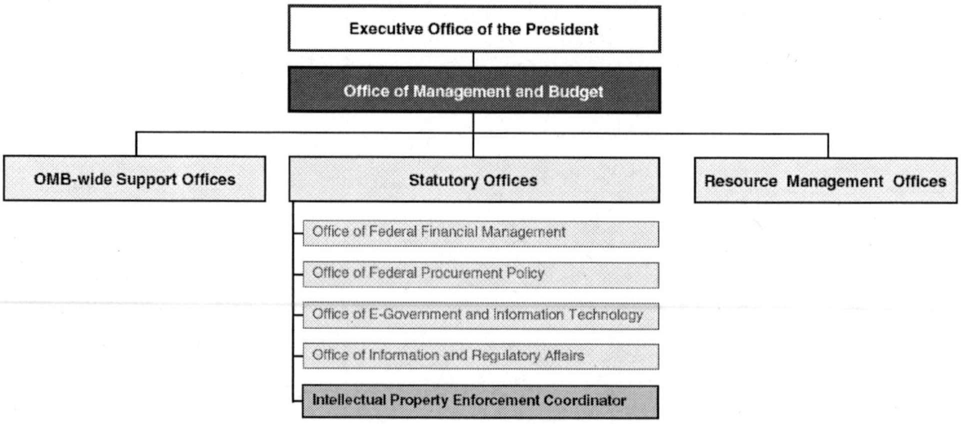

Source: Office of Management and Budget organization chart.

Figure 2. IPEC Located within OMB.

Office of the IPEC staff noted that because the office is located within OMB, it has had the opportunity to review and shape policy guidance and other policy statements provided by the departments and agencies involved in IP enforcement. For example, the office routinely participates in discussions on IP related issues when such issues are under consideration within the OMB. Staff reported that the office provides policy input on the drafts of IP related materials under review, such as Federal Register notices, proposed rules, and memoranda. Further, the office has requested that federal agencies keep the office informed about all significant IP enforcement issues.

Interagency Advisory Committee Established and Chaired by the IPEC

Office of the IPEC staff reported that the IPEC has convened and chaired two meetings of the Interagency Intellectual Property Enforcement Advisory Committee. Staff reported that the committee is currently composed of the IPEC and Senate-confirmed representatives of the departments and offices listed in the PRO-IP Act (see figure 3).[18] They noted that two committee meetings, on February 2, 2010 and May 14, 2010, took place to discuss the formulation of the joint strategic plan. Staff also reported that the IPEC convened dozens of other meetings with agency officials from the member agencies to identify issues to be addressed in the strategy, to discuss recommendations for addressing each issue, and to develop plans for formulating and implementing each component of the joint strategic plan. Staff stated that committee members also participated in weekly teleconferences, and individual committee members and their designees communicate regularly in person and by phone and e-mail.

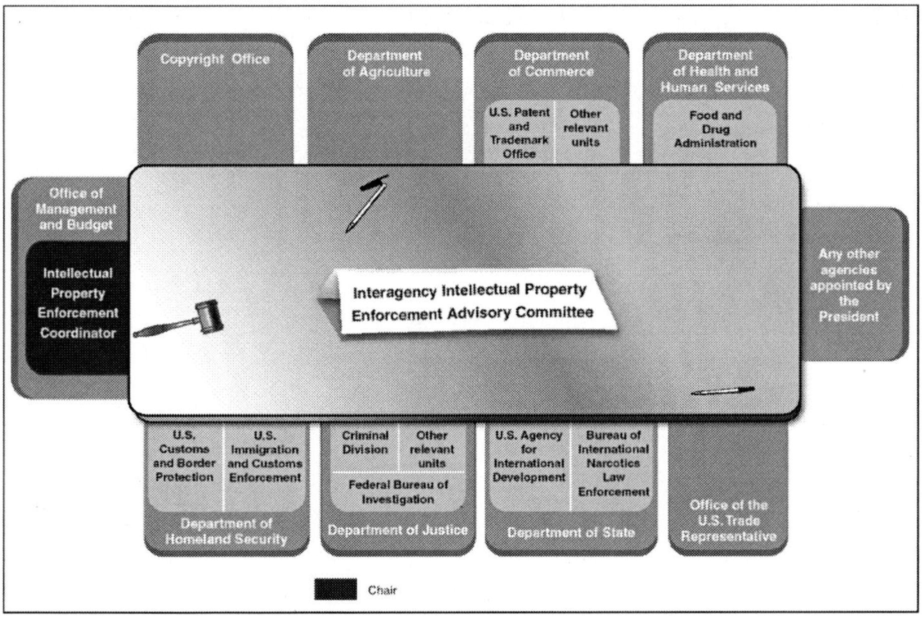

Source: GAO analysis Pro-IP Act; Art Resource s (clip art).

Figure 3. Interagency Intellectual Property Enforcement Advisory Committee Members as Provided by the PRO-IP Act.

> "The IPEC shall…chair the interagency intellectual property enforcement advisory committee…"
>
> "There is established an interagency intellectual property enforcement advisory committee composed of the IPEC, who shall chair the committee, and…Senate-confirmed representatives…of departments and agencies who a re involved in intellectual property enforcement…"
>
> "The advisory committee…shall develop the Joint Strategic Plan against counterfeiting and infringement..."
>
> Source: Section 301(b)(1)(A) & Section 301(b)(3)(A) and (B), P.L. 110-403.

The IPEC Coordinated and Assisted with Developing and Implementing the Joint Strategic Plan

Staff from the Office of the IPEC reported that the IPEC coordinated the development of the 2010 Joint Strategic Plan on Intellectual Property Enforcement and has begun assisting departments and agencies involved in implementing the plan. Staff reported that after the IPEC was confirmed, she brought the departments and agencies involved in IP enforcement together to draft the joint strategic plan. They said that, the IPEC, as the chair of the Interagency Intellectual Property Enforcement Advisory Committee, and the Office of the IPEC have actively coordinated the efforts of these departments, agencies, and White House offices to identify and prioritize IP enforcement issues, and then to develop action plans to address the issues. Staff reported that in addition to convening formal Interagency Intellectual Property Enforcement Advisory Committee meetings, the IPEC convened several dozen meetings and many other communications with participating agency officials.

> "The IPEC shall…coordinate the development of the Joint Strategic Plan against counterfeiting and infringement by the advisory committee…"
>
> "During the development of the joint strategic plan, the IPEC shall…provide assistance to, and coordinate the meetings and efforts of, the appropriate officers and employees of departments and agencies represented on the advisory committee… who are involved in intellectual property enforcement..."
>
> Source: Section 301(b)(1)(B) & Section 303(c)(1), P.L. 110-403.

Office of the IPEC staff reported that during the development of the joint strategic plan, they met with experts from various industry sectors to hear their views regarding the mechanisms of infringement and how illegal products are made, transported, and sold, as well as to collect information regarding the mechanisms for preventing infringement and its detection. Staff reported that they met with hundreds of companies, trade associations, and other organizations representing a diverse range of stakeholders[19] who shared their experience and expertise on IP enforcement issues. While the majority of these meetings took place in Washington, D.C., the IPEC also traveled around the country to hear from industries affected by IP infringement such as counterfeiting and piracy. The office also issued a Federal

Register notice seeking comments from the public, including the private sector, on IP infringement and asking for its help in shaping the administration's strategy. Staff reported receiving more than 1,600 responses and reviewing each response.

> "During the development of the joint strategic plan, the IPEC...may consult with private sector experts in intellectual property enforcement in furtherance of providing assistance to the members of the advisory committee..."
>
> Source: Section 303(c)(2), P.L. 110-40 3.

Staff from the Office of the IPEC also reported that the administration has already begun the process of assisting departments and agencies with implementation of the joint strategic plan. Staff reported that before the plan was issued the office met with the agencies responsible for the subject matter covered by each of the action items to formulate a detailed plan for implementing each action item.

> "The IPEC shall...assist, at the request of the departments and agencies...in the implementation of the Joint Strategic Plan..."
>
> Source: Section 301(b)(1)(C), P.L. 110-403.

IPEC Reporting on IP Enforcement Programs

The IPEC has reported to the President and Congress on the status of domestic and international IP enforcement programs through the 2010 joint strategic plan. Two sections in the plan provide descriptions of the domestic and international IP enforcement programs undertaken by the agencies with significant IP enforcement responsibilities.[20] Many of the action items listed in the plan also include a description of existing programs and recommend ways in which the U.S. government can improve its efforts under those programs. For example, one action item titled *Comprehensive Review of Existing Intellectual Property Laws to Determine Needed Legislative Changes* describes in detail the administration's plan to conduct an initial review of existing laws to identify any gaps in enforcement authorities.

Staff from the Office of the IPEC reported that the IPEC plans to submit the first annual report to Congress on the activities of the Interagency Intellectual Property Enforcement Advisory Committee, including the advisory committee's progress towards implementing the joint strategic plan, in December 2010. Staff noted that a December 2009 annual report was not submitted as required by the PRO-IP Act because the IPEC was not confirmed until December 4, 2009.

> "The IPEC shall...report to the President and report to Congress, to the extent consistent with law, regarding domestic and interna tional intellectual property enforcement programs..."

> "The IPEC shall…report to Congress… on the implementation of the Joint Strategic Plan, and make recommendations, if any and as appropriate, to Congress for improvements in Federal intellectual property laws and enforcement efforts…"
>
> "Not later than December 31 of each calendar year beginning in 2009, the IPEC shall submit a report on the activities of the advisory committee during the preceding fiscal year. The annual report shall be submitted to Congress, and disseminated to the people of the United States…"
>
> Source: Section 301(b)(1)(E) and (F) & Section 304(a), P.L. 110-403.

Agencies Carried Out Duties Related to the Development of the Joint Strategic Plan

Staff from the Office of the IPEC reported that departments and agencies involved in IP enforcement worked collaboratively with the IPEC and carried out duties related to the development of the joint strategic plan, including designating personnel and sharing information.[21] The IPEC also worked with other offices within the White House, including the Office of Science and Technology Policy and the Domestic Policy Council, among others. Staff noted that at each stage of the development of the joint strategic plan, the designated personnel drew on their expertise to provide input on the ideas, recommendations, and drafts that the Office of the IPEC circulated among the departments and agencies. They also noted that the departments and agencies were forthcoming with agency information, including statistical information on their enforcement activities, to the extent that they were permitted to do so by law.

> "In the development and implementation of the joint strategic plan, the heads of the departments and agencies… shall…
>
> "… designate personnel with expertise and experience in intellectual property enforcement matters to work with the IPEC and other members of the advisory committee…
>
> "… share relevant department or agency information with the IPEC and other members of the advisory committee, including statistical information on the enforcement activities of the department or agency against counterfeiting or infringement, and plans for addressing the joint strategic plan, to the extent permitted by a l w, including requirements relating to confidentiality and privacy, and to the extent that such sharing of information is consistent with Department of Justice and other law enforcement protocols for handling such information."
>
> Source: Section 303(d)(1) and (2), P.L. 110-403.

2010 Joint Strategic Plan on Intellectual Property Enforcement Delivered

The Office of the IPEC delivered the 2010 Joint Strategic Plan on Intellectual Property Enforcement to the Congress on June 22, 2010. The PRO-IP Act was enacted on October 13, 2008, and called for the first joint strategic plan to be delivered to Congress within 1 year. However, as previously mentioned, the IPEC was not confirmed until December 4, 2009, after the date the first joint strategic plan was due to Congress. The Office of the IPEC reported making the 2010 joint strategic plan available to the public by placing it on the White House Web site.[22]

> "Not later than 12 months after the date of the enactment of this Act, and not later than December 31 of every third year thereafter, the IPEC shall submit the joint strategic plan to the Committee on the Judiciary a nd the Committee on Appropriations of the Senate, and to the Committee on the Judiciary and the Committee on Appropriations of the House of Representatives."
>
> "The joint strategic plan shall be posted for public access on the website of the White House, and shall be disseminated to the public through such other means as the IPEC may identify."
>
> Source: Section 303(b) and (g), P.L. 110-403.

2010 Joint Strategic Plan Generally Addressed PRO-IP Act Content Requirements, but Two Enhancements Could Improve Future Plans

In general, the 2010 Joint Strategic Plan on Intellectual Property Enforcement addressed each content requirement listed in the PRO-IP Act, but two enhancements could help to improve future plans: identifying implementing departments and agencies for all action items related to the priorities identified for carrying out the plan's objectives and establishing resource estimates necessary to fulfill those objectives. The purpose of the plan is to develop an interagency strategy to combat infringement of IP rights. Joint strategic plans are required every 3 years, and the first plan was released less than 7 months after the confirmation of the IPEC. This first plan included analysis by outside entities of the economic, health, and safety threats posed by violations of IP rights. The plan also provided a description of priorities (called "categories of focus") for carrying out the plan's objectives and a description of the means or "action items" to be employed to achieve these priorities. Additionally, the plan established five performance indicators for IP protection and enforcement and acknowledged that this initial list is subject to modification based on the U.S. government's experience collecting and analyzing indicators. While the act calls for the plan to identify implementing departments and agencies for all priorities, it did not identify implementing entities for all action items aligned to the priorities. For example, responsibilities for about a third of the action items were assigned to the U.S. government generally instead of to specific departments and agencies. In addition, the plan included a strategy for data collection and analysis needed to establish future resource estimates; however, it did not provide actual resource estimates needed to fulfill the priorities of the plan.

Threat Analysis of IP Rights Violations

The 2010 joint strategic plan included analysis by outside entities of the threat posed by violations of IP rights as called for under the PRO-IP Act. The IPEC issued a Federal Register notice in February 2010 to obtain public comments on the costs to the U.S. economy resulting from IP violations, and the threats to public health and safety created by infringement.[23] The IPEC received comments regarding costs to the U.S. economy resulting from infringement of IP rights, both direct and indirect, including impact on the creation or maintenance of jobs, and concerns that counterfeits are being found in products related to the nation's critical infrastructure, in defense technologies, and in life-saving medical equipment. The plan's appendix also included a summary of studies relevant to costs to the economy of the United States resulting from violations of IP laws, and the threats to public health and safety created by counterfeiting and infringement.[24]

> "Each joint strategic plan shall include…
>
> "…An analysis of the threat posed by violations of intellectual property rights, including the costs to the economy of the United States resulting from violations of intellectual property laws, and the threats to public health and safety created by counterfeiting and infringement…
>
> "…Such other information as is necessary to convey the costs imposed on the United States economy by, and the threats to public health and safety created by, counterfeiting and infringement, and those steps that the Federal Government intends to take over the period covered by the succeeding joint strategic plan to reduce those costs and counter those threats."
>
> Source: Section 303 (e)(5) and (8), P.L. 110-403.

Requirements Related to Enhancing Efforts of Foreign Governments

The 2010 joint strategic plan addressed all of the PRO-IP Act requirements related to enhancing efforts of foreign governments. The plan discussed improving the effectiveness of U.S. personnel stationed overseas to combat IP infringement and coordination of international capacity building and training. The plan also explicitly stated that the federal government will "focus capacity building and training efforts in those countries in which intellectual property enforcement is a high priority and where those efforts can be most effective." Furthermore, the plan described how the list of countries identified by the USTR under the Special 301 process[25]—that is, those countries that deny adequate IP rights protection—will be utilized by an interagency process to work with foreign governments to improve their practices related to IP and market access. Finally, the plan called for metrics to measure the effectiveness of the federal government's efforts to improve the laws and enforcement practices of foreign governments against counterfeiting and infringement. The plan stated that one of its goals is to "increase the number of criminal enforcement actions against IP infringers in foreign countries in general." The performance measures section of the plan also stated that "the IPEC, in coordination with [Department of State, Department of Commerce, U.S. Trade Representative] and other relevant agencies will report on changes in other countries in intellectual property protection."

> "The joint strategic plan shall include programs to provide training and technical assistance to foreign governments for the purpose of enhancing the efforts of such governments to enforce laws against counterfeiting and infringement. With respect to such programs, the joint strategic plan shall…
>
> "…seek to enhance the efficiency and consistency with which Federal resources are expended, and seek to minimize duplication, overlap, or inconsistency of efforts;
>
> "…identify and give priority to those countries where programs of training and technical assistance can be carried out most effectively and with the greatest benefit to reducing counterfeit and infringing products in the United States market, to protecting the intellectual property rights of United States persons and their licensees, and to protecting the interests of United States persons otherwise harmed by violations of intellectual property rights in those countries;
>
> "…in identifying [such priorities], be guided by the list of countries identified by the United States Trade Representative[in the Special 301 Process]; and
>
> "…develop metrics to measure the effectiveness of the Federal Government's efforts to improve the laws and enforcement practices of foreign governments against counterfeiting and infringement."
>
> Source: Section 303(f)(1)-(4), P.L. 110-403.

Description of Priorities and Means

In addition, the 2010 joint strategic plan described the priorities identified for carrying out the objectives[26] of the plan, as well as the means to be employed to achieve these priorities. Staff from the Office of the IPEC confirmed that the plan's "six categories of focus" represent the "priorities" called for in the act. Therefore, the plan's priorities for the federal government related to IP enforcement are: (1) leading by example, (2) increasing transparency, (3) ensuring efficiency and coordination, (4) enforcing IP rights internationally, (5) securing the United States' supply chain, and (6) building a data-driven government. The plan explicitly lays out 33 action items that the federal government plans to take under each of these six priorities. Staff from the Office of the IPEC also confirmed that the plan's "action items" provide information on the "means" to be employed to achieve the plan's priorities. For example, a description of a priority called "Securing Our Supply Chain" stated that "… the U.S. Government will work to secure supply chains to stem the flow of infringing products through law enforcement efforts and through enhanced cooperation with the private sector." There were eight action items under this priority, including *Mandated Use of Electronic Track and Trace for Pharmaceuticals and Medical Products* and *Increased*

Enforcement Efforts to Guard Against the Proliferation of Counterfeit Pharmaceuticals and Medical Devices. (See app. III for a list of the plan's priorities and action items.)

> "Each joint strategic plan shall include...
> "...A description of the priorities identified for carrying out the objectives in the joint strategic plan, including activities of the Federal Government relating to intellectual property enforcement.
> "...A description of the means to be employed to achieve the priorities, including the means for improving the efficiency and effectiveness of the Federal Government's enforcement efforts against counterfeiting and infringement."
>
> Source: Section 303 (e)(1) and (2), P.L. 110-403.

Strategies for Ensuring Coordination Included

The 2010 joint strategic plan included strategies for ensuring coordination among the departments and agencies responsible for carrying out the strategy. First, the plan identified the agencies that the IPEC worked with during the development of the plan: (1) OMB; (2) DOJ, including the FBI; (3) Department of Commerce, including International Trade Administration and U.S. Patent and Trademark Office; (4) USTR; (5) Department of State; (6) Department of Homeland Security, including Customs and Border Protection and Immigration and Customs Enforcement; (7) Department of Health and Human Services, including the Food and Drug Administration; (8) U.S. Department of Agriculture; and (9) the U.S. Copyright Office.[27]

> "Each joint strategic plan shall include... A strategy for ensuring coordination among the departments and agencies...which will facilitate oversight by the executive branch of, and accountability among, the departments and agencies responsible for carrying out the strategy."
>
> Source: Section 303(e)(7), P.L. 110-403

The plan also included coordination strategies to be used during the implementation of the plan. For example, "Ensuring Efficiency and Coordination" was one of the plan's priorities and included the following action items: (1) *Coordination of National Law Enforcement Efforts to Avoid Duplication and Waste*; (2) *Coordination of Federal, State, and Local Law Enforcement*; (3) *Coordination of Training for State and Local Law Enforcement and Prosecutors*; (4) *Improve the Effectiveness of Personnel Stationed Overseas to Combat Intellectual Property Infringement*; (5) *Coordination of International Capacity Building and Training*; and (6) *Establishment of a Counterfeit Pharmaceutical Interagency Committee*. Furthermore, coordination strategies for implementing agencies were also included in the plan's other priorities. For instance, an action item under the plan's "Increasing Transparency" priority stated that "...USTR, in coordination with the IPEC, will initiate an interagency process to assess opportunities to further publicize and potentially expand on the

[Notorious Markets][28] list in an effort to increase public awareness and guide related trade enforcement actions."

Initial List of Performance Measures Established

The 2010 joint strategic plan established five performance indicators for IP protection and enforcement: (1) law enforcement actions, (2) seizures, (3) training and outreach, (4) increased IP protection in other countries, and (5) public perceptions of IP rights. The plan stated that measuring and reporting the effectiveness of the plan conveys to the public the impact of the federal government's work and helps the government to continue to expand effective enforcement activities and fix or curtail ineffective ones. The plan stated that the list of key performance indicators is "an initial list of key performance indicators for IP enforcement, primarily measuring government activities." The plan also stated that "as the U.S. Government as a whole gains experience collecting and analyzing these indicators, further modifications or additional measures may follow." The plan noted "that the goal—reduced infringement of IP rights—is difficult to accurately measure, in large part, because infringers, like other types of thieves, try to hide their actions." GAO's guidance[29] on performance measures within a national strategy recommends discussing the importance of implementing parties' establishing priorities, milestones, and performance measures to help ensure accountability. Moreover, GAO's guidance on key attributes of successful performance measures[30] recommends aligning performance measures with agency-wide goals or, in this case, the priorities of plan.

> "Each joint strategic plan shall include...The performance measures to be used to monitor results under the joint strategic plan during the following year."
>
> Source: Section 303(e)(4), P.L. 110-403.

Implementing Entities Not Identified for all Action Items Aligned to Priorities

Although most action items listed under the plan's priorities identified specific departments and agencies to be involved in their implementation, it was not done in all cases. Because each of the plan's priorities was comprised of multiple action items, the identification of implementing departments or agencies was made at the action item level.

> "Each joint strategic plan shall include... An identification of the departments and agencies that will be involved in implementing each priority..."
>
> Source: Section 303(e)(6), P.L. 110-403.

In most cases, the actions items identified specific departments and agencies responsible for implementation of those items. For instance, an action item entitled *Establishment of a*

U.S. Government-Wide Working Group to Prevent U.S. Government Purchase of Counterfeit Products stated,

> The IPEC will convene this working group, whose members will include the National Security Council (NSC), Department of Defense (DOD)/Acquisition, Technology and Logistics (AT&L), National Aeronautics and Space Administration (NASA), General Services Administration (GSA), [Department of Commerce], Small Business Administration (SBA), [Department of Homeland Security], and other participants as may be identified by the IPEC.

The plan added, "The working group shall be led by the IPEC, the Administrators of GSA and Federal Procurement Policy, and the Undersecretary of Defense for AT&L at DOD."

However, 12 out of 33 action items assigned implementation to the U.S. government generally instead of to specific departments and agencies. For example, the action item *Improved Transparency in Intellectual Property Policy-Making and International Negotiations* stated that "the U.S. Government will enhance public engagement through online outreach, stakeholder outreach, congressional consultations and soliciting feedback through advisory committees, official comment mechanisms such as Federal Register notices, notices of proposed rulemaking and notices of inquiry."[31]

Staff from the Office of the IPEC stated that not all action items in the joint strategic plan identified departments and agencies because it was not appropriate to assign specific entities, but rather it was appropriate to assign the U.S. government. However, the action item *Improve the Effectiveness of Personnel Stationed Overseas to Combat Intellectual Property Infringement* is an example of an action item that was assigned to the U.S. government generally, but could have been assigned to specific departments and agencies. Two GAO reports[32] described the federal agencies that have personnel posted overseas who conduct activities related to IP enforcement and protection and their respective roles and responsibilities. This suggests that any or all of these specific departments and agencies could have been identified as entities to be involved in implementing this action item. GAO's guidance[33] on organizational roles, responsibilities, and coordination within a national strategy recommends identifying the specific federal departments, agencies, or offices involved and, where appropriate, the different sectors, such as state, local, private, or international sectors. By not assigning implementation of all action items to specific departments and agencies, the departments and agencies involved in IP enforcement cannot be held accountable for carrying out the plan's strategy.

Resource Estimates to Implement Plan Not Included

While the 2010 joint strategic plan included a strategy for data collection and analysis needed to establish resource estimates, the plan did not include actual estimates of the resources needed to fulfill the plan's priorities because data collection and analysis are still in progress. The plan stated, "In order to better track resource baselines and inform future resource allocations dedicated to IP enforcement, the IPEC will collect annually the amount of U.S. Government resources spent on IP enforcement personnel, technologies, programs and other efforts." The plan also stated that the IPEC has already begun collecting data for fiscal year 2010 through a budget data request, whereby agencies report the amount of resources they dedicated to human capital and programs, identified metrics used in measuring IP enforcement successes, and provided planned and estimated expenditures for future years. The plan asserted that the IPEC will continue coordinating the budget data request annually, and will request the same data and metrics to allow for cross and multi-year comparisons.

> "Each joint strategic plan shall include… Estimates of the resources necessary to fulfill the priorities..."
>
> Source: Section 303(e)(3), P.L. 110-403.

GAO's guidance[34] on how to develop a national strategy recommends that plans address what the strategy will cost, the sources and types of resources and investments needed, and where those resources and investments should be targeted. Furthermore, GAO's guidance suggests the inclusion of a discussion of the types of resources required, such as budgetary, human capital information, information technology, research and development, procurement of equipment, or contract services. Staff from the Office of the IPEC stated that because data collection and analysis on current federal resources spent on IP enforcement by these agencies are still in progress, the plan cannot yet estimate the resources needed. However, the plan and Office of the IPEC staff did not specify whether resource estimates would be established in time for the next joint strategic plan, nor did they specify whether these resource estimates would be aligned to the priorities of the plan. By including resource estimates needed to fulfill the priorities in future plans, the IPEC and departments and agencies involved in IP enforcement will be able to communicate to Congress about resources available to support the joint strategic plan and to work towards effective resource allocation.

CONCLUSIONS

The PRO-IP Act of 2008 recognized the importance of protecting and enforcing IP rights by providing for additional IP enforcement resources, requiring key agencies to report on their IP enforcement efforts and establishing the Office of the IPEC within the Office of the President to coordinate federal IP enforcement efforts. Although IP protection and enforcement is challenging and complex, DOJ, the FBI, and the Office of the IPEC have made progress in implementing provisions of the act, including increasing staff and enhancing training, reporting, and planning. The Office of the IPECs' development of the first joint strategic plan represents an important step to providing an integrated strategy to protecting and enforcing IP rights.

While the current joint strategic plan generally addresses all content requirements listed in the PRO-IP Act, two enhancements could help to improve future plans. Most significantly, the existing plan does not always assign implementation responsibility to specific departments or agencies for the action items that align with the plan's priorities. Accountability is a significant element in any plan and is a requirement of the PRO-IP Act. Agency accountability is impaired when specific assignments for priority action items are not assigned to the IPEC and departments and agencies involved. In addition, the plan addresses the need to develop resource estimates to fulfill the plan's priorities by describing initial steps being taken to collect information on resources from the various agencies. However, future plans would benefit from the inclusion of actual resource estimates that are aligned to priorities, which would help the IPEC and departments and agencies involved in IP enforcement communicate to Congress about resources available to support the joint strategic plan and work towards effective resource allocation. The IPEC and the Interagency Intellectual Property Enforcement Advisory Committee will have an opportunity to address these issues when it issues future joint strategic plans, which are required by the PRO-IP Act.

RECOMMENDATIONS FOR EXECUTIVE ACTION

To meet the PRO-IP Act's content requirements related to the Joint Strategic Plan on Intellectual Property Enforcement and increase effectiveness and accountability, we recommend that the Intellectual Property Enforcement Coordinator, in consultation with the Interagency Intellectual Property Enforcement Advisory Committee, take the following actions when developing the 2013 plan and subsequent plans:

- assign implementation of all of the plan's priorities and related action items to specific departments and agencies; and
- provide estimates of the resources needed to carry out the priorities of the plan.

APPENDIX I. SCOPE AND METHODOLOGY

To determine the status of the implementation of the requirements of the Prioritizing Resources and Organization for Intellectual Property Act of 2008 (PRO-IP Act) that are assigned to the Office of the Intellectual Property Enforcement Coordinator (IPEC), the Department of Justice (DOJ), and the Federal Bureau of Investigation (FBI), we examined the PRO-IP Act to identify those requirements assigned to these offices and met staff and officials from these offices to discuss their implementation efforts. We requested that the IPEC, DOJ, and the FBI provide us with a written description of the status of their efforts and describe any challenges they faced related to implementing each requirement. Because of time limitations, we did not independently verify all agency statements, but attributed their statements accordingly. We compared each office's efforts to the requirements called for in the act to determine the status of their implementation and then met with staff from the Office of the IPEC, and officials from DOJ and the FBI to clarify our observations. We determined the data used in this report were sufficiently reliable for our purposes.

To compare the 2010 Joint Strategic Plan on Intellectual Property Enforcement to the content requirements detailed in the PRO-IP Act, we evaluated content from the plan against each content requirement listed in applicable provisions of the act to determine which content requirements were addressed. To determine whether the plan addressed the act's requirement to identify the departments and agencies that will be involved in implementing each priority, we reviewed each of the six priorities (also called "categories of focus") and the action items aligned to them. Because each priority was comprised of the multiple action items, the identification of the implementing agencies and departments were made at the action item level. For purposes of our analysis, we categorized the identification of implementing agencies for each of the plan's 33 action items as one of the following:

- *Specific.* Included in their description the identification of the specific departments and agencies responsible for implementing the action item.
- *Broad.* Did not include identification of the specific departments or agencies responsible for implementing the action item, but rather generally assigned implementation, for example, to the "Federal Government," "Federal Agencies," or "Federal law enforcement agencies."
- *Both.* Included both specific identification of the departments or agencies responsible for implementing the action item and generally assigned implementation to the "Federal Government," "Federal Agencies," or "Federal law enforcement agencies."
- *Neither.* Did not include either specific identification of the departments or agencies responsible for implementing the action item and did not generally assign implementation to the "Federal Government," "Federal Agencies," or "Federal law enforcement agencies."

APPENDIX II. 2010 JOINT STRATEGIC PLAN ON INTELLECTUAL PROPERTY ENFORCEMENT PRIORITIES AND RELATED ACTION ITEMS

Leading by Example
• Establishment of a U.S. government-wide working group to prevent U.S. Government purchase of counterfeit products
• Use of legal software by federal contractors
Increasing Transparency
• Improved transparency in intellectual property policy-making and international negotiations
• Increased information sharing with rightholders
• Communication with victims/rightholders
• Reporting on best practices of our tra ding partners
• Identify foreign pirate web sites as part of the Special 301 process
• Tracking and reporting of enforcement activities
• Sharing of exclusion order enforcement da ta
• Enhanced communications to strengthen Section 337 enforcement
Ensuring Efficiency and Coordination
• Coordination of national law enforcement efforts to avoid duplication and waste
• Coordination of federal, st ate, and local law enforcement
• Coordination of tra ining for state and local law enforcement and prosecutors
• Improve the effectiveness of personnel stationed overseas to combat intellectual property infringement

(Continued)

• Coordination of international capacity building and training
• Establishment of a cou nterfeit pharmaceutical interagency committee
Enforcing Our Rights Internationally
• Combat foreign-based and foreign-controlled web sites that infringe american intellectual property right s
• Enhance foreign law enforcement cooperation
• Promote enforcement of U.S. intellect ual property rights through trade policy tools
• Special 301 "action plans"
• Strengthen intellectua l property enforcement through international organizations
Securing Our Supply Chain
• FDA notification requirement for counterfeit pharmaceuticals and other medical products
• M andated use of electronic tra ck and trace for pharmaceuticals and medical products
• Increased enforcement efforts to guard against the proliferation of counterfeit pharmaceuticals and medical devices
• Penalty relief for vol untary disclosure
• Penalize exporter s of infringing goods
• Streamline bonding requirements for circumvention devices
• Fa cilitating cooperation to reduce intellectual property infringement occurring over the internet
Establish and implement voluntary protocols to help reduce illegal internet pharm a cies
Building a Data-Driven Government
• U.S. Government resources spent on intellectual property enforcement
• Assessing the economic impact of intellectual property-intensive industries
• Comprehensive review of existing intellectual property laws to determine needed legislative changes
• Supporting U.S. businesses in overseas markets

Source: 2010 Joint Strategic Plan on Intellectual Property Enforcement.

APPENDIX III. STAFF ACKNOWLEDGMENTS

Staff Acknowledgments

In addition to the contact named above, Christine Broderick, Assistant Director; Martin DeAlteriis; Karen Deans; Timothy Fairbanks; Etana Finkler; Justine Lazaro; and Ernie Jackson made key contributions to this report.

End Notes

[1] P.L. 110-403.

[2] Title III and IV of the P.L. 110-403.

[3] A copyright provides protection for literary and artistic works such as books, musical compositions, computer software, and cinematographic works (movies). A copyright is a property right in an original work of authorship that arises automatically upon creation of such a work and belongs, in the first instance, to the author. A patent protects an invention by giving the inventor the right to exclude others from making, using, or

selling a new, useful, or nonobvious invention during a specific term. Trademarks are words, phrases, logos, or other graphic symbols used by manufacturers or merchants to identify their goods and distinguish them from others. Other types of intellectual property include trade secrets, industrial designs, and geographic indications. Geographic indications are names used to identify products with quality, reputation, or other characteristics attributable to the origin of the product.

[4] Intellectual Property: Observations on Efforts to Quantify the Economic Effects of Counterfeit and Pirated Goods. GAO-10-423 (Washington, D.C.: Apr. 12, 2010).

[5] This division also investigates computer intrusions and child pornography.

[6] The National Intellectual Property Rights Coordination Center is the U.S. government's clearing house for investigations into counterfeiting and piracy. The National Intellectual Property Rights Center was created to promote sharing of information, resources and personnel between the U.S government agencies responsible for combating counterfeiting, piracy and related IP rights crime. The center is located in Arlington, VA.

[7] In September 1999, Congress authorized NIPLECC (P.L. 106-58).

[8] The council's membership included officials from: U.S. Customs and Border Protection; U.S. Immigration and Customs Enforcement; the Departments of Commerce, State, and Justice; the U.S. Patent and Trademark Office; and the Office of the U.S. Trade Representative. Department of Justice and the U.S. Patent and Trademark Office were co-chairs.

[9] (P.L. 108-447).

[10] GAO, *Intellectual Property: Strategy for Targeting Organized Piracy (STOP) Requires Changes for Long-term Success*, GAO-07-74 (Washington, D.C.: Nov. 8, 2006).

[11] Economic, High-Tech, and Cyber Crime Prevention grants were authorized under the Consolidated Appropriations Act, 2008 (P.L. 110-161).

[12] This program is authorized by the Omnibus Consolidated Appropriations Act, 2010 (P.L. 111-117)

[13] Omnibus Appropriations Act, FY 2009 (P.L. No. 111-118)

[14] In fiscal year 2010, the FBI reported a total of 51 agents dedicated to IP, of which 46 of these agents were assigned to 22 of DOJ's 25 CHIP units. The remaining 5 agents were assigned to the National Intellectual Property Rights Center to assist CCIPS. FBI officials noted that the placement of these IP-dedicated agents within the Intellectual Property Rights Unit and FBI field offices was coordinated with, and approved by, the Office of the Deputy Attorney General.

[15] FBI officials reported that the three agents in the Intellectual Property Rights Unit were also actively charging IP investigations at the end of August 2010.

[16] The U.S. Attorney General's Organized Crime Council was created by executive order in 1969 and directed the U.S. Attorney General to lead a government-wide response to organized crime. The council is chaired by the Deputy U.S. Attorney General and consists of the Assistant U.S. Attorney General for the Criminal Division and the leaders of nine participating federal law enforcement agencies.

[17] DOJ, *PRO-IP Act First Annual Report 2008-2009* (Oct. 13, 200).

[18] The PRO-IP Act listed the following as the Senate-confirmed representatives of the departments and agencies who are involved in intellectual property enforcement, and who are, or are appointed by, the respective heads of those departments and agencies: (1) The Office of Management and Budget; (2) Relevant units within the Department of Justice, including the Federal Bureau of Investigation and the Criminal Division; (3) The United States Patent and Trademark Office and other relevant units of the Department of Commerce; (4) The Office of the United States Trade Representative; (5) The Department of State, the United States Agency for International Development, and the Bureau of International Narcotics Law Enforcement; (6) The Department of Homeland Security, United States Customs and Border Protection, and United States Immigration and Customs Enforcement; (7) The Food and Drug Administration of the Department of Health and Human Services; (8) The Department of Agriculture; and (9) Any such other agencies as the President determines to be substantially involved in the efforts of the Federal Government to combat counterfeiting and infringement. The act also listed the Register of Copyrights, or a senior representative of the United States Copyright Office appointed by the Register of Copyrights as a member of the advisory committee.

[19] Office of the IPEC staff stated that the IPEC and staff met with many stakeholders including: pharmaceutical and medical device companies; software, hardware, and videogame makers; information technology companies; high technology companies, including those specializing in green technologies; biotech companies; photographers; book publishers; musicians; composers; publishers; songwriters; performers; recording studios; movie and television companies; unions; industrial manufactures; manufactures of automobile and aviation parts; cement companies; makers of consumer products; product safety certifiers; sports companies; the apparel industry; and makers of luxury goods.

[20] These sections were titled "Agencies' Intellectual Property Enforcement Missions" and "Agencies' 2010 Major Intellectual Property Enforcement Activities to Date."

[21] Agencies working with the Office of the IPEC included: (1) OMB; (2) DOJ, including the FBI; (3) Department of Commerce, including International Trade Association and U.S. Patent and Trademark Office; (4) U.S. Trade Representative; (5) Department of State; (6) Department of Homeland Security, including Customs and Border Protection and Immigration and Customs Enforcement; (7) Department of Health and Human Services,

including the Food and Drug Administration; (8) U.S. Department of Agriculture; and (9) the U.S. Copyright Office.

[22] The 2010 Joint Strategic Plan on Intellectual Property Enforcement can be found at http://www.whitehouse.gov/omb/intellectualproperty/.

[23] 75 Fed. Reg. 8137 (Feb. 23, 2010).

[24] The plan states that the appendix is intended as a summary of submissions and studies and is not intended to be a U.S. government endorsement of any specific study, methodology, or data.

[25] "Special 301" refers to certain provisions of the Trade Act of 1974, as amended by the 1988 Omnibus Trade and Competitiveness Act (P.L. 100-418), that require USTR to annually identify foreign countries that deny adequate and effective protection of intellectual property rights or fair and equitable market access for U.S. persons who rely on intellectual property protection. USTR identifies these countries with substantial input from interested persons and in consultation with U.S. agencies, and publishes the results of its reviews in an annual report.

[26] As stated in the PRO-IP Act, the plan's objectives included: (1) reducing counterfeit and infringing goods in the domestic and international supply chain; (2) identifying and addressing unjustified impediments to effective enforcement action activities involving sale of counterfeit or infringing goods; (3) ensuring that information is identified and shared among relevant departments and agencies; (4) disrupting and eliminating domestic and international counterfeiting and infringement networks; (5) strengthening the capacity of other countries to protect and enforce IP rights; (6) working with other countries to establish international standards and policies for the effective protection and enforcement of IP rights; and (7) protecting IP rights overseas.

[27] The plan added that "the IPEC worked with other offices, including the Office of the Vice President, the Office of Science and Technology Policy, the Domestic Policy Council and the White House Counsel's Office."

[28] The 2009 Special 301 report features a "Notorious Markets List" that lists examples of marketplaces, including those on the Internet that have been the subject of enforcement action, or may merit further investigation for possible IP infringements, or both. The list represents a selective summary of information reviewed during the Special 301 process; it is not a finding of violations of law.

[29] GAO, *Combating Terrorism: Evaluation of Selected Characteristics in National Strategies Related to Terrorism*, GAO-04-408T (Washington, D.C.: Feb. 3, 2004).

[30] GAO, *Drug Control: DOD Needs to Improve Its Performance System to Better Manage and Oversee Its Counternarcotics Activities*, GAO-10-835 (Washington, D.C.: July 21, 2010).

[31] This action item was under the priority "Increasing Transparency."

[32] GAO, *Overseas U.S. Government Personnel Involved in Efforts to Protect and Enforce Intellectual Property Rights*, GAO-09-402R (Washington, D.C.: Feb. 26, 2009) and *Intellectual Property: Enhanced Planning by U.S. Personnel Overseas Could Strengthen Efforts*, GAO-09-863 (Washington, D.C.: Sept. 30, 2009).

[33] GAO-04-408T.

[34] GAO-04-408T.

In: Intellectual Property
Editor: Nicholas D. Melark

ISBN: 978-1-61470-506-2

Chapter 5

INTELLECTUAL PROPERTY: OBSERVATIONS ON EFFORTS TO QUANTIFY THE ECONOMIC EFFECTS OF COUNTERFEIT AND PIRATED GOODS

United States Government Accountability Office

WHY GAO DID THIS STUDY

In October 2008, Congress passed the Prioritizing Resources and Organization for Intellectual Property Act of 2008 (PRO-IP Act), to improve the effectiveness of U.S. government efforts to protect intellectual property (IP) rights such as copyrights, patents, and trademarks. The act also directed GAO to provide information on the quantification of the impacts of counterfeit and pirated goods. GAO (1) examined existing research on the effects of counterfeiting and piracy on consumers, industries, government, and the U.S. economy; and (2) identified insights gained from efforts to quantify the effects of counterfeiting and piracy on the U.S. economy.

GAO interviewed officials and subject matter experts from U.S. government agencies, industry associations, nongovernmental organizations, and academic institutions, and reviewed literature and studies quantifying or discussing the economic impacts of counterfeiting and piracy on the U.S. economy, industry, government, and consumers. GAO is making no recommendations in this report.

WHAT GAO FOUND

According to experts and literature GAO reviewed, counterfeiting and piracy have produced a wide range of effects on consumers, industry, government, and the economy as a whole, depending on the type of infringements involved and other factors. Consumers are particularly likely to experience negative effects when they purchase counterfeit products they believe are genuine, such as pharmaceuticals. Negative effects on U.S. industry may include lost sales, lost brand value, and reduced incentives to innovate; however, industry effects vary widely among sectors and companies. The U.S. government may lose tax revenue, incur IP enforcement expenses, and face risks of counterfeits entering supply chains with national security or civilian safety implications. The U.S. economy as a whole may grow more slowly because of reduced innovation and loss of trade revenue. Some experts and literature also identified some potential positive effects of counterfeiting and piracy. Some consumers may knowingly purchase counterfeits that are less expensive than the genuine goods and experience positive effects (consumer surplus), although the longer-term impact is unclear due to reduced incentives for research and development, among other factors.

Three widely cited U.S. government estimates of economic losses resulting from counterfeiting cannot be substantiated due to the absence of underlying studies. Generally, the illicit nature of counterfeiting and piracy makes estimating the economic impact of IP infringements extremely difficult, so assumptions must be used to offset the lack of data. Efforts to estimate losses involve assumptions such as the rate at which consumers would substitute counterfeit for legitimate products, which can have enormous impacts on the resulting estimates. Because of the significant differences in types of counterfeited and pirated goods and industries involved, no single method can be used to develop estimates. Each method has limitations, and most experts observed that it is difficult, if not impossible, to quantify the economy-wide impacts. Nonetheless, research in specific industries suggest that the problem is sizeable, which is of particular concern as many U.S. industries are leaders in the creation of intellectual property.

Negative Effects of Counterfeiting and Piracy, by Stakeholder.

Stakeholders	Negative effects
Consumers	Health and safety risks, low quality goods
Industries	Lost sales and brand value, increased IP protection costs
U.S. government	Lost tax revenue, increased enforcement costs, and risks to supply chains with national security or safety implications
U.S. economy	Lower growth and innovation, declining trade with countries having weak IP rights enforcement

Source: GAO analysis.

ABBREVIATIONS

BSA	Business Software Alliance
CBP	Customs and Border Protection
DHS	Department of Homeland Security
FAA	Federal Aviation Administration
FBI	Federal Bureau of Investigation
FDA	U.S. Food and Drug Administration
FTC	Federal Trade Commission
HHS	Department of Health and Human Services
IP	intellectual property
ITC	International Trade Commission
OECD	Organization for Economic Cooperation and Development

PRO-IP ACT	Prioritizing Resources and Organization for Intellectual Property Act of 2008
RIMS II	Regional Input-Output Modeling System
TRIPS	Agreement on Trade-Related Aspects of Intellectual Property Rights
USTR	Office of the U.S. Trade Representative
WTO	World Trade Organization

April 12, 2010

The Honorable Patrick J. Leahy
Chairman
The Honorable Jeff Sessions
Ranking Member
Committee on the Judiciary
United States Senate

The Honorable John Conyers, Jr.
Chairman
The Honorable Lamar S. Smith
Ranking Member
Committee on the Judiciary
House of Representatives

In October 2008, Congress passed the Prioritizing Resources and Organization for Intellectual Property Act of 2008 (PRO-IP Act) (P.L. 110-403), to strengthen and improve the effectiveness of U.S. government efforts to protect the intellectual property (IP) of U.S. industries and IP rights holders. In the PRO-IP Act, Congress noted that U.S. IP industries have created millions of highly skilled, high-paying U.S. jobs and continue to represent a major source of creativity, innovation, economic growth, and competitiveness.

The PRO-IP Act directed GAO to provide information on the quantification of the impacts of counterfeit and pirated goods on the economy and industries of the United States to help the U.S. government better protect the IP of rights holders.[1] Our work: (1) examined existing research on the effects of counterfeiting and piracy on consumers, industries, government, and the U.S. economy; and (2) identified insights gained from efforts to quantify the effects of counterfeiting and piracy on the U.S. economy.

To address these objectives, we interviewed officials and representatives from U.S. government agencies, industry associations, nongovernmental organizations, academic institutions, and a multilateral organization, and we reviewed documents and studies quantifying or discussing the impacts of counterfeiting and piracy on the U.S. economy, industry, government, and consumers. We met with officials and reviewed documents from the Departments of Justice (Justice), Homeland Security (DHS), Commerce (Commerce), and Health and Human Services (HHS), the Office of the U.S. Trade Representative (USTR), and the International Trade Commission (ITC). We conducted a literature search of studies and estimates of the economic impact of IP infringements published since 1999 to examine various aspects of the economic impacts of counterfeiting and piracy, and to identify other insights about the role IP plays in the U.S. economy.[2] Among the studies we reviewed was the Organization for Economic Cooperation and Development's (OECD) 2008 report, *The Economic Impact of Counterfeiting and Piracy*.[3] Although this study was global rather than focused on the U.S. economy, its unique nature and prominence as the most comprehensive attempt to quantify the impacts of counterfeiting and piracy warranted its inclusion within our reviews. We also interviewed subject matter experts from a range of governmental, nongovernmental, academic and industry sources, and OECD officials to discuss efforts to quantify the economic impacts of counterfeiting and piracy and to obtain their views on the range of impacts of counterfeits and piracy, insights on counterfeiting activities and markets, and the role of IP in the U.S. economy. Unless otherwise noted, in our discussion of the impacts and insights on counterfeiting and piracy, we do not distinguish between imported counterfeit and pirated goods and those produced domestically. The literature we reviewed and experts we spoke with focused primarily on imported counterfeit goods rather than those produced within the United States. We determined that the U.S. government did not systematically collect data and perform analysis on the impacts of counterfeiting and piracy on the U.S. economy and, based on our review of literature and interviews with experts, we concluded that it was not feasible to develop our own estimates or attempt to quantify the economic impact of counterfeiting and piracy on the U.S. economy. We shared a copy of the draft report with officials from Commerce, DHS, HHS, Justice, ITC, USTR, and the Office of the U.S. Intellectual Property Enforcement Coordinator to obtain technical comments. We received comments from the DHS and Justice, and the Office of the U.S. Intellectual Property Enforcement Coordinator and made changes as appropriate.

We conducted our work from April 2009 to April 2010 in accordance with all sections of GAO's Quality Assurance Framework that are relevant to our objectives. The framework requires that we plan and perform the engagement to obtain sufficient and appropriate evidence to meet our stated objectives and to discuss any limitations to our work. We believe that the information and data obtained, and the analysis conducted, provide a reasonable basis for any findings and conclusions in this product. For additional details regarding our scope and methodology, see appendix I.

BACKGROUND

Importance of Protection for Innovators Has Long Been Recognized in the United States

The importance of patents and other mechanisms to enable inventors to capture some of the benefits of their innovations has long been recognized in the United States as a tool to encourage innovation, dating back to Article 1 of the U.S. Constitution and the 1790 patent law. Ensuring the protection of IP rights encourages the introduction of innovative products and creative works to the public. Protection is granted by guaranteeing proprietors limited exclusive rights to whatever economic reward the market may provide for their creations and products.

Today, eight federal agencies and entities within them undertake the primary U.S. government activities in support of IP rights. These agencies and entities include Commerce, HHS, DHS, Justice, ITC, State, USTR, the Copyright Office, and entities such as Customs and Border Protection (CBP), the U.S. Patent and Trademark Office, and the Federal Bureau of Investigation (FBI).

In addition to domestic efforts for protecting IP, the U.S. government participated actively in negotiating the World Trade Organization's (WTO) Agreement on Trade-Related Aspects of Intellectual Property Rights (TRIPS), which came into force in 1995 and broadly governs the multilateral protection of IP rights. Under TRIPS, all WTO member countries are obligated to establish laws and regulations that meet a minimum standard for protecting various areas of IP rights. It also provides for enforcement measures for members. One of USTR's priorities in recent years has been negotiating free trade agreements. Since 2000, USTR has completed negotiations for free trade agreements that have entered into force with Australia, Bahrain, Central America,[4] Chile, Jordan, Morocco, Oman, Peru, and Singapore.[5] According to officials at USTR, these agreements offer protection beyond that required in TRIPS.[6]

Intellectual property is an important component of the U.S. economy, and the United States is an acknowledged global leader in the creation of intellectual property. According to the USTR, "Americans are the world's leading innovators, and our ideas and intellectual property are a key ingredient to our competitiveness and prosperity." The United States has generally been very active in terms of advocating strong IP protection and encouraging other nations to improve these systems for two key reasons. First, the U.S. has been the source of a large share of technological improvements for many years and, therefore, stands to lose if the associated IP rights are not respected in other nations. Secondly, a prominent economist noted that IP protection appears to be one of the factors that has helped to generate the enormous growth in the world economy and in the standard of living that has occurred in the last 150 years. This economist pointed out that the last two centuries have created an unprecedented surge in growth compared to prior periods. Among the factors attributed to creating the conditions for this explosion in economic growth are the rule of law, including property rights and the enforceability of contracts.[7]

While these conditions are clearly important for generating economic growth, determining the contributions of innovation to economic growth at the level of the overall economy has been a challenging task. Economists have used a variety of techniques to better understand the role of innovation in growth, and historical evidence shows that growth rates have periodically been driven upward by major technological improvements, beginning with the industrial revolution and the role of electricity, and continuing with the current revolution in information technology.[8]

Common Protections Related to IP

Generally, individual countries grant and enforce IP rights. IP is any innovation, commercial or artistic, or any unique name, symbol, logo, or design used commercially. IP rights protect the economic interests of the creators of these works by giving them property rights over their creations.[9]

- *Copyright.* A set of exclusive rights subsisting in original works of authorship fixed in any tangible medium of expression now known or later developed, for a fixed period of time. For example, works may be literary, musical, or artistic.

- *Trademark.* Any sign or any combination of signs capable of distinguishing the source of goods or services is capable of constituting a trademark. Such signs— in particular, words (including personal names), letters, numerals, figurative elements, and combinations of colors, as well as any combination of such signs— are eligible for registration as trademarks.
- *Patent.* Exclusive rights granted to inventions for a fixed period of time, whether products or processes, in all fields of technology, provided they are new, not obvious (involve an inventive step), and have utility (are capable of industrial application).

"Pirated copyright goods" refer to any goods that are copies made without the consent of the right holder or person duly authorized by the right holder. "Counterfeit goods" refer to any goods, including packaging or bearing without authorization, a trademark that is identical to a trademark validly registered for those goods, or that cannot be distinguished in its essential aspects from such a trademark, and that, thereby, infringes the rights of the owner of the trademark in question. According to the U.S. Food and Drug Administration (FDA), "counterfeit drugs" are defined under U.S. law as those sold under a product name without proper authorization, where the identity of the source drug is knowingly and intentionally mislabeled in a way that suggests that it is the authentic and approved product.[10]

Counterfeiting and Piracy Cover a Wide Range of Goods

CBP data show that between fiscal years 2004 and 2009, the domestic value and number of U.S. seizures of counterfeit goods imported from other countries have fluctuated.[11] These seizures have been concentrated among certain types of products. For example, seizures of footwear, wearing apparel, and handbags accounted for about 57 percent of the aggregate domestic value of goods seized in those 6 years. Table 1 shows the percent of total domestic value for different types of commodities seized as well as the domestic value of all goods seized and total number of seizures. The value of wearing apparel and cigarette seizures generally declined, while the value of pharmaceutical seizures generally increased. Several factors influence trends in seizure values. For example, values of seized goods can vary from year to year due to counterfeiters' responses to changes in marketplace demand or enforcement actions. For instance, in fiscal year 2006, a federal enforcement investigation resulted in the seizure of 77 cargo containers of counterfeit Nike Air Jordan shoes and one container of counterfeit Abercrombie & Fitch clothing. The estimated domestic value of these goods was about $19 million, representing about 12 percent of the total domestic seizure value that year. In addition, the level of federal border enforcement effort varies across ports, resulting in different seizure rates, which is discussed in a later section of this report.

According to CBP data, seized counterfeit goods are dominated by products from China. During fiscal years 2004 through 2009, China accounted for about 77 percent of the aggregate value of goods seized in the United States. Hong Kong, India, and Taiwan followed China, accounting for 7, 2, and 1 percent of the seized value, respectively. CBP data indicate certain concentrations of counterfeit production among these countries: in 2009, about 58 percent of the seized goods from China were footwear and handbags; 69 percent of the seized goods from Hong Kong were consumer electronics and watch parts; 91 percent of the seized goods from India were pharmaceuticals and perfume; and 85 percent of seized goods from Taiwan were computers and consumer electronics. CBP data show that goods were also seized frequently from Russia, Korea, Pakistan, Vietnam, and certain Southeast Asian countries. Unlike imported counterfeits, there is little information on the extent and sources for domestically produced counterfeits. According to the Congressional Research Service, the United States is especially concerned with foreign counterfeits of U.S. intellectual property. Compared to foreign countries, counterfeits produced in the United States are estimated to be relatively low.

Table 1. DHS Seizures of IP-Infringing Goods, Expressed as a Percentage of Total Domestic Value of Goods Seized Annually, Fiscal Years 2004–2009.

Dollars in millions							
Commodity	**2004 (percentage)**	**2005 (percentage)**	**2006 (percentage)**	**2007 (percentage)**	**2008 (percentage)**	**2009 (percentage)**	**Reported percentage of 2004-2009 totals**
Footwear	1	10	41	40	38	38	32
Wearing apparel	37	17	16	14	9	8	15
Handbags/wallets/ backpacks	17	16	9	7	11	8	11
Consumer electronics	6	9	5	8	8	12	9
Computers/ hardware	1	5	9	5	3	5	5
Pharmaceuticals	-	2	1	6	10	4	5
Cigarettes	17	10	-	-	2	1	4
Media	4	-	4	4	2	4	3
Watches/parts	2	3	2	-	-	6	2
Toys/electronic games	3	9	-	-	-	2	2
Batteries	2	-	-	-	1	1	1
Sunglasses/parts	-	-	-	2	3	1	1
Perfumes	-	3	-	1	2	1	1
Jewelry	-	-	-	-	-	4	1
Headwear	-	-	2	-	-	-	-
Health care	-	-	2	-	-	-	-
All other commodities	10	15	8	14	10	3	9
Total domestic value of all seizures	**$139**	**93**	**155**	**197**	**273**	**261**	**$1,118**
Total number of seizures	**7,255**	**8,022**	**14,675**	**13,657**	**14,992**	**14,841**	**73,442**

Source: GAO analysis of CBP data.

Note: Where percentages are not provided, CBP either did not report the commodity as a separate category in a given year or the percentage seized of the commodity was less than 1 percent of the total domestic value of all commodities seized. Seizures of these commodities may be included in the "All other commodities" category. The percentage values may not add up to 100 percent due to rounding.

Another significant aspect of IP infringement is the piracy of digital copyrighted products, which is not captured by CBP seizure data. The development of technologies that enable the unauthorized distribution of copyrighted works is widely recognized as leading to an increase in piracy. The rapid growth of Internet use, in particular, has significantly contributed to the increase. Digital products are not physical or tangible, can be reproduced at very low cost, and have the potential for immediate delivery through the Internet across virtually unlimited geographic markets. Sectors facing threats from digital piracy include the music, motion picture, television, publishing, and software industries. Piracy of these products over the Internet can occur through methods including peer-to-peer networks, streaming sites, and one-click hosting services. There is no government agency that systematically collects or tracks data on the extent of digital copyright piracy.

These technological developments, along with an increase in the sophistication of packaging for counterfeit goods, have changed the nature of counterfeiting and piracy substantially in recent years. Industry associations with whom we met commented that technological changes and increased sophistication among counterfeiters have affected their businesses significantly.

Table 2. Potential Direct Effects of IP Infringements in the United States by Stakeholder.

Stakeholders	Potential effects
Consumers	Negative effects • Damage to health and safety • Costs incurred when product fails due to lower quality of counterfeit good
	Positive Effects • Perceived benefits from lower prices of counterfeit and pirated goods
Industry	Negative effects • Lost sales • Lost brand value or damage to public image • Cost of IP protection • Decreased incentive to invest in research and development
	Positive effects • Increased sales of legitimate goods based on consumer "sampling" of pirated goods
Government	Negative effects • Lost tax revenue due to illegal sales of counterfeit and pirated goods • Cost of IP enforcement • Risks of counterfeits entering supply chains with national security or civilian safety implications
Economy as a whole	Negative effects • Lower economic growth as a result of reduced incentives to innovate • Lost revenue from declining U.S. trade in countries with weak IP rights regimes

Source: GAO analysis of data collected through interviews with experts and literature reviewed.

Note: These effects may differ greatly in magnitude by industry and stakeholder, with specific impacts depending on which product or industry is being discussed.

Counterfeiting and Piracy Have a Wide Range of Effects on U.S. Consumers, Industry, Government, and the Economy

According to experts we spoke with and literature we reviewed, counterfeiting and piracy have produced a wide range of effects on consumers, industry, government, and the economy as a whole, depending on the type of infringements involved and other factors. Most of the information and views we obtained from our interviews and literature review focused on the significant direct negative effects of counterfeiting and piracy on stakeholders, including health and safety risks, lost revenues, and increased costs of protecting and enforcing IP rights. However, some experts and literature point out that certain stakeholders may experience some positive effects from counterfeits and piracy, though there is little information available on potential positive effects. Table 2 summarizes the positive and negative effects by stakeholder, based on our discussions with experts and literature we reviewed.

Consumer Effects Include Danger to Health and Safety

A commonly cited concern about counterfeit trade is that certain types of counterfeit goods can have harmful effects on consumers' health and safety, causing serious illness or death. Experts we spoke with and literature we reviewed identified certain counterfeit products, such as pharmaceuticals, automotive parts, electrical components, toys, and household goods, as having potentially damaging health and safety effects. According to experts we spoke with, a key characteristic of these types of counterfeit goods, which distinguishes their effects from other types of counterfeiting or piracy, is that U.S. consumers are likely to have been deceived about the origin of the product. In addition, some studies and an expert reported that counterfeiters have increasingly diversified beyond their traditional products, such as luxury goods, to more functional products such as baby shampoo and household cleaners, and will continue to expand their product portfolios since the profit incentives are large. Examples of the types of counterfeit products that may have negative health and safety effects on consumers are presented below.

- Counterfeit pharmaceuticals may include toxic or nonactive ingredients, correct ingredients in incorrect quantities, or other mislabeling. These products can be ineffective in treating ailments or may lead to adverse reactions, drug resistance, or even death.[12] The FDA has specifically highlighted and issued warnings to U.S. consumers on the dangers of buying prescription drugs over the Internet.
- Counterfeit automotive products may be substandard. A representative of a U.S. automotive parts supplier stated that it tested a supply of counterfeit timing belts that did not meet industry safety standards and could potentially impair the safety of vehicles.
- Counterfeit or pirated software may threaten consumers' computer security. The illegitimate software, for example, may contain malicious programming code that could interfere with computers' operations or violates users' privacy.

Effects Vary Across Industries and Include Lost Sales and Reduced Incentives to Innovate

Counterfeit or pirated products that act as substitutes for genuine goods can have a wide range of negative effects on industries, according to experts we spoke with and literature we reviewed. These sources further noted that the economic effects vary widely among industries and among companies within an industry. The most commonly identified effect cited was lost sales, which leads to decreased revenues and/or market share. Many industries lose sales because of consumers' purchases of counterfeit and pirated goods, particularly if the consumer purchased a counterfeit when intending to purchase a genuine product. In such cases, the industry may lose sales in direct proportion to the number of counterfeit products that the deceived consumers purchased. Industries in which consumers knowingly purchase counterfeits as a substitute for the genuine good may also experience lost sales. For example, recording companies have lost sales on a wide scale as a result of pirated music distributed over the Internet and producers of high-end fashion goods have lost sales from purchases of counterfeit goods made to look similar to genuine products.

Lost revenues can also occur when lower-priced counterfeit and pirated goods pressure producers or IP owners to reduce prices of genuine goods. In some industries, such as the audiovisual sector, marketing strategies must be adjusted to minimize the impact of counterfeiting on lost revenues. Movie studios that use time-related marketing strategies—introducing different formats of a movie after certain periods of time—have reduced the time periods or "windows" for each format as a countermeasure, reducing the overall revenue acquired in each window. Experts stated that companies may also experience losses due to the dilution of brand value or damage to reputation and public image, as counterfeiting and piracy may reduce consumers' confidence in the brand's quality. Consumers who are unaware that a product is counterfeit may blame the manufacturer of the legitimate good for negative effects of the fake. Some manufacturers learn of the existence of counterfeit versions of their products from returns of inferior counterfeit goods.

Companies are affected in additional ways. For example, to avoid losing sales and liability issues, companies may increase spending on IP protection efforts. In addition, experts we spoke with stated that companies could experience a decline in innovation and production of new goods if counterfeiting leads to reductions in corporate investments in research and development. Another variation in the nature of the effects of counterfeiting and piracy is that some effects are experienced immediately, while others are more long-term in nature, according to the OECD. The OECD's 2008 report cited loss of sales volume and lower prices as short-term effects, while the medium- and long-term effects include loss of brand value and reputation, lost investment, increased costs of countermeasures, potentially reduced scope of operations, and reduced innovation.

Finally, one expert emphasized to us that the loss of the IP rights is much more important than the loss of revenue. He stated that the danger for the United States is in the accelerated "learning effects"—companies learn how to produce and will improve upon these goods. They will no longer need to illegally copy a given brand—they will be in the aftermarket. He suggested that companies should work to ensure their competitive advantage in the future by inhibiting undesired knowledge transfer.

U.S. Government Loses Tax Revenue, Incurs Enforcement Expenses, and Faces Risks to Supply Chains

Many of the experts we interviewed identified lost tax revenue as an effect of counterfeiting and piracy on governments. IP owners or producers of legitimate goods who lose revenue because of competition from counterfeiters pay less in taxes. The U.S. government also incurs costs due to IP protection and enforcement efforts. Researchers have found anecdotal evidence that organized criminal and terrorist organizations are involved in counterfeiting and piracy. A 2009 RAND Corporation study, for example, presented case studies showing the involvement of organized crime or terrorist groups involved in film piracy to generate funding for their activities.[13] Because criminal networks are involved, government law enforcement priorities may be affected since more resources are devoted to combating these networks. Researchers have identified economic incentives that have contributed to the increase in counterfeiting and piracy in recent years. Economic incentives include low barriers to entering the counterfeiting and piracy business, potentially high profits, and limited legal sanctions if caught.

The federal government also incurs costs to store and destroy counterfeit and pirated goods. Seized goods have to be secured, as they have potential value but cannot be allowed to enter U.S. commerce. Storage may be prolonged by law enforcement actions, but the goods are generally destroyed or otherwise disposed of when they are determined to be illegal and are no longer needed. According to CBP officials, as seizures have increased, the agency's storage and destruction costs have grown and become increasingly burdensome. CBP reported that it spent about $41.9 million to destroy seized property between fiscal years 2007 and 2009.

Counterfeits also pose a threat to the reliability of supply chains that have national security or civilian safety significance. According to a recent Commerce report, counterfeit electronics parts have infiltrated U.S. defense and industrial supply chains and almost 40 percent of companies and organizations—including the Department of Defense—surveyed for the report have encountered counterfeit electronics.[14] Commerce reported that the infiltration of counterfeit parts into the supply chain was exacerbated by weaknesses in inventory management, procurement procedures, and inspection protocols, among other factors. The Federal Aviation Administration (FAA) tracks and posts notifications of incidents of counterfeit or improperly maintained parts entering airline industry supply chains through its Suspected Unapproved Parts Program in an effort to improve flight safety. The FAA program has identified instances of counterfeit aviation parts, as well as fake data plates and history cards to make old parts look new. FAA's program highlights the risks that counterfeit parts pose to the safety of commercial aircraft.

The U.S. Economy May Experience Slower Growth

The U.S. economy as a whole may grow at a slower pace than it otherwise would because of counterfeiting and piracy's effect on U.S. industries, government, and consumers. According to officials we interviewed and OECD's 2008 study, to the extent that companies experience a loss of revenues or incentives to invest in research and development for new products, slower economic growth could occur. IP-related industries play an important role in the growth of the U.S. economy and contribute a significant percentage to the U.S. gross domestic product. IP-related industries also pay significantly higher wages than other industries and contribute to a higher standard of living in the United States. To the extent that counterfeiting and piracy reduce investments in research and development, these companies may hire fewer workers and may contribute less to U.S. economic growth, overall. The U.S. economy may also experience slower growth due to a decline in trade with countries where widespread counterfeiting hinders the activities of U.S. companies operating overseas.

In addition to the industry effects, the U.S. economy, as a whole, also may experience effects of losses by consumers and government. An economy's gross domestic product could be measured as either the total expenditures by households (consumers), or as the total wages paid by the private sector (industry). Hence, the effect of counterfeiting and piracy on industry would affect consumers by reducing their wages, which could reduce consumption of goods and services and the gross domestic product. Finally, the government is also affected by the reduction of economic activity, since fewer taxes are collected.

Certain Stakeholders May Experience Positive Economic Effects of Counterfeiting and Piracy

Some experts we interviewed and literature we reviewed identified potential positive economic effects of counterfeiting and piracy. Some consumers may knowingly purchase a counterfeit or pirated product because it is less expensive than the genuine good or because the genuine good is unavailable, and they may experience positive effects from such purchases. For example, consumers in the United States and other countries purchase counterfeit copies of high-priced luxury-branded fashion goods at low prices, although the products' packaging and sales venues make it apparent they are not genuine. Consumers may purchase movies that have yet to be released in theaters and are unavailable in legitimate form. Lower-priced counterfeit goods may exert competitive pressure to lower prices for legitimate goods, which may benefit consumers. However, according to the OECD, the longer-term impact for consumers of falling prices for legitimate goods is unclear, as these changes may affect the speed of innovation.

There are also certain instances when IP rights holders in some industries might experience potentially positive effects from the knowing consumption of pirated or counterfeit goods. For example, consumers may use pirated goods to "sample" music, movies, software, or electronic games before purchasing legitimate copies, which may lead to increased sales of legitimate goods. In addition, industries with products that are characterized by large "switching costs," may also benefit from piracy due to lock-in effects. For example, some experts we spoke with and literature we reviewed discussed how consumers after being introduced to the pirated version might get locked into new legitimate software because of large switching costs, such as a steep learning curve, reluctance to switch to new products, and search costs incurred by consumers to identify a new product to use.

Some authors have argued that companies that experience revenue losses in one line of business—such as movies—may also increase revenues in related or complementary businesses due to increased brand awareness. For instance, companies may experience increased revenues due to the sales of merchandise that are based on movie characters whose popularity is enhanced by sales of pirated movies. One expert also observed that some industries may experience an increase in demand for their products because of piracy in other industries. This expert identified Internet infrastructure manufacturers (e.g., companies that make routers) as possible beneficiaries of digital piracy, because of the bandwidth demands related to the transfer of pirated digital content. While competitive pressure to keep one step ahead of counterfeiters may spur innovation in some cases, some of this innovation may be oriented toward anticounterfeiting and antipiracy efforts, rather than enhancing the product for consumers.

LACK OF DATA HINDERS EFFORTS TO QUANTIFY IMPACTS OF COUNTERFEITING AND PIRACY

According to experts we spoke with and literature we reviewed, estimating the economic impact of IP infringements is extremely difficult, and assumptions must be used due to the absence of data. Assumptions, such as the rate at which consumers would substitute counterfeit goods for legitimate products, can have enormous impacts on the resulting estimates and heighten the importance of transparency. Because of the significant differences in types of counterfeit and pirated goods and industries involved, no single method can be used to develop estimates, and each method has limitations. Nonetheless, research in specific industries suggest that the problem is sizeable. Most experts we spoke with and the literature we reviewed observed that despite significant efforts, it is difficult, if not impossible, to quantify the net effect of counterfeiting and piracy on the economy as a whole.

Lack of Data Is the Primary Challenge for Quantifying Economic Impacts of Counterfeiting and Piracy

Quantifying the economic impact of counterfeit and pirated goods on the U.S. economy is challenging primarily because of the lack of available data on the extent and value of counterfeit trade. Counterfeiting and piracy are illicit activities, which makes data on them inherently difficult to obtain. In discussing their own effort to develop a global estimate on the scale of counterfeit trade, OECD officials told us that obtaining reliable data is the most important and difficult part of any attempt to quantify the economic impact of counterfeiting and piracy. OECD's 2008 report, *The Economic Impact of Counterfeiting and Piracy*, further states that available information on the scope and magnitude of counterfeiting and piracy provides only a crude indication of how widespread they may be, and that neither governments nor industry were able to provide solid assessments of their respective situations. The report stated that one of the key problems is that data have not been systematically collected or evaluated and, in many cases, assessments "rely excessively on fragmentary and anecdotal information; where data are lacking, unsubstantiated opinions are often treated as facts."

In cases in which data on counterfeits are collected by federal agencies, such as CBP or FAA, it is difficult to know how complete the data are. For example, it is difficult to determine whether CBP's annual seizure data in table 1 reflect the extent and types of counterfeits entering the United States in any given year, the counterfeit products that were detected, or the level of federal border enforcement effort expended. FAA's notifications on counterfeit parts through its Suspect Unapproved Parts Program rely, in part, on reported incidents or complaints from members of the aviation community.

Commerce and FBI officials told us they rely on industry statistics on counterfeit and pirated goods and do not conduct any original data gathering to assess the economic impact of counterfeit and pirated goods on the U.S. economy or domestic industries. However, according to experts and government officials, industry associations do not always disclose their proprietary data sources and methods, making it difficult to verify their estimates. Industries collect this information to address counterfeiting problems associated with their products and may be reluctant to discuss instances of counterfeiting because consumers might lose confidence. OECD officials, for example, told us that one reason some industry representatives were hesitant to participate in their study was that they did not want information to be widely released about the scale of the counterfeiting problem in their sectors.

Assumptions are Used to Compensate for the Lack of Data

Because of the lack of data on illicit trade, methods for calculating estimates of economic losses must involve certain assumptions, and the resulting economic loss estimates are highly sensitive to the assumptions used. Two experts told us that the selection and weighting of these assumptions and variables are critical to the results of counterfeit estimates, and the assumptions should, therefore, be identified and evaluated. Transparency in how these estimates are developed is essential for assessing the usefulness of an estimate. Two key assumptions that typically are required in calculating a loss estimate from counterfeit goods include the substitution rate used by consumers and the value of counterfeit goods.

- *Substitution rate*. The assumed rate at which a consumer is willing to switch from purchasing a fake good to the genuine product is a key assumption that can have a critical impact on the results of an economic loss estimate. For example, if a consumer pays the full retail price for a fake movie thinking that it is the genuine good, an assumption can be made that a legitimate copy would have been bought in the absence of the fake product, representing a one-to-one substitution rate. However, this one-to-one substitution rate requires three important conditions: (1) the fake good is almost identical in quality to the genuine one; (2) the consumer is paying full retail price for the fake product; and (3) the consumer is not aware he is purchasing a counterfeit product. When some of these conditions are not met (e.g., the consumer paid a significantly lower price for the counterfeit), the likelihood that the consumer would have purchased the genuine product at full price is not clear. Substitution rates also vary by industry, since factors such as product quality, distribution channels, and information available about the product can differ significantly.
- *Value of fake goods*. Valuation of the fake goods constitutes another set of assumptions that has a significant impact. There are several measures of value that can be used, such as the production cost, the domestic value, or the manufacturer's suggested retail price. For example, CBP announced in a January 2010 press release that it had seized 252,968 DVDs with counterfeit trademarks. The agency reported

that the manufacturer's suggested retail price of the shipment was estimated to be more than $7.1 million and the domestic value was estimated at $204,904. Officials from the International Trade Commission stated that counterfeits are very difficult to price and estimates of economic impact would benefit from including a range of prices, from the spot price of the fake on the street corner at the bottom to the manufacturer's suggested retail price at the top.

The level or extent of deception that consumers face is also an important factor to consider when developing assumptions for the substitution rate and value of the fake goods. If a consumer is completely deceived, it could be reasonable to assume a one-to-one substitution rate (i.e., the purchase of a legitimate good in lieu of the counterfeit one) and a full retail price (i.e., the manufacturer's suggested retail sales price). Price, packaging, and location of the transaction are the most important signs to the consumer indicating the legitimacy of a good. Many of the experts we interviewed said that a one-to-one substitution rate is not likely to exist in most circumstances where counterfeit goods are significantly cheaper than the legitimate goods. Some experts also noted that the level of consumer deception varies across industries. For example, consumers who purchase counterfeit pharmaceuticals are more likely to be deceived, particularly when the counterfeit good is sold through the same distribution channel as the genuine product. Some experts observed that few, if any, consumers would willingly purchase a pharmaceutical product they knew might be counterfeit.[15] However, the extent of deception among consumers of audiovisual products is likely lower because sales venues for counterfeit audiovisual goods tend to be separate from the legitimate ones. Unless the assumptions about substitution rates and valuations of counterfeit goods are transparently explained, experts observed that it is difficult, if not impossible, to assess the reasonableness of the resulting estimate.

Three Widely Cited Estimates Sourced to U.S. Agencies Cannot Be Substantiated

Three commonly cited estimates of U.S. industry losses due to counterfeiting have been sourced to U.S. agencies, but cannot be substantiated or traced back to an underlying data source or methodology. First, a number of industry, media, and government publications have cited an FBI estimate that U.S. businesses lose $200-$250 billion to counterfeiting on an annual basis. This estimate was contained in a 2002 FBI press release, but FBI officials told us that it has no record of source data or methodology for generating the estimate and that it cannot be corroborated. Second, a 2002 CBP press release contained an estimate that U.S. businesses and industries lose $200 billion a year in revenue and 750,000 jobs due to counterfeits of merchandise. However, a CBP official stated that these figures are of uncertain origin, have been discredited, and are no longer used by CBP. A March 2009 CBP internal memo was circulated to inform staff not to use the figures. However, another entity within DHS continues to use them. Third, the Motor and Equipment Manufacturers Association reported an estimate that the U.S. automotive parts industry has lost $3 billion in sales due to counterfeit goods and attributed the figure to the Federal Trade Commission (FTC). The OECD has also referenced this estimate in its report on counterfeiting and piracy, citing the association report that is sourced to the FTC. However, when we contacted FTC officials to substantiate the estimate, they were unable to locate any record or source of this estimate within its reports or archives, and officials could not recall the agency ever developing or using this estimate. These estimates attributed to FBI, CBP, and FTC continue to be referenced by various industry and government sources as evidence of the significance of the counterfeiting and piracy problem to the U.S. economy.

No Single Approach for Quantifying Impacts of Counterfeiting and Piracy Can Be Used, but Different Studies Indicate Problem Is Sizeable

There is no single methodology to collect and analyze data that can be applied across industries to estimate the effects of counterfeiting and piracy on the U.S. economy or industry sectors. The nature of data collection, the substitution rate, value of goods, and level of deception are not the same across industries. Due to these challenges and the lack of data, researchers have developed different methodologies. In addition, some experts we interviewed noted the methodological and data challenges they face when the nature of the problem has changed substantially over time. Some commented that they have not updated earlier estimates or were required to change methodologies for these reasons. Nonetheless, the studies and experts we spoke with suggested that counterfeiting and piracy is a sizeable problem, which affects consumer behavior and firms' incentives to innovate. The most commonly used methods to collect and analyze data, based on our literature review and interviews with experts, are presented below.

Extrapolation of Enforcement Seizure Data

Seizure data from CBP is one of the few types of hard data sources available and is often used to extrapolate the level of counterfeit and pirated trade. This approach provides hard evidence of the minimum quantity of counterfeit goods, but a major limitation is that levels of border enforcement efforts can vary. For example, in our study of seizures made by the CBP field offices, we calculated "seizure rates" for the top 25 U.S. ports, based on the dollar value of IP seizures at each port compared to the dollar value of IP-related imports there. These ports accounted for over 75 percent of the value of all IP-related imports into the United States in fiscal year 2005.[16] We found that the top 3 ports seized over 100 times more IP counterfeits than the lowest 5 of these ports per dollar of IP-related imports. As a result, it appears that the importance of IP enforcement and the skill of the personnel at the ports have significant impact on the level of seizures. This suggests that seizure data might be useful as a floor, but are not indicative of the actual level of U.S. imports of counterfeit goods.

A study conducted by the Los Angeles County Economic Development Corporation, *A False Bargain: The Los Angeles County Economic Consequences of Counterfeit Products,* [17] used extrapolation of seizure data as one of its three approaches to estimate the economic impact of counterfeits.[18] The authors noted that the key variable in extrapolating seizure data from CBP was to determine CBP's success rate in interdicting illegal goods, which they acknowledged was "unknowable." One of the study's estimates that used CBP seizures to extrapolate the value of counterfeit and pirated goods in Los Angeles County calculated a range between $1 billion and $4.6 billion in 2005. This range was based on different assumptions used for seizure rates and other variables.

Another challenge when extrapolating seizure data is determining the dollar value to assign to the seized good, which can have a significant impact on the magnitude of the estimates. For example, in 2009, CBP seized a shipment of counterfeit sunglasses from China and reported an estimated total domestic value at $12,146 and a manufacturer's suggested retail price at $7.9 million.

Surveys of Supply and Demand

Researchers have conducted surveys to gather data on the consumption or sales patterns of counterfeit or pirated goods. The main advantage of this method is that it can also show consumers' behavior in terms of their preferences. For example, a survey could collect information on the consumer's willingness to pay for a counterfeit good; the number of counterfeit units purchased in a determined period of time; the minimum expected quality; the necessary price reduction of the legitimate good to avoid the consumer's purchase of the counterfeit good; the knowledge of sanctions if caught purchasing the counterfeit good; and the knowledge of potential "side effects" due to the purchase of fake goods. However, a survey can be a labor-intensive project and can cost in the millions of dollars. Moreover, one expert stated that the bias in surveys is hard to identify. For example, he commented that students, who are often the subjects in surveys of illegal file sharing, may either not admit that they are engaging in illegal activity, or may admit to such behavior because it may be popular for this demographic.

The Business Software Alliance publishes piracy estimates based on a set of annual surveys it conducts in different countries.[19] Based on its survey results, the industry association estimated the U.S. piracy rate at 20 percent for business software, carrying a loss of $9 billion in 2008. This study defined piracy as the difference between total installed software and legitimate software sold, and its scope involved only packaged physical software. While this study has an enviable data set on industries and consumers located around the world from its country surveys, it uses assumptions that have raised concerns among experts we interviewed, including the assumption of a one-to-one rate of substitution and questions on how the results from the surveyed countries are extrapolated to nonsurveyed countries.

Another example of the use of surveys is the study by the Motion Picture Association, which relied on a consumer survey conducted in several countries.[20] This study found that U.S. motion picture studios lost $6.1 billion to piracy in 2005. It is difficult, based on the information provided in the study, to determine how the authors handled key assumptions such as substitution rates and extrapolation from the survey sample to the broader population.

In a smaller-scale example of a survey method, Rob and Waldfogel[21] surveyed students in American universities during parts of 2003 and 2004, asking not only about the amount of music albums they purchased and illegally downloaded, but also the titles and their valuation for the albums they purchased and illegally downloaded. Their main findings are: (1) downloading reduces legitimate purchases by individuals by 20 percent in the sample, that is, every five music downloads substitute one legitimate purchase; (2) on average, respondents downloaded music that they valued one-third to one-half less than their legitimately purchased music, suggesting that some of the music that was downloaded would never have been purchased as an album; and (3) while downloading reduces per capita expenditures by $25, it raises per capita consumers' surplus by $70. The study indicated that downloading illegal music can have a positive effect on total consumer welfare. However, as explained by the authors, this experiment cannot be generalized; the data consist of a snapshot of undergraduate students' responses, which is not representative of the general population.

As previously discussed, Commerce recently conducted a survey of 387 companies and organizations participating in U.S. defense and industrial supply chains and reported that almost 40 percent of them encountered counterfeit products between 2005 and 2008.[22] The report focused on basic electronic parts and components, including microcircuits and circuit boards, throughout the entire electronics industrial base in the United States. The report noted that these parts are key elements of electronic systems that support national security missions and control essential commercial and industrial operations. Information provided by these companies and organizations also demonstrated an increase in the number of reported counterfeit incidents from 3,868 in 2005 to 9,356 in 2008. Some of these counterfeit incidents could include DOD-qualified parts and components.

Use of Economic Multipliers to Estimate Effects on the U.S. Economy

Economic multipliers show how capital changes in one industry affect output and employment of associated industries. Commerce's Bureau of Economic Analysis guidelines make regional multipliers available through its Regional Input-Output Modeling System (RIMS II). These multipliers estimate the extent to which a one-time or sustained change in economic activity will be attributed to specific industries in a region.[23] Multipliers can provide an illustration of the possible "induced" effects from a onetime change in final demand. For example, if a new facility is to be created with a determined investment amount, one can estimate how many new jobs can be created, as well as the benefit to the region in terms of output (e.g., extra construction, manufacturing, supplies, and other products needed). It must be noted that RIMS II multipliers assume no job immigration or substitution effect. That is, if new jobs are created as a result of investing more capital, those jobs would not be filled by the labor force from another industry.

In the case of estimating the effect of counterfeiting and piracy, RIMS II economic multipliers are applied to U.S. industry loss figures, which have been derived from other studies, and used to calculate the harm on employment and output due to reduced investments. Using the RIMS II multipliers in this setting does not take into account the two-fold effect: (1) in the case that the counterfeit good has similar quality to the original, consumers have extra disposable income from purchasing a less expensive good, and (2) the extra disposable income goes back to the U.S. economy, as consumers can spend it on other goods and services.

Most of the experts we interviewed were reluctant to use economic multipliers to calculate losses from counterfeiting because this methodology was developed to look at a one-time change in output and employment. Nonetheless, the use of this methodology corroborates that the effect of counterfeiting and piracy goes beyond the infringed industry. For example, when pirated movies are sold, it damages not only the motion picture industry, but all other industries linked to those sales.

The Institute of Policy Innovation has commissioned three studies in the audiovisual industries using economic multipliers; the most expansive of the studies covers motion pictures, sound recordings, business and entertainment software, and video games for the year 2005.[24] This study found that losses in the U.S. economy due to piracy accounted for $58 billion in output, over 370,000 jobs, and $2.6 billion in tax revenue. It was calculated by taking industry estimates of loss revenue and applying the RIMS II multipliers to these figures.[25]

Other Data Collection and Modeling Methods

Several additional studies that we reviewed provided alternative data collection and modeling techniques to quantify the effect of counterfeiting on a specific industry or, in the case of the OECD, on world trade. The OECD, for example, adopted an approach of combining different methodologies to develop a single estimate. The OECD triangulated a combination of data sets: extrapolating seizure data provided by national customs authorities, comparing the seizure data to international trade data, and using these data in an econometric model. The seizure data were used to develop a model that would measure the magnitude of global counterfeit trade.

The OECD estimated that the magnitude of counterfeit and pirated goods in international trade could have accounted for up to $200 billion in 2005, and later updated this estimate to $250 billion based on 2005-2007 world trade data.[26, 27] As noted by the OECD, most of the international trade data were supplied by national governments and relevant industries, and the OECD did not independently assess the reliability of the figures. Its methodology is based on matching, to the best of its knowledge, the industry data with customs seizure data from the OECD members, acknowledging the limitations of working with customs seizure data. OECD heavily qualified this estimate, however, reporting that "the overall degree to which products are being counterfeited and pirated is unknown and there do not appear to be any methodologies that could be employed to develop an acceptable overall estimate." A second phase of the OECD project covered digital piracy, but did not attempt to quantify the effects.

In a more narrowly focused study on downloads of music, Oberholzer-Gee and Strumpf[28] used modeling to determine that illegal downloads have no effect on record sales. They concluded that, in contrast with industry estimates, declining sales over the period of 2000-2002 were not primarily caused by illegal downloads. The results were found after compiling a data set of illegal downloads from a prominent server and testing the variation between illegal downloads and legal sales in the United States of specific albums on a weekly basis for 17 weeks in the second half of 2002. This was done by modeling album sales as a function of the quantity of album downloads and other album specific characteristics. While this is an enviable data set of actual illegal downloads, the study has two main limitations: first, the study uses a static model which does not reflect the effect of downloads apart from the week the download occured. Second, the study only observed the supply side of music. Thus, it is not clear if consumers who are illegally downloading music would have purchased the genuine albums.

Hui and Png's[29] study provided another example that used modeling. This study estimated that piracy in the music industry caused revenue losses of 6.6 percent in 1998. The authors stated that their estimate is significantly less than the industry loss estimate. In particular, for the year 1998 in the United States, legitimate sales of CDs were 3.73 CDs per capita, and the average loss in sales per capita due to piracy was 0.044 CDs. The data set included CD prices, music CD demand, piracy level and country-specific characteristics for 28 countries, mostly provided by the International Federation of the Phonographic Industry.[30] The main limitation for this study was that it only covered physical piracy. While digital piracy was not a major concern during the time period sampled, it has become so for at least the last decade due to the Internet. Another limitation is that the study used piracy rates that assumed a one-to-one substitution rate, including those used by the Business Software Alliance.

Many experts we interviewed also agreed that general or partial equilibrium models would offer useful insights if the input data existed. These involve modeling the supply and demand of a good and simulating the effect of how counterfeiting affects the market for that good (in the case of a partial model) and the economy as a whole (for a general equilibrium model). The approach allows a systematic analysis of the problem, but depends on the quality of the data used to develop the models. The benefit of an equilibrium model is that assumptions can be tested based on the results obtained and modified if the results fall outside of established parameters. Experts agreed on the potential benefits of this approach, but recognized that data limitations make it currently close to impossible to implement. Officials from the International Trade Commission and other industry experts said that this would be their preferred approach to think of the problem in question, but they also acknowledged that data reliability is a major concern, as with the other methodologies.

"Rule of Thumb" for Measuring Counterfeit Trade as a Proportion of World Trade

According to experts we interviewed and the literature we reviewed, there is no evidence to support a "rule of thumb" that measures counterfeit trade as a proportion of world trade to estimate the amount of counterfeit trade that occurs in a local economy. The advantage of finding a so-called "rule of thumb" for counterfeit trade is that it can be applied generally and does not try to take into consideration the different rates of counterfeiting and piracy for each of the different industry sectors. However, as noted earlier, piracy rates differ enormously across industries, so it is not possible to generalize findings. Moreover, not all goods from world trade can be counterfeited or pirated.

The most commonly cited "rule of thumb" is that counterfeit trade accounts for 5 to 7 percent of world trade, which has been attributed to the International Chamber of Commerce. The Office of the Comptroller of the City of New York used this rule of thumb in its 2004 study to estimate the total dollar exchange of counterfeit goods in the United States and in New York State.[31] This study first applied a 6 percent rule (an average of 5 to 7 percent "rule of thumb") to the total value of world trade in 2003 ($7.6 trillion) to calculate the value of world trade that is made up of counterfeit goods, arriving at $456 billion.[32]

This rule of thumb was widely spread by a 1998 OECD report, although OECD and experts cautioned that this estimate was not verifiable and the source data were not independently calculated. In its 2008 report, *The Economic Impact of Counterfeiting and Piracy*, the OECD commented that the "metrics underlying the International Chamber of Commerce's estimates are not clear," nor is it clear what types of IP infringements are included in the estimate. In a 2009 update to the report, the OECD estimated the share of counterfeit and pirated goods in world trade as 1.95 percent in 2007, increasing from 1.85 percent in 2000. Many of the experts we interviewed also expressed skepticism over the estimate that counterfeit trade represents 5 to 7 percent of world trade.

Economy-Wide Impact of Counterfeiting and Piracy Is Unknown

While experts and literature we reviewed provided different examples of effects on the U.S. economy, most observed that despite significant efforts, it is difficult, if not impossible, to quantify the net effect of counterfeiting and piracy on the economy as a whole. For example, as previously discussed, OECD attempted to develop an estimate of the economic impact of counterfeiting and concluded that an acceptable overall estimate of counterfeit goods could not be developed. OECD further stated that information that can be obtained, such as data on enforcement and information developed through surveys, "has significant limitations, however, and falls far short of what is needed to develop a robust overall estimate." One expert characterized the attempt to quantify the overall economic impact of counterfeiting as "fruitless," while another stated that any estimate is highly suspect since this is covert trade and the numbers are all "guesstimates."

To determine the net effect, any positive effects of counterfeiting and piracy on the economy should be considered, as well as the negative effects. Experts held different views on the nature of potentially offsetting effects. While one expert we interviewed stated that he did not believe there were any positive effects on the economy due to counterfeiting and piracy, other experts stated that there were positive effects and they should be assessed as well. Few studies have been conducted on positive effects, and little is known about their impact on the economy. Although some literature and experts suggest that negative effects may be overstated, in general, literature and experts indicate the negative effects of counterfeiting and piracy on the U.S. economy outweigh the positive effects. Since there is an absence of data concerning these potential effects, the net effect cannot be determined with any certainty.

The experts we interviewed also differed regarding the extent to which net effects of counterfeiting and piracy could be measured in certain parts of the economy. For example, one expert we spoke with has conducted research that found that employment numbers may be lost to the U.S. economy when copyright industries lose business due to piracy. Other experts we interviewed stated that, in their view, employment effects are unclear, because employment may decline in certain industries or rise in other industries as workers are hired to produce counterfeits. Another expert told us that effects of piracy within the United States are mainly redistributions within the economy for other purposes and that they should not be considered as a loss to the overall economy. He stated that "the money does not just vanish; it is used for other purposes." Other experts we spoke with focused more on the difficulties of aggregating the wide variety of effects on industries into a single assessment.

We are sending copies of this report to interested congressional committees; the Secretaries of Commerce, Health and Human Services, and Homeland Security; the Attorney General; the Chairman of the International Trade Commission; the U.S. Trade Representative, and the Intellectual Property Enforcement Coordinator. This report will also be available at no charge on GAO's Web site at http://www.gao.gov.

If you or your staffs have any questions about this report, please contact me at (202) 512-4347 or yagerl@gao.gov. Contact points for our Offices of Congressional Relations and Public Affairs may be found on the last page of this report.

Loren Yager
Director, International Affairs and Trade

Appendix I. Objectives, Scope, and Methodology

The Prioritizing Resources and Organization for Intellectual Property Act of 2008 (PRO-IP Act) directed GAO to conduct a study on the quantification of the impacts of imported and domestic counterfeits on the U.S. manufacturing industry and the overall economy of the United States. After conducting initial research, we determined that the U.S. government did not systematically collect data and perform analysis on the impacts of counterfeiting and piracy on the U.S. economy, and concluded that it was not feasible to generate our own data or attempt to quantify the economic impact of counterfeiting or piracy on the U.S. economy based on the review of existing literature and interviews with experts. In addition, we noted that many of the existing studies and literature on economic effects address both counterfeiting and piracy. Based on discussions with staff from the House and Senate Judiciary Committees, we agreed that we would (1) examine existing research on the effects of counterfeiting and piracy on consumers, industries, government, and the U.S. economy; and (2) identify insights gained from efforts to quantify the effects of counterfeiting and piracy on the U.S. economy. To address both of these objectives, we interviewed officials and representatives from industry associations, nongovernmental organizations, academic institutions, and U.S. government agencies and the multilateral Organization for Economic Cooperation and Development (OECD). We also reviewed documents and studies quantifying or discussing the impacts of counterfeiting and piracy on the U.S. economy, industry, government, and consumers.

Specifically, we reviewed quantitative and qualitative studies published since 1999 of the economic impact of intellectual property (IP) infringements to examine the range of impacts of counterfeiting and piracy on various stakeholders (both positive and negative) and to identify other insights about the nature of counterfeit markets, approaches to developing estimates, and the role IP plays in the U.S. economy. We identified these reports and studies through a literature search and discussions with representatives from industry associations, nongovernmental organizations, academic institutions, U.S. government agencies, and the OECD to obtain their views on the most relevant studies to review. Our literature review also included the OECD studies that examined the economic impact of counterfeiting and piracy. Although the OECD studies are global in scope rather than focused on the U.S. economy, their unique nature and prominence as the most comprehensive attempt to quantify the impacts of counterfeiting and piracy warranted their inclusion within our scope. See the bibliography for a partial list of references we consulted. We did not assess or evaluate the accuracy of quantitative estimates or other data found in these studies. We reviewed the studies primarily to obtain information on the range of effects from counterfeiting and piracy, different methods and assumptions used in determining effects, and insights gained from these efforts. In selecting studies for review, we sought to include a range of industries and methodologies. In some cases, we interviewed the authors of these reports to obtain additional information.

We conducted structured interviews with subject matter experts to obtain their views on efforts to quantify the economic impacts of counterfeiting and piracy and methodological approaches, the range of impacts of counterfeits and piracy, and insights on counterfeiting activities and markets. We identified experts through a literature review and discussions with relevant government officials, industry and consumer representatives, academics, and other stakeholders. These subject matter experts were selected from a population of individuals from government, academia, industry, and professional organizations. More specifically, our criteria for selecting experts to interview included:

- type and depth of experience, for instance, whether the expert had authored a widely referenced study or article on the topic, and whether the expert was referred to us by at least one other interviewee as someone knowledgeable about the topic;
- relevance of published work to this engagement;
- representation of a range of perspectives;
- representation of relevant organizations and sectors including, where applicable, representatives from government, academia, industry, and professional organizations; and
- other subject matter experts' recommendations.

We developed a common list of structured interview questions that we asked of each of the experts. We pretested our questions with two of our initial respondents and refined our questions based on their input. The structured interviews included questions on definitions of counterfeit and pirated goods; effects of counterfeiting and piracy; and their views on methodologies and studies that quantify the effects of counterfeiting and piracy, as well as assumptions used. Individuals or organizations that we met with for these structured interviews are listed below:

- Business Software Alliance (BSA)
- Peggy Chaudhry, Villanova University
- International Trade Commission
- Joe Karaganis, Social Science Research Council
- Keith Maskus, University of Colorado
- OECD
- Felix Olberholzer-Gee, Harvard University
- Stephen Siwek, Economists Inc.
- John Spink, Michigan State University
- Thorsten Staake, ETH Zurich, Department of Management, Technology, and Economics
- Office of the U.S. Trade Representative
- Alan Zimmerman, City University of New York

We also met with representatives from other industry associations and other organizations outside of the structured interview process in order to gain more in-depth information and additional perspectives on both of our objectives. In addition, we interviewed U.S. agency officials and reviewed documents from the Departments of Justice, Homeland Security, Commerce, and Health and Human Services, the Office of the U.S. Trade Representative, and the International Trade Commission. U.S. agency documents that we reviewed included counterfeiting and piracy studies, press releases, and other documents. For background purposes, we updated CBP data on counterfeit seizures and costs to store and destroy seized counterfeit goods from our 2007 report, *Intellectual Property: Better Data*

Analysis and Integration Could Help U.S. Customs and Border Protection Improve Border Enforcement Efforts (GAO-07-735). To assess the reliability of the seizure data, we reviewed our prior work that reported on seizure data, examined them for internal consistency, and discussed with CBP how the data are collected and reviewed. We found the data to be sufficiently reliable for background purposes of reporting trends in law enforcement seizures. We shared a copy of the draft report with officials from the Departments of Commerce, Justice, Homeland Security, Health and Human Services, the Office of the U.S. Trade Representative, the International Trade Commission, and the Office of the U.S. Intellectual Property Enforcement Coordinator to obtain technical comments. We received comments from the Departments of Homeland Security and Justice, and the Office of the U.S. Intellectual Property Enforcement Coordinator and made changes as appropriate.

The PRO-IP Act also directed us to report on the nature and scope of IP statutory and case laws and the extent that they are being used to investigate and prosecute acts of trafficking and counterfeits. As agreed with Congressional committees, this part of the mandate was addressed by our 2008 report, *Intellectual Property: Federal Enforcement Has Generally Increased, but Assessing Performance Could Strengthen Law Enforcement Efforts* (GAO-08-157).

We conducted our work from April 2009 to April 2010 in accordance with all sections of GAO's Quality Assurance Framework that are relevant to our objectives. The framework requires that we plan and perform the engagement to obtain sufficient and appropriate evidence to meet our stated objectives and to discuss any limitations to our work. We believe that the information and data obtained, and the analysis conducted, provide a reasonable basis for any findings and conclusions in this product.

APPENDIX II. STAFF ACKNOWLEDGMENTS

Staff Acknowledgements

In addition to the contact named above, Christine Broderick, Assistant Director; Jeremy Latimer; Catherine Gelb; Pedro Almoguera; Shirley Brothwell; Karen Deans; Matthew Jones; and Diahanna Post made key contributions to this report. In addition Virginia Chanley and Ernie Jackson provided technical assistance.

BIBLIOGRAPHY

Studies and Literature on the Nature of Counterfeiting and Piracy and Their Economic Effects

Studies and Government Estimates We Reviewed that Quantify Economic Impacts on the U.S. Economy or Industry Sectors

[1] Business Software Alliance (BSA), *Sixth Annual BSA-IDC Global Software 08 Piracy Study*, Washington, D.C.: BSA, May 2009.

[2] Customs and Border Protection. *Press Release, May 29, 2002*, Washington, D.C.: May 2002 http://www.cbp.gov/xp/cgov/newsroom/news_releases/archives/legacy/2002/52002/05292002.xml (accessed April 4, 2009).

[3] Federal Bureau of Investigation. *Press Release,* July 17, 2002, Washington, D.C.: July 2002 http://www.fbi.gov/pressrel/pressrel02/outreach071702.htm (accessed March 30, 2010).

[4] Freeman, Gregory, Nancy D. Sidhu & Michael Montoya. (2007). *A False Bargain: The Los Angeles County Economic Consequences of Counterfeit Products.* Los Angeles, Calif.: Los Angeles County Economic Development Corporation, February.

[5] Hui, Kai-Lung & Ivan Png. (2003). "Piracy and the Legitimate Demand for Recorded Music," *Contributions to Economic Analysis & Policy*, vol. 2, issue 1, article 11.

[6] International Chamber of Commerce. (2010). *Counterfeiting Intelligence Bureau,* London: 2010. http://www.icc-ccs.org/index.php?option=com_content&view=article&id= 29&Ite mid=39 (accessed March 30).

[7] Consulting, L. E. K. (2006). *The Cost of Movie Piracy*, sponsored by the Motion Picture Association.

[8] Motor & Equipment Manufacturers Association (MEMA). (2005). *Stop Counterfeiting of Automotive and Truck Parts.* MEMA.

[9] Oberholzer-Gee, Felix & Koleman Strumpf. (2007). "*The Effect of File Sharing on Record Sales: An Empirical Analysis*," *Journal of Political Economy*, vol. *115*, no. 1.

[10] Organisation for Economic Cooperation and Development (OECD). (2008). *The Economic Impact of Counterfeiting and Piracy.* Paris: OECD.

[11] OECD. (2009). *Magnitude of Counterfeiting and Piracy of Tangible Products: An Update*, Paris: OECD, November.

[12] OECD & *Piracy of Digital Content.* (2009). Paris: OECD.

[13] Rob, Rafael & Joel Waldfogel. (2006). "*Piracy on the High C's: Music Downloading, Sales Displacement, and Social welfare in a Sample of College Students," Journal of Law and Economics*, vol. *XLIX*, (Apri).

[14] Siwek, Stephen E. (2007). *The True Cost of Copyright Industry Piracy to the U.S. Economy*, Institute for Policy Innovation (IPI), IPI Center for Technology Freedom, Policy Report 189, (October).

[15] Thompson, William C. Jr. (2004). *Bootleg Billions: The Impact of the Counterfeit Goods Trade on New York City*, City of New York, Office of the Comptroller, November.

Other Literature We Reviewed

[1] Baumol, William J. (2002). The Free Market Innovation Machine: Analyzing the Growth Miracle of Capitalism. Princeton and Oxford: Princeton University Press.

[2] Chaudhry, Peggy & Alan Zimmerman. (2009). The Economics of Counterfeit Trade: Governments, Consumers, Pirates, and Intellectual Property Rights. Berlin: Springer.

[3] Fink, Carsten & Carlos M. (2009). Correa, The Global Debate on the Enforcement of Intellectual Property Rights and Developing Countries. International Centre for Trade and Sustainable Development. Issue Paper No. 22, February.

[4] Forzley, Michele. (2003). Counterfeit Goods and the Public's Health and Safety. International Intellectual Property Institute.
[5] Horan, Amanda, Christopher Johnson & Heather Sykes. (2005). Foreign Infringement of Intellectual Property Rights: Implications for Selected U.S. Industries. No. ID-14, U.S. International Trade Commission, Office of Industries Working Paper, October.
[6] Mansfield, Edwin. (1968). Industrial Research and Technological Innovation. New York, N.Y.: W.W. Norton.
[7] RAND Corporation. (2009). Film Piracy, Organized Crime, and Terrorism, RAND Safety and Justice Program and the Global Risk and Security Center, (Santa Monica, Calif.).
[8] Rosenberg, Nathan. (1994). Exploring the Black Box: Technology, Economics, and History, Cambridge, United Kingdom: Cambridge University Press.
[9] Schumpeter, J.A. (1939). Business Cycles: A Theoretical, Historical and Statistical Analysis of the Capitalist Process, New York: McGraw-Hill.
[10] Siwek, Stephen E. (2005). Engines of Economic Growth: Economic Contributions of the US Intellectual Property Industries. Washington, D.C.: Economists Incorporated.
[11] Staake. (2009). Thorsten, Frederic Thiesse and Elgar Fleisch, "The Emergence of Counterfeit Trade: A Literature Review," *European Journal of Marketing,* Vol. *43* No. 3/4.
[12] Staake, Thorsten and Elgar Fleisch. (2008). Countering Counterfeit Trade: Illicit Market Insights, Best-Practice Strategies, and Management Toolbox. Berlin: Springer.
[13] U.S. Department of Commerce. (2010). Bureau of Industry and Security, Office of Technology Evaluation. Defense Industrial Base Assessment: Counterfeit Electronics. Washington, D.C., January.
[14] U.S. Department of Commerce. (1997). Bureau of Economic Analysis and Economics and Statistics Administration, Regional Multipliers. A User Handbook for the Regional Input-Output Modeling System (RIMS II) 3rd ed., Washington, D.C..

End Notes

[1] The PRO-IP Act also directed GAO to report on the nature and scope of IP statutory and case laws and the extent that they are being used to investigate and prosecute acts of trafficking and counterfeits. As agreed with congressional committees, this part of the mandate was addressed by GAO's report, *Intellectual Property: Federal Enforcement Has Generally Increased, but Assessing Performance Could Strengthen Law Enforcement Efforts,* GAO-08-157 (Washington, D.C.: Mar. 11, 2008).

[2] See the Bibliography for a list of studies and estimates that we reviewed.

[3] Organisation for Economic Cooperation and Development (OECD), *The Economic Impact of Counterfeiting and Piracy*. Paris: OECD, 2008.

[4] Participants in the Central America Free Trade Agreement are Costa Rica, the Dominican Republic, El Salvador, Guatemala, Honduras, Nicaragua, and the United States.

[5] The United States also has signed free trade agreements with Colombia, Korea, and Panama, but Congress must enact legislation to approve and implement each individual agreement in order for them to go into effect. Prior to 2000, two other free trade agreements had entered into force: the U.S.-Israel Free Trade Agreement (entered into force in 1985) and the North American Free Trade Agreement between Canada, Mexico, and the United States (entered into force in 1994).

[6] For example, these protections include adherence to new World Intellectual Property Organization Internet treaties, a longer minimum time period for copyright protection, additional penalties for circumventing technological measures controlling access to copyrighted materials, transparent procedures for protection of trademarks, stronger protection for well-known marks, patent protection for plants and animals, protection

against arbitrary revocation of patents, new provisions dealing with domain name disputes, and increased enforcement measures.

[7] William J. Baumol, *The Free-Market Innovation Machine: Analyzing the Growth Miracle of Capitalism.* (Princeton, N.J.: Princeton University Press, 2002).

[8] Edwin Mansfield, *Industrial Research and Technological Innovation.* (New York, N.Y.: W.W. Norton, 1968); Nathan Rosenberg, *Exploring the Black Box: Technology, Economics, and History.* (Cambridge, United Kingdom: Cambridge University Press, 1994); J. Schumpeter, *Business Cycles, A Theoretical and Statistical Analysis of the Capitalist Process.* (New York, N.Y.: McGraw-Hill, 1939).

[9] In addition to copyrights, trademarks, and patents, two other IP protections are trade secrets and geographical indications. Trade secrets are defined as any type of valuable information, including a formula, pattern, compilation, program device, method, technique, or process that gains commercial value from not being generally known or readily obtainable; and for which the owner has made reasonable efforts to keep secret. Geographical indications are defined as indications that identify a good as originating in a country, region, or locality, where a given quality, reputation, or other characteristic of the good is essentially attributable to its geographic origin. Definitions used in this report for the various types of IP are provided by the U.S. Patent and Trademark Office.

[10] Counterfeit drugs under this definition may include products without the active ingredient, with an insufficient quantity of the active ingredient, with the wrong active ingredient, or with packaging that falsely suggests the drug was manufactured by an FDA-approved manufacturer.

[11] CBP data represent seizures made by CBP or Immigration and Customs Enforcement. CBP measures IP activity two ways: number of seizure actions and estimated domestic value of goods seized. The number of goods in one seizure action can range from a few items shipped via international mail to hundreds of boxes in an ocean-going cargo container. Domestic value is calculated as the landed cost plus profit (the cost of the merchandise when last purchased, plus all duties, fees, broker's charges, profit, unlading charges, and U.S. freight charges to bring the good to the importer's premises), a value generally lower than the price at which the goods might sell to the final consumer.

[12] For example, the FDA in recent years has found cases of a counterfeit HIV/AIDS drug that contained nonsterile tap water instead of an active ingredient; a fake schizophrenia medication that contained aspirin; a counterfeit influenza vaccine; and a misbranded cough suppressant that caused the death of five consumers.

[13] RAND Corporation, *Film Piracy, Organized Crime, and Terrorism,* RAND Safety and Justice Program and the Global Risk and Security Center, (Santa Monica, Calif., 2009).

[14] Commerce, Bureau of Industry and Security, Office of Technology Evaluation, *Defense Industrial Base Assessment: Counterfeit Electronics* (Washington, D.C., January 2010).

[15] A FDA official told us that most of the fake pharmaceutical purchases were made through the Internet, where consumers were seeking drugs without prescription.

[16] This method enabled us to perform a better comparison across ports by reducing the influence of non-IP-related imports, as well as eliminating the impact of the fact that some ports handle many times the volume of imports compared to other ports. For a more detailed explanation of U.S. custom seizure data and our analysis see GAO, *Intellectual Property: Better Data Analysis and Integration Could Help U.S. Customs and Border Protection Improve Border Enforcement Efforts*, GAO-07-735 (Washington, D.C.: Apr. 26, 2007).

[17] Gregory Freeman, Nancy D. Sidhu, and Michael Montoya, *A False Bargain: The Los Angeles County Economic Consequences of Counterfeit Products.* (Los Angeles, Calif.: Los Angeles County Economic Development Corporation, February 2007).

[18] The authors used the extrapolation method in combination with two other methods as tests of reasonableness.

[19] Business Software Alliance (BSA), *Sixth Annual BSA-IDC Global Software 08 Piracy Study.* (Washington, D.C.: BSA, May 2009).

[20] L.E.K. Consulting, *The Cost of Movie Piracy*, sponsored by the Motion Picture Association, 2006.

[21] Rafael Rob and Joel Waldfogel, *Piracy on the High C's: Music Downloading, Sales Displacement, and Social Welfare in a Sample of College Students*. Journal of Law and Economics, vol. XLIX, April 2006.

[22] Commerce, Bureau of Industry and Security, Office of Technology Evaluation, *Defense Industrial Base Assessment: Counterfeit Electronics* (Washington, D.C., January 2010).

[23] Commerce, Bureau of Economic Analysis and Economics and Statistics Administration, *Regional Multipliers. A User Handbook for the Regional Input-Output Modeling System (RIMS II)* 3rd ed., Washington, D.C.: 1997.

[24] Stephen E. Siwek, *The True Cost of Copyright Industry Piracy to the U.S. Economy*, Institute for Policy Innovation (IPI), IPI Center for Technology Freedom, Policy Report 189, (October 2007).

[25] In some cases, the author adjusted the industry estimates of loss revenue in order to make them comparable across industries.

[26] The OECD estimate was limited to internationally traded hard goods and did not include digital piracy or counterfeit goods produced and consumed within the same country.

[27] OECD, *Magnitude of Counterfeiting and Piracy of Tangible Products: An Update*, Paris: OECD, November 2009.

[28] Felix Oberholzer-Gee and Koleman Strumpf, *The Effect of File Sharing on Record Sales: An Empirical Analysis.* Journal of Political Economy, vol. 115, no. 1, 2007.

[29] Kai-Lung Hui and Ivan Png, *Piracy and the Legitimate Demand for Recorded Music*, Contributions to Economic Analysis & Policy, Volume 2 Issue 1, Article 11, 2003.

[30] The piracy rates used in the study were provided by the International Federation of the Phonographic Industry and Business Software Alliance for music cassettes and business computer software, respectively.

[31] William C. Thompson, Jr., *Bootleg Billions: The Impact of the Counterfeit Goods Trade on New York City,* (New York City Office of the Comptroller, November 2004).

[32] This study does not specify which industries are covered or whether it includes piracy, and does not explain the linear proportion between trade and counterfeiting for the world or the United States.

CHAPTER SOURCES

Chapter 1 – This is an edited, reformatted and augmented version of Congressional Research Service Report RL34292, dated February 17, 2011.

Chapter 2 – This is an edited, reformatted and augmented version of Congressional Research Service Report R40607, dated June 14, 2010.

Chapter 3 – This is an edited, reformatted and augmented version of Congressional Research Service Report R41391, dated August 31, 2010.

Chapter 4 – This is an edited, reformatted and augmented version of United States Government Accountability Office Report GAO-11-39, dated October 2010.

Chapter 5 – This is an edited, reformatted and augmented version of United States Government Accountability Office Report GAO-10-423, dated April 2010.

INDEX

A

B

C

D

E

F

G

H

R

S

T

U

V

W